FROM DARKNESS TO LIGHT

Discover the Secret of Who You Really Are, and Heal Your Body, Mind and Spirit

DESPO PISHIRI

BALBOA.PRESS

A DIVISION OF HAY HOUSE

Balboa Press books may be ordered through booksellers or by contacting:

Balboa Press
A Division of Hay House
1663 Liberty Drive
Bloomington, IN 47403
www.balboapress.com
844-682-1282

Print information available on the last page.

ISBN: 978-1-9822-6537-3 (sc)
ISBN: 978-1-9822-6539-7 (hc)
ISBN: 978-1-9822-6538-0 (e)

Library of Congress Control Number: 2021904588

Balboa Press rev. date: 05/13/2021

CONTENTS

DEDICATION

Dedicated to my beloved brother Loucas, the most loving, kind and generous human being, who crossed to the spirit side as I was finishing the first draft of this book. I miss him every day but knowing that he is in a better place gives me comfort.

THANK YOU

To my wonderful sons: you are my Alpha and my Omega. Thank you for choosing me to be your mother on your earthly journey.

To my husband of 30 years, who put up with me during my ups and downs and supported me in this spiritual journey. Thank you for your unconditional love.

To my parents, who are no longer in the physical world: thank you for the values that you instilled in us, despite the hardships that you went through to raise all nine of us.

We all have a Guardian Angel loving us unconditionally and looking after us. Sometimes it happens that our Guardian Angel is another human being. Gladys, my friend, thank you for guiding me onto this path. Without you, I would not have even contemplated writing this book.

ACKNOWLEDGEMENTS

Without my husband, Mario, publishing this book would not have been possible. He spent endless hours editing and correcting. It is always a challenge writing a book in a language other than one's mother tongue. It most definitely required a native English speaker to look at it before it went to a publisher. When he first read it, he said, *"It needs restructuring. There is a lot of work to be done"*. As you can imagine, I was offended! I only wanted someone to proofread it, and didn't expect to be told that it needed *"restructuring"*! I was concerned that his *"restructuring"* would change the message, but at the same time, there is no one I trust more than my husband. When he sent me the edited version, I was pleasantly surprised to see how skilfully he had edited the book. I will be eternally grateful to you Mario, my life partner and best friend. Thank you!

My beautiful, kind, determined and creative friend Myriam Hara, did such a wonderful job with the illustrations for this book, and did so with so much enthusiasm and love. Myriam, I am very grateful for all your hard work and the positive energy that you directed into this book.

Dr. Gary O'Neill, thank you for your invaluable input in proofreading this book. You have ironed out mistakes and polished this book in an incredibly effective way.

To all Balboa Press employees involved in the production of this book, I am grateful for your patience and kindness. Every step of the way during this journey of publishing my first book, you have guided me, provided valuable advice and patiently answered numerous questions. Your professionalism and patience has made this book possible. Thank you!

HIGHLIGHT

The intention of this book is to share my personal experience and discuss a range of subjects, including reincarnation, spiritual learning, past lives, the soul and the physical body, etc. As such, this book may offer theories and principles which may be different to conventional religious teachings.

It is necessary for the reader to approach this book with an open mind and objective outlook. The intention is to reinforce the message of love, compassion and tolerance inherent in the three religions, Hinduism, Buddhism and Christianity, and not to criticise or change in any way the teachings and messages contained in the holy books of these religions. Stressing the similarities between the three religions is a key theme of this book and will only reinforce their teachings.

The reader does not have to believe or follow any religion to read this book. The key requirement is an open and inquisitive mind, and an objective approach free from any prejudices or preformed judgments. It is my hope that you will find the contents useful and enlightening.

CHAPTER 1

Introduction

Awaking from Ignorance

"Anyone for coffee or tea?", I asked. After a heavy Christmas lunch, it was time for dessert and a hot cup of something relaxing. Christmas is a very special time for my family. Although I love cooking for family and friends, it is unfortunate that Christmas is now all about food and gifts; but we still enjoy quality time together.

A few minutes later we were all enjoying a hot cup of tea with not-so-light Christmas goodies. *"Has anyone read* Many Lives, Many Masters*?"* (See Reference List 1 - R1), Gladys asked. *"What is it all about?"* I replied. *"Reincarnation",* another friend said. I love subjects like this. They are thought-provoking and stimulating. I had heard about reincarnation but was not sure what it was exactly and how it could relate to me. I made a note of the name of the book and a few weeks later bought it and read it in three days.

Not to spoil the book for people that have not read it, but half-way through the book, something happened to me. It's difficult for someone that has not experienced this to understand what I felt. It was an internal shift, an awakening from ignorance of who I really am. It was as if I saw the light at the end of the tunnel. Everything suddenly made sense. Just like that, my fears and insecurities vanished, and

I did not care what people thought of me. *"I am not my body"*, I thought. *"I am my soul, my spirit"*. This was a eureka moment. All of a sudden there were two of us: my body and my soul. My body is unimportant; it dies and the soul returns with another body. The body is just like a school uniform or a suit that the soul uses to experience and learn in this earthly school. I must clarify that *awakening* is not the same as *enlightenment.* I am not an enlightened person or a saint. This will all become clearer in the following pages.

Eighteen months earlier, I had left my corporate job after nearly having a nervous breakdown. My marriage was falling apart, I had neglected my family and I was in a deep depression. With my husband's support, I decided it was best for all of us if I took a break from corporate life and focused on getting my life back together. It was the right decision. Although not completely healed by the time of this Christmas lunch, I was a lot better. During these eighteen months, I had spent a lot of time questioning my purpose in life. Why was I here? Did I exist to live and die and nothing else? Was there a purpose in our existence? I felt deep inside that there was more to life than existing and passing without contributing something to society. I felt that I had contributed nothing.

I was brought up in a conservative family with traditional Eastern Mediterranean values. A woman's place was in the house. Ours was not a religiously conservative upbringing, and we were not raised to strictly follow the way of the Church. I was, however, perhaps more so than the other members of my family, drawn to the teachings of Jesus and his message of love and forgiveness. I believed in God, but at the same time, religion scared me. When I was young, we were taught that our sins would lead to eternal suffering in the fires of Hell. That was an awful thought for my young mind, and I was really not looking forward to death! In my young mind, I was asking: "Who is counting our sins? What if the spirit that is counting makes a small mistake and I end up in Hell instead of Heaven? Is there some kind of a scale that someone will use to weigh our sins?". This sounded

2

like a better idea, perhaps fairer than counting. We were also told that once we die, we would go into some kind of *'sleep'* waiting for Judgement Day (G6). I thought that life would be very boring in the spirit world. How many millions of years would I have to wait? Death was not welcome at all. The spirit side was not appealing.

As I was growing up, I found that I had become more withdrawn, more introverted. Social interaction and mixing with other people required effort and I just did not understand the point of life. What is the meaning and purpose? We live and die and go to Hell for our sins and that's it? How unfair is this? What kind of loving and compassionate God wants his children to burn for eternity? All of this did not make any sense.

After reading *Many Lives, Many Masters* and the other five books written by Dr. Brian Weiss, my doubts and concerns have been answered - I felt liberated. In the Gospel of John (8:32), Jesus said, *"The truth will set you free"*. That's exactly how I felt. I felt that, somehow, I had been given *'secret'* knowledge that had set me free.

I started reading the religious scriptures of the other major religions, including the Holy Quran, Bhagavad Gita, Dhammapada, and lastly the Bible. I intentionally left the Bible to last. The original Bible was written in ancient Greek and I intended to read this side by side with the English version because I suspected that some of the original meaning would have been lost in translation.

MY JOURNEY BEGINS

Within months of reading *Many Lives Many Masters*, I enrolled myself in a clinical hypnotherapy and other specialist healing courses. When I started this journey, I did not know the path that I was going to take and wasn't even sure if I wanted to do this professionally. All I had in mind was to help my family and friends.

These courses provided me with a wide range of tools, and I realised then that this was what I wanted to do. I started practising more seriously.

A particular client, for the purposes of this book I will call her Jane (not her real name), came to me for a session. I had many sessions with Jane, and although she was feeling fine, she had some mental blockages that she wanted to analyse. I decided to explore these through Higher Self Therapy. This is a technique whereby we talk directly to a Higher Self which directly responds to the questions raised. I will explain the concept of Higher Self in the next section.

I guided her into a trance and followed the guidelines for the Higher Self Therapy. It was the first time I had performed Higher Self Therapy at a professional level. I had previously practised in a study class, but this was not the same as having to perform the technique with a real client. I was a little nervous but well prepared, and it helped that Jane was a hypnotherapist's dream client. She quicky moved into a deep trance and responded well to the therapy.

When preparing for such a session, I agree what to ask the Higher Self with my client. The questions could be related to belief blockages, physical ailments, life learnings and so on. Jane and I agreed on five questions.

We quickly connected with Jane's Higher Self. I was channelling the interaction through her and was surprised how the modulation of her voice changed when the Higher Self was communicating. Jane's Higher Self was irritated with her *'slow learning'* life after life. I provided reassurance that she was eager to learn, but we needed its help to progress her learning. At my request, the Higher Self agreed to answer the questions, and the next thirty minutes or so were unforgettable. The information I was given on how to heal Jane, and the details provided to me, were unexpected. I was also guided to perform past life regression to find information regarding her past lives and her karmas (G7) that she had carried forward to this life, and how those karmas were causing blockages in this life.

Towards the end of the session, the exchange went as follows:

D: So, are you saying that if I guide her to a past life, she will find more information about her learnings and her blockages?

JHS: Correct, but you must speak to your green light first.

D: What do you mean by that?

JHS: Your light is here to talk to you.

D: Ah, you mean my Higher Self?

JHS: Correct.

D: How do you suggest I do this? Do you mean I should get someone to hypnotise me so that I can also talk to my Higher Self?

JHS: No. I will go and your Higher Self will come.

D: Ah OK … through Jane?

JHS: Correct.

D: Great. Thank you for letting me communicate with you and I really appreciate all the information you have provided. Jane will be very happy. Can we come back to you again for more information in the future?

JHS: Yes.

D: OK, thank you. You can move back now and thank you again. Please let me know when my Higher Self is here.

There was a pause of about 10 seconds.

HS: You are more powerful than most people (higher selves don't engage in casual talk and polite dialogue; they get straight to the point! The voice modulation changed again; the voice was deeper, a bit more 'mellow' than Jane's Higher Self).

D: Who am I speaking to?

HS: I am you!

It was such a surprise. I never expected that I could communicate with my own Higher Self. I had read several books written by other hypnotherapists, but I had not read of a case of hypnotherapists channelling their own Higher Self.

D: Ah … thanks for coming forward. I have many questions to ask you!

HS: I know. You are helping so many people.

D: How? I can't recall helping people. I have only recently started down this path.

HS: You have been helping people all your life and the lives before this one. You just don't realise it. You heal people with your voice; your power is in your voice. Your name will remain in the scriptures.

D: That's good to know, even though I don't feel powerful at all. I have done and said things that I have regretted, and I am feeling guilty for so many things.

HS: Those are forgiven. We send people and situations into your life for your learning.

D: That's a relief! What did you mean by 'scriptures'? I am not a holy person.

HS: You will write.

D: Ah … you mean my name will be known through writing a book?

HS: Correct. You will write and help so many people.

D: I have always wanted to write, but I am not the creative type. What do you think I should write about?

HS: It will come to you.

D: So, are you saying that ideas will come to me … perhaps through my reading?

HS: Correct. We will guide you through it.

D: Thanks. Jane's Higher Self said that I am a green light. What does that mean?

HS: You are a healer, an evolved soul. Your energy is lime green colour.

D: I understand. Am I on the right path then?

HS: Oh yes. You have healed people in all your lives, and you are healing people in this life.

D: It's good to know that I am on the right path. It gives me comfort. I wonder if you can give me some information about a health issue.

HS: Yes, I can.

D: I have been having problems with my legs for a long time and this is making me anxious. I can't sleep well at night. What is causing this?

HS: Past life trauma.

D: Do you mean the way I died in a previous life?

HS: Correct.

D: How did I die?

HS: You were tortured.

D: That sounds terrible. Was I a man or a woman?

HS: A man.

D: What was my name?

HS: Artemis. I see you are wearing something shining on your chest. I can't find a word for it. (My Higher Self is looking for words in Jane's vocabulary).

D: Which year was it?

HS: I can't see which year it is in physical time, but it was a very long time ago.

D: Okay. Now that I am aware of this, will these problems with my legs go away? I am really suffering with this.

HS: But you are already feeling better!

D: I am, but not completely well. Can you tell me how I can get completely cured? (I felt embarrassed since in the past few months I had indeed seen improvement. I felt like a child caught lying!)

HS: It will go away in good time.

This conversation on my development and personal issues carried on for a while. In this book, I will only refer to parts of the transcripts relating to my learnings, in order to explain how my Higher Self guided me in writing this book.

The soul colour can vary, depending on the level of evolution and the spiritual path of a person. For more information relating to soul colours, an excellent reference is Dr. Michael Newton's book *Destiny of Souls* (R19). This book will provide clarity and understanding regarding this concept.

It is important to understand that an *'evolved'* soul does not mean an enlightened soul. There are millions of evolved souls on earth. An evolved soul is one that has progressed and is closer to the end of their *'education'*. To provide an educational analogy, this is comparable to a student who has completed his/her secondary education but who still needs to carry out undergraduate and postgraduate university studies.

Higher Self, Your Spiritual Extension

The Higher Self is an extension of the individual; each one of us has a Higher Self. The soul is essentially a quantity of energy that is too large to be accommodated in the physical body. A fraction of the soul, therefore, reincarnates and the rest of the soul remains on the spirit side, monitoring and guiding the reincarnated part of the soul through its journey. This is illustrated in Figure 1.

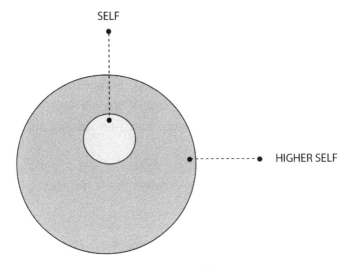

Figure 1: Higher Self Analogy

Higher selves have their own personalities, just like us. Some of them are strict and borderline rude, while others are funny or serious. They can come out with comments such as: "She is lazy!", "He is a slow learner", "She lacks empathy", "He is arrogant", "She needs to be humble".

Our higher selves want the best for us and are only interested in our spiritual development. At the same time, they want us to be happy and enjoy our experience in this earthly school. They may say things, which leads to the need to negotiate with them.

Our higher selves have access to our past lives and all information about us. They have access to the 'akashic' records, the universal 'database' where all our knowledge, memories and experiences are stored. Think of this as comparable to the Cloud we use to back up our computer data. I learnt, during my studies and work, that the spirit side is very sophisticated and complex.

Higher selves are not allowed to interfere with our free will. They are also monitored by other beings of higher vibration, within a *'hierarchy'* of sorts on the spirit side.

As an example of this hierarchy, my Higher Self once referred to *"two higher bodies in this room"*, meaning we were not alone, and our conversation was being monitored. Sometimes when I ask a question, they might say that they cannot answer - not because they don't want to but because in that instance they are not allowed to.

Our higher selves never leave us. When we get a hunch or a gut feeling, this is them guiding us. Always put some trust in your gut feelings.

In a religious context, there is no concept of The Higher Self in Christianity; it is not mentioned anywhere in the Bible.

The Buddha rejected the concept of The Higher Self since Buddhism is based on the concept of Anatta or *'non-self'*, the principle of impermanence, meaning that there is no underlying substance called the soul.

The concept of Higher Self is associated with Hinduism. Atman, meaning *'self'*, is the Inner Self, the Soul. (आत्मन्) which is eternal, omnipotent and intelligent. Atman is our true, Divine Self, the highest part of our being.

In the Bhagavad Gita (G2), Krishna says to Arjuna:

> *As space, though present everywhere, remains by reason of its subtlety unaffected, so the Self, though present in all forms, retains its purity unalloyed. (Bhagavad Gita 13:33)*

In the passage above, Krishna explains the relationship of the Higher Self with our Physical Self, the Ego.

Upon reviewing the first draft of this book, I was concerned that the reader may not fully understand the concept of Higher Self. When I was talking to my Higher Self, I asked if my interpretation of this concept was accurate. The response was as follows:

> *You can elaborate a little more. Think about it as a source of energy. Imagine that you have an electrical device; for this to work you need a source of energy and this comes from the electricity network that you access via a wall socket that you connect the device's plug to. You are the device, and your Higher Self is the infinite source of energy.*

I hope the above explanation helps to better understand this concept.

• CHAPTER 2 •

Introduction to Spirituality

What is Spirituality?

In recent years spirituality has become an *'in'* concept. I hear people say, *"I have become more spiritual"*. But what is spirituality? Is your and my understanding of the meaning of spirituality the same? Perhaps not. People define the meaning of *'spirituality'* to suit their own beliefs and perceptions.

Spirituality is a process which turns the person *'inside out'*, acting with the *'spirit'* rather than the physical body. The soul is entrapped in the physical body. Our physical needs are keeping us completely focused on our physical form. Consumerism and materialism have become a burden to our spirituality. We are bombarded with thousands of commercials each day and we want, want, want. In other parts of the book I have written about how Eastern religions use yoga and meditation for spiritual growth. In Western society it is very common, and I could say fashionable, to practice yoga and meditation. Yoga and meditation alone does not lead to spiritual growth.

Religion was created by man, for the purpose of helping us achieve our goal of reaching Heaven, Nirvana (G11), the Source, or whatever else our respective religions call it. Jesus, Krishna and the Buddha did not create Christianity, Hinduism and Buddhism. The great masters were teachers. They were teaching the path of enlightenment to their disciples, and their disciples were to continue their work after they moved back to the spirit side.

Religion may have started with good intentions. I can only speak for Christianity, the religion I was born into. There are many people, myself included, who have become disillusioned with the present day Christian Church. In its current form (with varying degrees depending on the denomination) the institution has become a forum for liturgies, sermons, services such as Holy Communion, weddings, funerals, baptisms (See Glossary - G1) and other such services, and has moved away from its original purpose of providing spiritual guidance.

In my country the service is delivered in ancient Greek, which, for someone who has not studied it, is like any other foreign language; not easy to understand. It has been two thousand years since Jesus's ascension, and the Greek Orthodox Church is yet to translate the Bible into a language that the majority of people understand. Even though there are modern Greek translations in existence, the Church is still using the ancient Greek scriptures. Its defence is that the translation would alter the meaning of the scriptures. This may be true; however, the Greek New Testament is already a translation from the original Aramaic, which Jesus and his disciples spoke. In different parts of this book, I will provide examples of translation discrepancies. The original Old Testament was written in Hebrew. The English version of the Bible has gone the opposite way. Approximately 450 versions exist today. You can imagine the translation discrepancies, especially translating from a language that is no longer commonly used, ancient Greek. The first translation of the Bible into English was attempted by William Tyndale in the early 16th century, who worked from ancient Greek and Hebrew texts. This did not end well for him; his work was condemned and banned by the Church and the translated copies were set on fire. Tyndale himself was accused of mistranslating the texts in order to promote anticlericalism and heretical views, and was tried and executed.

While I am sure that the majority of priests are kind-hearted people, who are driven to priesthood for the right reasons, and truly live and breathe the true teachings of Jesus, it is natural that there will be exceptions. To become a priest, a pujari, a brahmana, or the equivalent in any religion is a significant responsibility. The primary commitment should be to help the people to move to a new spiritual level. Mechanically going through the motions of only providing services, sermons and liturgies does not help anyone. The religious representative should be out among the people, feeding the poor, visiting people in prisons, and actively promoting love and forgiveness.

> *For I was hungry, and you gave Me food; I was thirsty and you gave Me drink; I was a stranger and you took Me in; I was naked and you clothed Me; I was sick and you visited Me; I was in prison and you came to Me. (Matthew 25:35-36)*

This is what Jesus wants from all of us, especially from the clergy, who need to lead by example and spread the message of *love and forgiveness.*

In recent years in the Western world, we have seen an increasing number of people turning to Hinduism, Buddhism, and other Eastern religions. What is driving this attraction to the East? Why is Christianity losing ground? Is there any evidence of attempts to re-interpret Buddhism and Hinduism, in the same way that the early Christian Church did with the teachings of Jesus? For example, Jesus was from the Middle East and unlikely to have been blonde and blue-eyed, whereas religious icons show Jesus with typical Middle Eastern features, Hollywood movies and western literature portray him as light-skinned, blonde, and blue-eyed.

The Triangle of Hinduism, Buddhism and Christianity

In this book, I use the *'triangle'* of the three religions - Hinduism, Buddhism and Christianity. It would be very difficult to draw comparisons with more religions, and the added complexity will not significantly add to the intent of this book and may even create confusion. The triangle I have drawn in Figure 2 is a very simple graphical representation of what these three religions offer to our spirituality.

I believe that a combination of the teachings of the great masters from these three religions will accelerate our spiritual growth. I was told by my Higher Self that I have to bring the religions together but at the same time provide the facts. When I was discussing my ideas about the book with my Higher Self I asked if criticising the Christian Church in my book would be wrong? My Higher Self said:

> *It's not wrong. It's not the first time you have done this.*
> *Five hundred years ago, you were persecuted for the*
> *same reason. You rubbed their noses the wrong way!*

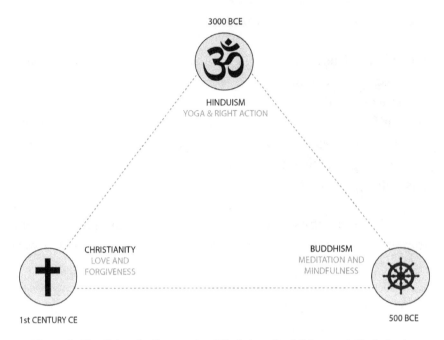

Figure 2: The Triangle Connecting Hinduism, Buddhism and Christianity

Note: The religions were placed based on the age of the religion.

Apparently, I had another painful death in that life. My Higher Self refused to give me details this time. I was told that when the time is right, I will be given more details. I was advised to be *"more diplomatic"* when writing this book, and not to repeat the mistakes of five hundred years ago. This book is not intended to insult the Christian Church. Religious institutions have a critical role to play in our spiritual development but need to change the focus from ceremony to genuine practice, and this is a key message of this book.

All religions were formed to help people progress spiritually. Hinduism is the oldest of the three religions, and for thousands of years has advanced knowledge of the metaphysical side of our existence, which has been recorded in great detail. Religion is not only theology and philosophy; it is also science. During my research, I discovered the teachings of Sri Yukteswar Giri, in his book *Holy*

Science (R2), originally published in 1894. He was the Guru of Paramhansa Yogananda, the author of *The Autobiography of a Yogi* (R3).

In the introduction of this book Sri Yukteswar Giri begins with the following:

> *The purpose of this book is to show as clearly as possible that there is an essential unity in all religions; that there is no difference in the truths inculcated by the various faiths; that there is but one method by which the world, both external and internal, has evolved; and that there is but one Goal admitted by all scriptures. But this basic truth is one not easily comprehended. The discord existing between the different religions and ignorance of men, make it almost impossible to lift the veil and have a look at this grand verity. The creeds foster a spirit of hostility and dissension; ignorance widens the gulf that separates one creed from another. Only a few specially gifted persons can rise superior to the influence of their professed creeds and find absolute unanimity in the truths propagated by all great faiths.*

Sri Yukteswar Giri compared passages from Hindu and Christian scriptures. He did so in a scientific way, by applying to both Hindu and Christian scriptures the metaphysical knowledge that had been recorded thousands of years previously, and using this knowledge as the basis for a scientific discussion.

What is particularly interesting is the graph he inserted in the book (Figure 3 below) with which, in a purely scientific way, he explains the relationship between physical and subtle bodies (G20), and their relationship with the soul. Sri Yukteswar Giri started by quoting the relevant passages from the Sutras (G21) and then providing his reasoning.

He describes how the different elements of both subtle and physical bodies interact with each other, by creating positive and negative electricities and magnetism, which then become neutralised. This process becomes the *'key'* to the soul's liberation from the body and its return back to its Source.

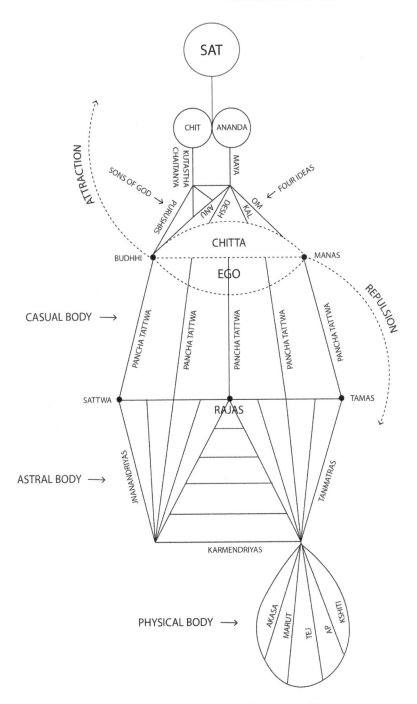

Figure 3: Holy Science by Sri Yukteswar Giri

A simplified, non-scientific way of explaining this concept is included in Chapter 8.

The extract below provides an example of Sri Yukteswar Giri's writings. You are not alone if you find this complicated and incomprehensible; I also initially struggled with it, but with some effort I understood the general principle. Those amongst you with more scientific minds, might have a clearer perspective.

> *The Atom, under the influence of 'Chit' ('universal knowledge') forms the 'Chitta' or the 'calm state of mind', which when spiritualised is called 'Buddhi', 'Intelligence'. Its opposite is 'Manas', 'Mind', in which lives the 'Jiva', 'the self', with 'Ahamkara', 'Ego', the idea of separate existence.*

> *Chitta, the spiritualised Atom, in which Ahamkara (the idea of separate existence of Self) appears, has five manifestations (aura electricities). They (the five aura electricities) constitute the causal body or Purusha. The five electricities, 'Pancha Tattwa', from their attributes, 'Gunas' – 'Sattwa' (positive), 'Rajas' (neutralised), and 'Tamas' (negative) produce 'Jnanandriyas' (organs of sense), 'Karmendriyas' (organs of action), and 'Tanmatras' (objects of sense). These fifteen attributes plus Mind and Intelligence constitute the seventeen 'fine limbs' of the subtle body, the 'Lingasariya'.*

> *The aforesaid five objects which are the negative, attributes of the five electricities, being combined produce the idea of gross matter in its five forms: 'Kshiti', solids; 'Ap', liquids; 'Tehas', fire, 'Marut', gaseous substances, and 'Akasa', ether.*

These five forms of gross matter and the aforesaid fifteen attributes, together with Manas, Mind, sense consciousness; Buddhi, discriminatory Intelligence; Chitta, The Heart or power of feeling; and Ahamkara, the Ego, constitute the twenty-four principles of creation.

This is the scientific explanation and would therefore be easier to grasp by those with knowledge of the scientific principles involved. Such scientifically minded readers would greatly benefit from reading Sri Yukteswar Giri's book.

Krishna's Path to Enlightenment

Krishna, according to Hindu tradition, was born more than 3000 years before Jesus and 2500 years before the Buddha. He is depicted as a blue-skinned man with a flute. Krishna befriended a prince called Arjuna and became his counsel; the Bhagavad Gita is a record of their philosophical discussions, in much the same way as the Christian gospels define the philosophical basis of Christianity. Bhagavad Gita is the holy book of the Hindus. Hinduism has several religious figures and scriptures; however, for the purposes of this book, I will be mainly referring to the Bhagavad Gita and the teachings of Krishna.

When Paramhansa Yogananda, the author of *The Autobiography of a Yogi,* moved to the United States in 1920, he was on a mission to spread Kriya Yoga to the west. Yogananda not only succeeded in achieving this goal but he also developed a powerful correlation between Christianity and Hinduism in his autobiography and in the subsequent publication of his two-volume 1700-page book *The Second Coming of Christ* (R8). His excellent interpretation of the New Testament and its parallels with The Bhagavad Gita and other Hindu religious scriptures, is a literary masterpiece. While reading these books I could not help but reflect on the fact that I was being taught Christianity, my religion from birth, by a Hindu. Not in my wildest dreams did I ever think this possible. I felt humbled and grateful; perhaps without Yogananda's insightful knowledge, I would not have considered going down the path which led me to writing this book.

Paramhansa Yogananda, by spreading Kriya Yoga to the west, wanted to give the Western World another *'path'* to spirituality. He had no intention of replacing Christianity and the teachings of Jesus. He wanted people to understand that Jesus has given us a path and complimenting the teachings of Jesus with Kriya Yoga would accelerate that path to enlightenment.

Understanding the True Meaning of Yoga

So, what is yoga? Is it a type of exercise? Not quite. Everyone's purpose in life is to reach enlightenment, regardless of the religion each of us follow. This even applies to those of us who don't believe in any religion. In Hinduism, yoga is the path to enlightenment. By becoming enlightened, the individual breaks the cycle of death and rebirth, which we call reincarnation, and is not required to be born again.

Yoga is an ancient belief system from India which dates back to around 3000 BCE. It is a discipline intended to accelerate the spiritual development of the individual. The word Yoga (Sanskrit: योग) is derived from the Sanskrit (G18) root *'Yuj'*, meaning *'to join'* or *'to unite'*. As per the Yogic scriptures, the practice of yoga leads to the *union* of the individual consciousness with that of the Universal Consciousness.

The spiritual process, depending on the type of yoga, may include *'asanas'* (various physical poses), *'pranayamas'* (breath control), *'mantras'* (sacred sounds), *'mudras'* (meaning *'seal'* or *'gesture'*), and meditation. Yoga is not a form of exercise. It's a scientific spiritual process which leads to enlightenment.

In the West, there are hundreds of different types of modern yoga which are primarily used for fitness purposes. Even though yoga is an excellent means of exercise (we will discuss its benefits at a later stage), this predominant focus on physical fitness ignores the spiritual aspects and does not lead to spiritual growth. Meditation is another practice that has become popular in modern western society, but as with the Western application of yoga, meditation alone will not lead to spiritual growth. Yogis live a monastic life for twenty or more years in order to achieve enlightenment.

Hinduism is not only about yoga. Krishna has provided Three Paths in the Bhagavad Gita.

The Path of Action – Karma Yoga

> *O Arjuna! All honour to him whose mind controls his senses, for he is thereby beginning to practise Karma-Yoga, the Path of Right Action, keeping himself always unattached. (Bhagavad Gita 3:7)*

The spiritual seeker should practice 'selfless action' for the benefit of others, and totally devote himself or herself to helping others without any personal motives.

The Path of Wisdom – Dnyana Yoga

> *There is nothing in the world so purifying as wisdom; and he who is a perfect saint finds that at last in his own Self. He who is full of faith attains wisdom, and he too who can control his senses, having attained*

that wisdom, he shall ere long attain Supreme Peace.
(Bhagavad Gita 4:38-39)

This is the path of achieving enlightenment through knowledge. Working with his or her Guru, the seeker obtains knowledge about the true nature of our existence.

The Path of Love – Bhakti Yoga

But if thou canst not fix thy mind firmly on Me, then, My beloved friend, try to do so by constant practice. And if thou are not strong enough to practice concentration, then devote thyself to My service, do all thine acts for My sake, and thou shalt still attain the goal. (Bhagavad Gita 12:9-10)

This path requires the devotee to show absolute love and devotion to God. This should be done through meditation. Krishna also explains that this might be difficult for some people who are not able to fully meditate. He stresses that if seekers act according to his teachings, they will still reach enlightenment.

This is what Krishna means when he says, *"devote thyself to My service, do all thine acts for My sake, and thou shalt still attain the goal".*

The Bhagavad Gita is full of examples referring to principles and behaviours associated with devotion, eventually leading to enlightenment. Some are included below:

Desire, aversion, pleasure, pain, sympathy, vitality and the persistent clinging to life, these are in brief the constituents of changing Matter. Humility, sincerity, harmlessness, forgiveness, rectitude, service of the Master, purity, steadfastness, self-control;

Renunciation of the delights of sense, absence of pride, right understanding of the painful problem of birth and death, of age and sickness; Indifference, non-attachment to sex, progeny or home, equanimity in good fortune and in bad. (Bhagavad Gita 13:7-10)

Fearlessness, clean living, unceasing concentration on wisdom, readiness to give, self-control, a spirit of sacrifice, regular study of the scriptures, austerities, candour, harmlessness, truth, absence of wrath, renunciation, contentment, straightforwardness, compassion towards all, uncovetousness, courtesy, modesty, constancy, valour, forgiveness, fortitude, purity, freedom from hate and vanity; these are his who possesses the Godly Qualities, O Arjuna! Hypocrisy, pride, insolence, cruelty, ignorance belongs to him who is born of the godless qualities. Godly qualities lead to liberation; godless to bondage. Do not be anxious, Prince! Thou hast the Godly qualities. (Bhagavad Gita 16:1:6)

Speech that hurts no one, that is true, is pleasant to listen to and beneficial, and the constant study of the scriptures – this is austerity in speech. Serenity, kindness, silence, self-control, and purity – this is austerity of mind. (Bhagavad Gita 17:15-16)

Serenity, self-restraint, austerity, purity, forgiveness, as well as uprightness, knowledge, wisdom and faith in God – these constitute the duty of a spiritual Teacher. (Bhagavad Gita 18:42)

Therefore, we should not mistake Hinduism as a religion based purely on yoga. In the three passages above Krishna describes the qualities a person should possess to become enlightened. The references above, from Bhagavad Gita, are comparable with the teachings of Jesus and the Buddha. The three religions complement each other by the common messaging from their respective teachings.

Jesus's Path to Enlightenment

In Christianity, the path to Heaven is through living a moral and ethical life and following the ten commandments given to Moses by God.

Prior to studying Jesus's path to enlightenment, it is important to understand the Christian view of the concept of Salvation. Salvation is what in Hinduism and Buddhism is referred to as 'Liberation'.

The narrative of the Christian Church that Jesus died on the Cross for our salvation, is widely misunderstood. Jesus's Jewish name was Yeshua, which means *'salvation'.* Yes, Jesus died for our salvation, but his purpose was not to *'erase'* human sin or our karmas. Jesus had come to show us the way. At no time during his teachings did he say that his mission or goal was atonement for human sin. The four examples below are well-known passages from the New Testament and illustrate how Jesus's teachings could be misunderstood:

> *I am the light of the world. Whoever follows me will never walk in darkness but will have the light of life. (John 8:12)*

> *I am the bread of life. Whoever comes to me will never go hungry, and whoever believes in me will never be thirsty. (John 6:35)*

> *I am the good shepherd. The good shepherd lays down his life for the sheep. (John 10:11)*

> *I am the door. If anyone enters by me, he will be saved*
> *and will go in and out and find pasture. (John 10:9)*

In the above passages, Jesus describes the purpose of his incarnation. Jesus tells us that he has come to show us the way through darkness, to show us the way like a good shepherd who safely guides his sheep back to the farm. When Jesus said that he was the bread of life, he was referring to his message of *Love*, and those that understood his message would be spiritually fulfilled. Wisdom is the food of the soul; bread is the food of the physical body.

Jesus's death on the Cross was more than Salvation. It has given us three key teachings.

Jesus's First Teaching: Rebirth

Through his death and *'resurrection'*, or return of his soul to the physical body, Jesus wanted to demonstrate that it was possible for the soul to return and be reincarnated. In his case, it was the same body, but in almost all other cases of reincarnation, the soul returns into a new body to continue its learning. This can be compared to going to school. Students progress to a new grade if they have learnt their lessons or remain in the same grade if they have not. In this way, we all continue the cycle of death and rebirth until *'graduation day'*, when we have achieved all the learning that is required of us and don't have to return. Once a person reaches the highest level of spirituality or enlightenment, they can come back as volunteers, or return on a *'mission'*, in the same way as Jesus was sent to bring the message of love and show us the way through *'darkness'*. The passage below confirms that Jesus was sent on a mission:

> *Therefore, the disciples said to one another, "Has*
> *anyone brought Him anything to eat?" Jesus said to*
> *them, "My food is to do the will of Him who sent Me,*
> *and to finish His work." (John 4:33-34)*

There are many such examples in the New Testament of Jesus confirming that he was on a mission. He had become enlightened in previous reincarnations and was sent to do *'His work'*.

Jesus's Second Teaching: Divine Love

Jesus suffered a horrific and painful death to teach us ultimate Love. His crucifixion was prophesied. He was on a mission knowing that he would die a painful death. Jesus had a choice. He could have avoided death by giving up on his mission but chose not to and proceeded to the end. To die for what you believe in for those you love is the ultimate sacrifice.

Jesus's Third Teaching: Forgiveness

> *Father, forgive them, for they do not know what they do. (Luke 23:34)*

Isn't this the ultimate message of forgiveness? Jesus is asking God to forgive those who crucified him. They are in *darkness*. They don't know what they are doing. Then how do we judge those who commit crimes if they do not know what they are doing?

In March 2019, a man called Farid Ahmed lost his wife in the terrorist attack on the mosque in Christchurch, New Zealand. He chose to forgive the gunman.

> *I don't want to have a heart that is boiling like a volcano. A volcano has anger, fury, rage. It doesn't have peace. It has hatred. It burns itself within, and also it burns the surroundings. I don't want to have a heart like this.*

Ahmed understood that forgiveness is not about cutting loose the person that hurt you. He or she will have to learn from their mistakes, either in this life or in another. Ahmed understood that forgiveness is liberation of the soul, whereas hate is like a *'volcano'* that burns from the inside and does not allow the individual to find peace. What a wise man.

> *And whenever you stand praying, if you have anything against anyone, forgive him, that your Father in heaven may also forgive you your trespasses. But if you do not forgive, neither will your Father in heaven forgive your trespasses. (Mark 11:25-26)*

The passage above is explicit. When we are forgiving others, God forgives us. We cannot expect forgiveness when we are not able to forgive others.

Forgiveness and repentance play a central role in Jesus's path of enlightenment. We must learn to forgive others if we want to be forgiven.

Sins or karmas are not set in stone forever. They can be forgiven when the person learns from his or her mistakes. However, we cannot ask for forgiveness unless we have forgiven all the people that have wronged us. This is the key, otherwise we are carrying karmas from one life to another.

Detachment from Physical Needs

Another key element of Jesus's teachings is concerned with detachment from physical needs. Such detachment is ever more difficult in the 21st century when consumerism and materialism are ingrained in our daily lives. Detachment from physical needs usually takes place in the last phase of enlightenment. People in this phase naturally withdraw from life and disengage from *'things'* and dependence on other people.

> *Assuredly, I say to you that it is hard for a rich man to enter the kingdom of heaven. And again, I say to you, it is easier for a camel to go through the eye of a needle than for a rich man to enter the kingdom of God. (Matthew 19:23-24)*

For anyone who is unaware or does not believe in reincarnation or the link with Jesus's teachings, the passage above would appear harsh and rather rigid. While Jesus was teaching, a rich man told him that he was a good man because he followed the ten commandments and always helped others. Jesus told him that if he wanted to become enlightened in this life, he should sell all his belongings or distribute them to the poor, the message being that one cannot become enlightened while clinging to physical needs. The soul can only be liberated when it returns to its original state and the physical entity, the ego, has completely detached from physical needs. This is not easy for an average soul that is still working though their karmas, because complete detachment from physical needs is achieved in the last stage of enlightenment, after relevant karmas have been cleared in previous lives. Monks and yogis make a conscious decision to completely detach themselves from their physical needs. It comes to them naturally because they are in the last stages before enlightenment.

Another inference from the above statement is that wealthy individuals who manage businesses or are in positions of great responsibility, may consider themselves good people because they perceive that they treat their employees fairly and compassionately. However, sometimes to please executive management or shareholders they may have to make decisions that are not completely ethical. It does not mean that a rich person cannot eventually achieve enlightenment, just not in this life. Souls make their own decisions before reincarnating - where to be born, in which family, which country, which religion, which race, and so on. A rich person in this life may choose a less privileged life in the next incarnation in order to progress further spiritually.

My Higher Self said:

> *When the physical body dies, the soul goes into a community* (I interpret this as the spirit side) *to prepare for the next incarnation. Souls work in groups; they agree between themselves and they decide where and how to be born in the next incarnation.*

All souls will reach enlightenment, without exception. Some are fast learners and *'graduate'* faster, while others are slower learners and will take longer to complete their earthly education. Jesus spelled out the behaviours needed to achieve enlightenment; these will be covered in the coming chapters.

Buddha's Path to Enlightenment

The Buddha (meaning *'the enlightened one'*) lived some 500 or so years before Jesus. His name was Siddhartha Gautama, and he was born into a royal family in what is now Nepal. According to religious scriptures, Siddhartha was moved by the suffering he saw during one of his excursions among the common people, and even though he was married and had a child, at the age of 29 he left the palace and became a monk. The Buddha become enlightened at the age of 35 and died at the age of 80; he spent 45 years teaching the way to enlightenment.

In Buddhism, similar to Hinduism, the aim is to achieve Nirvana, the equivalent to the Christian Heaven.

In his book *Living Buddha, Living Christ* (R4), Thich Nhat Hahn, a Zen Buddhism religious leader, compares Buddhism and Christianity and highlights their similarities and common aims. I mentioned earlier in this book how humbled I am to have learnt so much about the teachings of Jesus from non-Christians.

In his book *The Heart of the Buddha's Teachings* (R5), Thich Nhat Hahn outlines the Buddhist path to enlightenment. He describes a conversation between the Buddha and a king:

> *One day when he was thirty-eight years old, the Buddha met King Prasenajit of Kosala. The king said, "Reverend, you are young, yet people call you 'The Highest Enlightened One'. There are holy men in our country eighty and ninety years old, venerated by many people yet none of them claims to be the highest enlightened one. How can a young man like you make such a claim?"*
>
> *The Buddha replied, "Your majesty, enlightenment is not a matter of age. A tiny spark of fire has the power to burn down the whole city. A small poisonous snake can kill you in an instant. A baby prince has the potentiality of a king. And a young monk has the capacity of becoming enlightened and changing the world."*

All souls are made equal, but some souls learn faster than others. There are people amongst us that are enlightened. Some people choose to accelerate their spiritual journeys by withdrawing from life and detaching from physical needs. Not all enlightened people are in monasteries, and not all people in monasteries are enlightened. Monastic life does not guarantee enlightenment. One must clear their karmas first. Similarly, there are people living amongst us that are aware they have reached enlightenment but are too humble to talk about it.

The person who serves you in a supermarket or restaurant, or perhaps even a very young child, may already be enlightened and living their final life on this planet. An enlightened person does not need to look and talk like a guru.

The Buddha's teachings are primarily centred on the suffering caused by desire. The Buddha taught that to achieve enlightenment we have to let go of all desires, physical and mental. As described previously for Hinduism and Christianity, physical detachment is usually experienced during the last stage prior to attaining Nirvana. Detachment from mental desires gradually progresses during the various incarnations. This will be described in detail in the coming chapters.

When the Buddha became enlightened, he made the following declaration:

> *Dear friends, with humans, gods, brahmans, monastics, and maras as witnesses, I tell you that if I have not experienced directly all that I have told you, I would not proclaim that I am an enlightened person, free from suffering. Because I myself, identified the causes of suffering, removed the causes of suffering, confirmed the existence of well-being obtained well-being, identified the path to well-being, have gone to the end of the path, and realised total liberation. I now proclaim to you that I am a free person.*

When one becomes enlightened their suffering ends because they have detached themselves from their physical and mental desires. This is self-evident from our own life experiences; the more we are attached to our needs and wants, the more pain and suffering we cause ourselves. Enlightened individuals do not envy people living a *'normal'* life. They pity them because they understand that a *'normal'* life is one of suffering.

The Buddha offered the Four Noble Truths which lead to the Eightfold Path (Figure 4), to help us let go of all our suffering and reach enlightenment. The Buddha left the comfort of the palace and lived in austerity for the rest of his life. This action may appear extreme to most people, but for him it was the right path to exchange his comfortable life and leave behind his wife and child. He was already living his last life on earth. It did not mean that he did not love his family, but he had no need to cling to people, physical desires, or a comfortable life. For him it was the natural action to take, as it is for monks and nuns who leave behind society as we know it to live a simple life separated from other people.

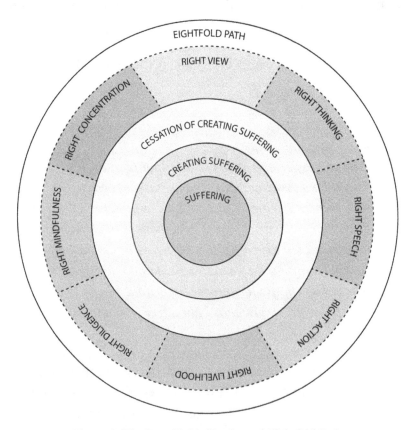

Figure 4: The Four Noble Truths and Eightfold Path

The Four Noble Truths

These relate to our suffering as follows:

1. **Dukkha** – Suffering. This is the state where people cling onto physical needs and are living a life of suffering.
2. **Samudava** – Creating Suffering. In this phase, the person identifies the root cause of suffering.
3. **Nirodha** – Cessation of Creating Suffering. In this phase, the person ceases actions that cause suffering.
4. **Marga** – the Eightfold Path to end suffering.

The Eightfold Path

The Eightfold Path to end suffering is the centrepiece of Buddhism.

1. **Right View:** The ability to distinguish wrong from right and understand that our actions have consequences.
2. **Right Thinking:** Our thoughts are the beginning of our suffering. Thinking leads to action and suffering.
3. **Right Mindfulness:** The heart of the Buddha's teachings. Be present. Clinging to the past and being buried in our thoughts keeps wounds open and prolongs our suffering.
4. **Right Speech:** Suffering caused by unmindful speech. We sometimes open our mouths and say things that hurt others but also cause us to suffer from our guilt.
5. **Right Action:** Not harming oneself or others; promoting non-violence.
6. **Right Diligence or Right Effort:** Not being consumed by physical possessions, food, sex, wealth, and other pleasures.
7. **Right Concentration:** The mind focuses on what is happening in the present moment.
8. **Right Livelihood:** Earning an honest living and exhibiting ethical and compassionate behaviours.

The Four Noble Truths and the Eightfold Path are at the heart of Buddhism, but these are not the only teachings of the Buddha. His teachings are detailed further in this book, and the similarities and linkages between the three religions will start to become clearer.

CHAPTER 3

The Institution of the Church

The Church

Throughout my life, I have experienced resentment towards Christianity from a wide variety of people, from close family and friends to casual acquaintances. For a long time, I could not understand where this resentment was coming from. In my mind, Jesus was preaching *love and forgiveness,* and how could anyone find fault with this pure message? However, I had not read the Bible fully, nor did I understand its deeper meaning. My knowledge came from what I was taught at school. My spiritual journey became more focused after speaking to my Higher Self, and this was when I started reading the scriptures of different religions, to develop an objective, unbiased view of the religion of my birth, and its relationship to other belief systems.

As I explained earlier in this book, it would have been a struggle reading the ancient Greek Bible. I placed the English New King James Bible and the ancient Greek version side by side and started reading both together, at the same time referring to translations of Aramaic and Hebrew versions when I needed to clarify points of uncertainty. I have also read many other theological texts from early Christianity and have approached Christianity not only from a theological perspective but also from a historical one.

So, what is the Church?

Ekklesia or Εκκλησία is a Greek word that literally means *'to call out'* or *'to bring together'* people in an *'assembly'*, which is a translation of the Hebrew word להק (qahal or synagogue). The English word *'church'* also derives from a Greek word, *'kyriakon'*, literally *'the House of the Lord'*.

After a turbulent beginning and a three-hundred-year period of persecution of Christians, in 313 CE Christianity was legalised across the Roman Empire by Constantine I, also known as Constantine the Great. Constantine himself converted to Christianity and formed the hierarchical institution of the Church. After his death, he and his mother Helena were canonised and proclaimed Saints.

Jesus had not intended for a religious organisation with a defined hierarchy to be created. It is very clear from his words that Jesus asked his disciples to travel and spread the message of love and forgiveness, and to continue his work of guiding souls *'out of darkness'*. The following passage provides evidence of his intent:

> *And He said to them, "Go into all the world and preach the gospel to every creature". (Mark 16:15)*

Saint Paul, in the following New Testament passage, explains that our body is the temple of the soul. We don't require physical man-made structures.

> *Do you not know that you are the temple of God and that the Spirit of God dwells in you? (1 Corinthians: 3:16)*

> *God, who made the world and everything in it, since He is Lord of heaven and earth, does not dwell in temples made with hands. Nor is He worshiped with*

*men's hands, as though He needed anything, since He
gives to all life, breath, and all things. (Acts 17:24-25)*

Our body is the temple of the soul. God resides within us and we do
not require temples or churches to communicate with Him.

The Bible

The Bible consists of two parts - the Old and the New Testament.
The Old Testament contains the religious scriptures written before
Jesus, and the New Testament is made up of the scriptures written
after his arrival on earth.

The Old Testament scriptures were written by prophets, who lived
well before the time of Jesus. It consists of the first five books of the
Pentateuch (Genesis, Exodus, Leviticus, Numbers and Deuteronomy),
and the books written by various prophets including Isaiah, Jeremiah,
Ezekiel and others. It also includes The Wisdom Books, such as the
Book of Job, the Book of Proverbs, Ecclesiastes, Psalms, and the
Song of Solomon.

The New Testament is the second part of the Bible with Jesus as
the central figure. It includes the four Gospels, written by Matthew,
Mark, Luke and John. The Gospels are stories around the life and
teachings of Jesus. Other New Testament texts include the Acts of
the Apostles, which describes the founding of the Christian Church
and its spread across the Roman Empire, the Epistles of Saint Paul
(letters attributed to Saint Paul) and the last book of the Revelation,
or Apocalypse (from the Greek meaning *'unveiling'*). This book is
an apocalyptic document written by Saint John which has attracted
much scepticism over the years because it is written in riddles and is
difficult to understand.

The Old Testament was originally written in Hebrew. The New
Testament was written in ancient Greek, although some scholars

insist that it was originally written in Aramaic, the language spoken by Jesus, while other scholars argue that it was written in Hebrew. The fact is that Jesus taught in Aramaic and was fluent in Hebrew, which was necessary for those who taught in the temple.

I have always wondered what has gone wrong with Christianity. Why are so many people turning their backs on the Christian Church? Why do so many people find solace in other religions, such as Buddhism and Hinduism?

It was a subject I always avoided in the past. I became irritated when I heard people blaming Jesus for the ills of the Church. I was not able to understand how the message of *love and forgiveness* has turned into two thousand years of monstrous abuse and bloodshed. With the creation of the inquisition, thousands of people considered as heretics were tortured and executed. Similarly, the Crusades were responsible for the deaths of 1.7 million people over a two-hundred-year period.

The Inquisition originated in France in the 12th century, to forcibly ensure that the principles of the Catholic Church were strictly adhered to, and to persecute and eliminate deviant beliefs from other Christian sects. The reach of the Inquisition spread from France across Europe and was active wherever the Catholic Church was present, with comparable levels of brutality in every country. The Portuguese and Spanish inquisitions, in addition to operating in their home countries and European possessions, set up inquisitorial courts across their empires in Africa, Asia, and the Americas. This practice lasted for almost seven hundred years and was responsible for thousands of people being tortured and executed, primarily by being burned alive, for practising *'heretical'* variations of Catholicism. If the inquisition existed today, anyone practising reiki, hypnosis and similar healing modalities, would be at risk of being branded heretics, witches or in league with the devil.

The New Testament teachings and message of love and forgiveness were clearly not the reason for these extreme reactions from the Catholic hierarchy. Rather, we should look to the Old Testament and the uncompromising and unforgiving language for dealing with perceived transgressions. Some examples are included below:

> *You shall not permit a sorceress to live. Whoever lies with an animal shall surely be put to death. He who sacrifices to any god, except to the Lord only, he shall be utterly destroyed. (Exodus 22:18-20)*

The above passage leaves no doubt about how those considered to be sorceresses or witches should be dealt with.

> *Then they entered into a covenant to seek the LORD God of their fathers with all their heart and with all their soul; and whoever would not seek the LORD God of Israel was to be put to death, whether small or great, whether man or woman. (2 Chronicles 15:12-13)*

The above Old Testament passage is an example of the religious intolerance towards those who did not believe in the scriptures.

Contrast the rigidity and intolerance of these two passages with New Testament writings and their message of love and forgiveness:

> *You have heard that it was said, 'An eye for an eye and a tooth for a tooth'. But I tell you not to resist an evil person. But whoever slaps you on your right cheek, turn the other to him also. (Matthew 5:38-39)*

Jesus preached non-violence. In the above passage from the Gospel of Matthew, he opposes the Old Testament reference in Exodus 21:24, *"eye for eye, tooth for tooth, hand for hand, foot for foot"*. Jesus believed aggression can be overcome with kindness. In a similar way, war can be avoided through diplomacy, and not by an aggressive approach which would lead to conflict escalation.

For almost two hundred years, from 1095 to 1272, the Crusades, a series of planned military expeditions to the Holy Land, which were initiated by Pope Urban II and directed by the Catholic Church for the purpose of reclaiming the Holy Land from Muslim rule, were responsible for the deaths of an estimated 1.7 million people, more than half a percent of the total estimated global population of 300 million. Such butchery in the name of religion was clearly at odds with the teachings of Jesus:

> *Blessed are the meek, for they shall inherit the earth.*
> *(Matthew 5:5)*

> *Blessed are the peacemakers, for they shall be called*
> *sons of God. (Matthew 5:9)*

> *But Jesus said to him, "Put your sword in its place,*
> *for all who take the sword will perish by the sword".*
> *(Matthew 26:52)*

Jesus clearly advocates peace and meekness. When Jesus says, *"all who take the sword will perish by the sword"*, he is referring to the karmic impact of cause and effect. When one causes pain to another person, it will come back round to him/her, in this life or another, not as a punishment but as a lesson to allow progression along the spiritual journey.

Some Old Testament books not only condone violence, but actually demand it.

> *You shall not sacrifice to the Lord your God an ox or*
> *a sheep in which is a blemish, any defect whatever,*
> *for that is an abomination to the Lord your God. If*
> *there is found among you, within any of your towns*

*that the Lord your God is giving you, a man or woman
who does what is evil in the sight of the Lord your
God, in transgressing his covenant, and has gone
and served other gods and worshiped them, or the
sun or the moon or any of the host of heaven, which
I have forbidden, and it is told you and you hear of
it, then you shall inquire diligently, and if it is true
and certain that such an abomination has been done
in Israel, then you shall bring out to your gates that
man or woman who has done this evil thing, and you
shall stone that man or woman to death with stones.
(Deuteronomy 17:1-5)*

The Old Testament is a source of historical context and one we should not ignore. However, the Christian Church needs to re-evaluate the contradictions between the intolerance of the Old Testament and the message of love and forgiveness of the New Testament. There are Old Testament texts which clearly contradict the message of Jesus and encourage violence. These texts have led to hundreds of years of misery and bloodshed and have associated the message of Jesus, one of love and forgiveness, with intolerance and death. How is it possible for two such extremely different messages to be reconciled in the teachings of one religion?

The passages below provide further examples from the Old Testament, for reflection when assessing these contradictions between the two parts of the Bible.

*Samaria is held guilty, for she has rebelled against
her God. They shall fall by the sword, their infants
shall be dashed in pieces, and their women with child
ripped open. (Hosea 13:16)*

43

Their children also will be dashed to pieces before their eyes; Their houses will be plundered and their wives ravished. (Isaiah 13:16)

When I have cut off your supply of bread, ten women shall bake your bread in one oven, and they shall bring back your bread by weight, and you shall eat and not be satisfied. And after all this, if you do not obey Me, but walk contrary to Me, then I also will walk contrary to you in fury; and I, even I, will chastise you seven times for your sins. You shall eat the flesh of your sons, and you shall eat the flesh of your daughters. (Leviticus 26:26-29)

O daughter of Babylon, who are to be destroyed, Happy the one who repays you as you have served us! Happy the one who takes and dashes Your little ones against the rock! (Psalms 137:8)

*And Moses said to them: "Have you kept all the women alive? Look, these women caused the children of Israel, through the counsel of Balaam, to trespass against the LORD in the incident of Peor, and there was a plague among the congregation of the LORD. Now therefore, kill every male among the little ones, and kill every woman who has known a man intimately. But keep alive for yourselves all the young girls who have not known a man intimately".
(Numbers 31:15-18)*

If a man commits adultery with the wife of his neighbour, both the adulterer and the adulteress shall surely be put to death. (Leviticus 20:10)

If a man is found lying with the wife of another man, both of them shall die, the man who lay with the woman, and the woman. So you shall purge the evil from Israel. (Deuteronomy 22:22)

Then you shall bring them both out to the gate of that city, and you shall stone them to death with stones, the young woman because she did not cry for help though she was in the city, and the man because he violated his neighbour's wife. So you shall purge the evil from your midst. (Deuteronomy 22:24)

That certain worthless fellows have gone out among you and have drawn away the inhabitants of their city, saying, 'Let us go and serve other gods,' which you have not known, then you shall inquire and make search and ask diligently. And behold, if it be true and certain that such an abomination has been done among you, you shall surely put the inhabitants of that city to the sword, devoting it to destruction, all who are in it and its cattle, with the edge of the sword. You shall gather all its spoil into the midst of its open square and burn the city and all its spoil with fire, as a whole burnt offering to the Lord *your God. It shall be a heap forever. It shall not be built again. None of the devoted things shall stick to your hand, that the* Lord *may turn from the fierceness of his anger and show you mercy and have compassion on you and multiply you, as he swore to your fathers. (Deuteronomy 13:13-18)*

The man who acts presumptuously by not obeying the priest who stands to minister there before the Lord *your God, or the judge, that man shall die. So you shall purge the evil from Israel. (Deuteronomy 17:12)*

The Son of God

Another controversy surrounding Christianity is the interpretation of Jesus as the Son of God. Jesus never said that he was the Son of God, but he referred to himself as the Son of Man, and there are numerous instances of this in the New Testament. In his physical state as Jesus, he is the son of Mary and Joseph. In his non-physical, spiritual capacity as the messenger of Love and the Light to show us the way through darkness, he is the Christ. He referred to God as his father, but he never called himself the Son of God.

In Psalms 89:26-28, God, referring to King David, says the following:

> He shall cry to Me, You are my Father, My God, and the rock of my salvation. Also I will make him My firstborn, The highest of the kings of the earth. (Psalms 89:26-27)

The title 'Son of God' was given to Jesus by his disciples. In those days, kings, prophets, and holy men were called Sons of God. Abraham and King David were also referred to as the Sons of God in the Old Testament. This is why Jesus's disciples called him the Son of God; this was a metaphorical reference, not a literal one.

> For God so loved the world that He gave His only **begotten** Son, that whoever believes in Him should not perish but have everlasting life. (John 3:16)

> Οὕτως γὰρ ἠγάπησεν ὁ θεὸς τὸν κόσμον, ὥστε τὸν υἱὸν τὸν **μονογενῆ** ἔδωκεν, ἵνα πᾶς ὁ πιστεύων εἰς αὐτὸν μὴ ἀπόληται ἀλλί ἔχῃ ζωὴν αἰώνιον. (John 3:16)

The English word 'begotten' means 'offspring' which was translated from the Greek word 'monogenes' (μονογενὴς) which has several meanings. It means the only child, or it could mean one of a kind or a special one. In fact, it really makes no difference what it means,

46

but what is likely to have transpired is that the translations from the original Greek version used an alternative interpretation of the word. Jesus never called himself the Son of God.

In various passages in the New Testament, Jesus says that those who achieve the highest level of spirituality will be called Sons of God. This is because, when the soul is liberated from the physical body, it returns and becomes one with God (or *the Source* in Hinduism). This is also the explanation of the following passage:

So God created man in His own image. (Genesis 1:27)

The Soul is a speck of God, pure Love, pure Bliss.

*And we have known and believed the love that God has for us. **God is love**, and he who abides in love abides in God, and God in him. (1 John 4:16)*

In the above New Testament passage Saint Paul, in his Epistle to Saint John said, "*God is Love*". He understood what the soul is and that the path back to God was through Love.

The words *'sons of God'* appear several times in the New Testament, in the context that those who achieve enlightenment will be of the same essence as God.

For you are all sons of God through faith in Christ Jesus. (Galatians 3:26)

Blessed are the peacemakers, for they shall be called sons of God. (Matthew 5:9)

When Jesus appears to Mary Magdalene after his resurrection, he says:

> *Do not cling to Me, for I have not yet ascended to My Father; but go to My brethren and say to them, I am ascending to My Father and your Father, and to My God and your God. (John 20:17)*

Jesus's reference in the above passage to *"My father and your Father, and my God and Your God"* is clear evidence that Jesus was not claiming to be God's only son.

When the disciples asked Jesus how they should pray, he gave them a prayer which starts:

> *In this manner, therefore, pray: "Our Father in heaven, Hallowed be Your name ….....". (Matthew 6:9)*

Why would Jesus give us a prayer that says, *'Our Father'* if he believed he was the only son, and why are there multiple references to sons of God, as opposed to one *'Son of God'*?

Turbulent Times for The Christian Church

Throughout its history, the Christian Church has experienced turbulent times and continues to face challenges.

The intolerance of the Catholic Church towards homosexuality, abortion and divorce, and the rigid stance towards not allowing women and married men to join the clergy has driven people away from the Church.

Some Christian denominations are more flexible towards female clergy, married priests, divorce and abortion. Clearly, there is a lack of consensus in the interpretation of the Bible between the different Christian denominations.

Such differences in the interpretations of the Bible were the main cause of the Great Schism in 1054 (Figure 5). These complex religious disputes resulted in mutual excommunications between the Latin Western and Greek Eastern parts of the Christian Church and caused the division of the Church into two distinct Catholic and Eastern Orthodox Churches.

The Protestant movement began in Germany in 1517 when Martin Luther, a professor of moral theology at the University of Wittenberg, published his *Ninety-Five Theses,* which ultimately led to the separation from the Catholic Church.

In England, King Henry VIII broke away from the Catholic Church and declared himself the head of Church of England in 1534, when Rome refused to allow him to divorce or declare void his marriage to Catherine of Aragon.

There is a multiplicity of Christian denominations such as Baptist, Anglican, Methodist, Presbyterian, Calvinist and many more, which have been founded over the years and exist today.

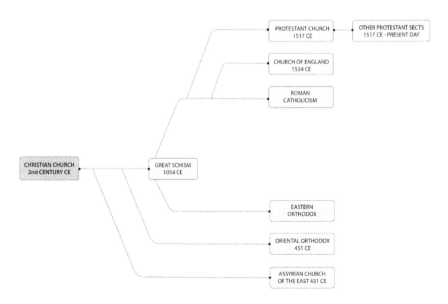

Figure 5: Major Branches of Christianity

The term *'Catholic'* comes from the Greek word καθολικός (*katholikos*) or *'the whole'*, meaning the religion that holds the *'whole truth'*. The Orthodox Church comes from the Greek word ορθοδοξία (*orthodoxia*) which means the *'correct religion'*. The Protestant churches come from the word *'protest'*, in reference to their resistance to the behaviours of the Catholic Church. I question how such names were selected by these Christian groups. They could have been called *'The Church of Love'* or *'The Church of Jesus'*, *'The Church of Liberation'* and so on. It is a rigid and uncompromising stance to reject all other religions and say that any one religion is the *correct one*, or the one that holds the *whole truth*, or the one that *protests* against another.

In his book *Crossing the Threshold of Hope* (R6), Pope John Paul II states that:

> *Christ is absolutely original and absolutely unique. If he were only a wise man like Socrates, if He were a 'prophet' like Mohammed, if He were 'enlightened' like Buddha, without any doubt He would not be what He is. He is the one mediator between God and humanity.*

Thich Nhat Hanh, in his book *Living Buddha, Living Christ*, makes reference to Pope John Paul's statement as follows:

> *This statement does not seem to reflect the deep mystery of the oneness of the Trinity. It also does not reflect the fact that Christ is also the Son of Man. All Christians, while praying to God address Him as Father. Of course, Christ is unique. But who is not unique? Socrates, Mohammed, the Buddha, you, and I are all unique. The idea behind the statement, however, is the notion that Christianity provides the only way of salvation and all other religious traditions*

are of no use. This attitude excludes dialogue and fosters religious intolerance and discrimination. It does not help.

Pope John Paul II tried to bring religions together and travelled more than any other Pope. It is clear from his actions throughout his celebrated life that he had no intention of denigrating or causing a rift with other religions. However, it is also evident that his book was intended for Christian readers and this statement could have been worded differently in a way that better accommodated the beliefs of other religions.

We cannot achieve peace when we take a position that our religion is *'the correct religion'* or the one that holds the *'whole truth'*. We cannot achieve peace when we say that Jesus is superior to Krishna and the Buddha. The above statement resulted in a threat by Sri Lankan Buddhists to boycott Pope John Paul II's 1995 visit to Sri Lanka. The Pope subsequently issued a declaration of his *"profound respect and sincere esteem"* for the Buddhist religion.

Jesus's main message has been greatly diluted. The path to enlightenment offered by Jesus has been lost in mistranslation, inflexibility, and inability to modernise the Church.

Christianisation

During the period of colonisation of the Americas and parts of Africa and Asia by the Spanish and Portuguese, the Catholic Church decreed that colonies were to be Christianised. Christian missionaries were tasked with converting the indigenous populations to Catholicism. They achieved this with varying degrees of success. Thich Nhat Hanh, the Buddhist spiritual leader, bitterly relates how Christian missionaries attempted to convert Asian Buddhists to Christianity.

The Native Americans in particular suffered greatly as a result of colonisation, and indigenous populations were decimated by diseases introduced from Europe. From the 1600s, Christian missionaries were on a mission to convert the native populations to Christianity. The Native Americans were portrayed as uneducated savages and the Europeans as sent by God to save their souls and lead them to a better world. Such attitudes persisted until well into the twentieth century, and are shocking by today's standards; how could anyone believe that Native Americans needed to be converted? They have always been very spiritual people. Does it matter that they don't believe in Jesus the way that Christians do?

Christianisation happened in most of the European colonies, and the peoples of many of today's nations resent Christianity for this reason.

Mother Teresa was once asked whether she was trying to convert people. She replied, *"Yes, I do convert. I convert you to be a better Hindu, a better Christian, and a better Muslim. When you have found God, it's up to you to do with Him what you want."* Does it really matter what religion we belong to? As long as we are loving, compassionate and caring human beings, why does anyone need to be converted to another religion?

A New Enemy for the Church

After centuries of misery and bloodshed in the name of Christianity, the Church has found a new enemy, Science.

Galileo Galilei (1564-1642) was an Italian astronomer, physicist and engineer who invented the pendulum clock, the thermometer, and the telescope.

In the early 17th century, Galileo challenged the Church with his theory that Earth orbited the sun and not the other way round, a theory that was influenced by the writings of the Greek philosopher

Aristotle over two thousand years earlier. In 1615, his theory of heliocentrism was referred to the Roman Inquisition. Galileo was urged *"to abandon completely the opinion that the sun stands still at the centre of the word and the Earth moves, and henceforth not to hold, teach, or defend it in any way whatever, either orally or in writing".*

Galileo refused to comply with the demands of the Church, who claimed that his writings were contrary to the Holy Scriptures. He was sentenced to house arrest and remained so for the rest of his life. It took the Catholic Church nearly 400 years to issue an apology, which was finally made by John Paul II in October 1996.

This was one example of the Church's intolerance to anything that appeared to contradict its rigid interpretation of the scriptures.

From the 16th century onwards, the scientific revolution, followed by the Age of Enlightenment and the industrial revolution, led to a gradual dilution of the power of the Church. The Church continued to oppose many of the scientific developments and theories but were not powerful enough to stop the tide of progress or punish the scientists themselves. They have progressively adopted a more mellow and pragmatic approach, but not without some instances of controversy. In 2009, Pope Benedict, while on a trip to Africa, declared that condoms would worsen the AIDS epidemic. During the Covid-19 epidemic, the Greek Orthodox Church announced that the virus would not be transmitted to believers who participated in the ritual of the Holy Communion. A recent Synod of the Greek Orthodox Church ruled that yoga is not compatible with Christianity: *"Yoga is a fundamental chapter in Hindu religion ... It is not a kind of physical exercise".* Even though they were not wrong about the Western understanding of yoga, why does the Church get involved with opinions about the practices and beliefs of other religions which are followed by many millions of people? Does yoga make people bad? Does yoga disturb our spiritual development? What is the meaning of *'not compatible'*?

Yoga can be very beneficial for spiritual growth if used properly. This is discussed further in Chapter 15.

Starting in the 1960s, the sexual liberation movement further challenged centuries old, entrenched positions taken by the Church. This social movement challenged traditional sexual behaviour, initially in the United States, followed by Europe. The movement aimed to promote sex outside of marriage and to overturn established norms relating to traditionally accepted heterosexual and monogamous relationships, as well as promoting the use of contraception, the right to abortion, and so on.

The Catholic Church's sexual abuse scandals, which first gained attention in the late 1980s, continue to this day. Approximately 1700 priests and other clergy members have been accused of sexual abuse involving thousands of innocent children, and have been largely covered up by the Catholic establishment. In 2001, Pope John Paul II issued an apology to the victims and referred to the abuses as *"a profound contradiction of the teachings and witness of Jesus Christ"*. The apology was long overdue, but the damage was done; decades of abuse and cover-up cannot be erased with an apology. Pope Benedict XVI, Pope John Paul II's successor, was himself accused of covering up the molestation of three boys in Texas. The scandal continues to haunt the Catholic Church to this day. Pope John Paul II promoted Theodore McCarrick to archbishop of Washington D.C. despite reports of sexual abuse. As a result of a lengthy investigation, Pope Frances asked McCarrick to step down.

We need to be careful not to stereotype all priests as sexual predators. The perpetrators are a small percentage of the total priesthood, but large enough to cause pain and lifelong trauma for thousands of individuals who were abused when they were children. Even a single case against one child should have been enough to trigger investigation, remorse and change in the Catholic Church. A vast majority of priests are genuine, well-meaning individuals who are committed to their spiritual calling, but they have lost the trust of the general population because of the inability of the Church to tackle this problem, instead of brushing it *under the carpet'.*

The Catholic Church demands clerical celibacy, and priests are not able to marry or partake in sexual relationships. Jesus did not create the institution of the Church and did not require his disciples and close followers to be unmarried. Celibacy is not a natural human state and the requirement for priests to abstain from marriage and sexual relations is a human creation and not a divine instruction.

The Greek Orthodox Church takes a different approach to the issue of marriage for the priesthood. The Church ordains both married and unmarried priests, however, unmarried priests cannot change their minds and later decide they want to marry. There is no turning back, and if a priest subsequently decides he wants to get married he has to leave the priesthood. Married priests cannot be promoted to the higher ranks of the Church. The Orthodox Church requires Bishops and Archbishops to observe celibacy, therefore only unmarried priests can be promoted to the higher ranks.

The Church must move with the times and consider allowing anyone to join the clergy, irrespective of gender, race, sexual persuasion, or marital status. The most important attribute is the individual's commitment to live by and spread the message of love and forgiveness. Physical characteristics are not relevant when determining a person's suitability to serve in the priesthood; our bodies are nothing more than a vehicle for our souls to progress in their learning.

Monastics who reach the last stage of their spiritual path are able to control their physical needs, because the kundalini energy (explained in Chapter 12) in their spinal cord, has moved from the bottom of the spine, the Root Chakra, towards the Third Eye Chakra. Therefore, abstinence from food, drink, sexual activity, and other such desires comes naturally to those who have evolved spiritually.

The Catholic Church continues not to allow women and married men to join the clergy, despite the ever-increasing shortage of priests. Pope John Paul II said:

> *The Church holds that it is not admissible to ordain women to the priesthood, for very fundamental reasons. These reasons include: the example recorded in the Sacred Scriptures of Christ choosing his Apostles only from among men; the constant practice of the Church, which has imitated Christ in choosing only men; and her living teaching authority which has consistently held that the exclusion of women from the priesthood is in accordance with God's plan for his Church.*

Pope John Paul II's comments above are inconsistent with the teachings of Jesus. The mother of Saint Mark was a follower of Jesus, and it is common knowledge that Mary Magdalene, Johanna and Susanna accompanied Jesus during his ministry. The reason he only selected men to be his disciples was more practical than political or theological. The role of women in those times was primarily to give birth and raise children, and they were not considered as equal to men. For this reason, it was not practical for Jesus to have chosen women as his disciples; the society of the time would not have been ready for this and the strength of Jesus's teachings would have been compromised. Furthermore, Jesus wanted his disciples to travel abroad after his death and continue his teachings and spreading his message of love and forgiveness. This is what happened; most of them went to Rome and other parts of the Roman Empire. Thomas travelled to India and Matthew to Ethiopia. Jesus foresaw his death and the suffering and persecution of his disciples. It would have been impractical for women disciples in those times to have travelled extensively and experienced that level of persecution.

The Rise of Atheism

Atheism has become a major movement with increasing numbers of adherents. Atheism is based on a Greek word άθεος (*atheos*), meaning '*without God*', and groups together those people that do not believe in any religion.

So, what drives people away from the Church?

Reason 1:

The primary reason is the religious institutions themselves. Atheism is a reaction against the excesses and failings of these institutions. The behaviours described in this book are the reason why people do not want to be associated with religious establishments. People are increasingly associating the Church and other religious institutions with inflexibility and intolerance, and a stubborn refusal to change with the times and embrace the advances in technology and science, and the changes to the social fabric.

Reason 2

The second reason for the rise in atheism is the incompatibility of religion with many people's lifestyles, in particular with reference to their addiction to consumerism and materialism. This has its roots in the 18th century and the beginning of the industrial revolution. For the first time in history, the common people had access to '*things*', as a result of the mass production of goods that were readily transportable and were therefore available at affordable prices. This fixation with goods has exponentially increased in recent years with the development of the internet, which has digitally expanded promotion and marketing activities and increased the power of persuasion to purchase. Such tools have become a potent weapon for luxury goods retailers to drive a culture of linking such products with social status, and an obsessive need by all levels of society to acquire branded goods at all costs. The sad truth is that many people mistakenly believe that leading a comfortable life and progressing spiritually are mutually exclusive, which is absolutely not the case. The reason for this misunderstanding is people's perception, based on the teachings of some religious institutions, that the scriptures are very restrictive and intolerant to those who have wealth and the ability to live comfortably.

Reason 3

The third group of atheists are mainly scientists and intellectuals that cannot accept anything that has not been proven. So many theories and scientific beliefs have been proven wrong over the centuries, and many things also remain unexplained. Why is it that people cannot believe something that has not been proven, and that for them, faith alone is not a reason to believe? If something has not been proven, it does not mean that it is not true, and there are many examples of things that were thought to have been proven in the past that have subsequently been disproven. For example, prior to the 6th century BCE, people thought that the earth was flat and that if one travelled far enough, he or she would fall off the edge of the world! It was only a few hundred years ago that the accepted theory of the sun orbiting around earth was rejected by Galileo, at considerable risk to himself; Galileo's theory is now universally accepted. Until relatively recently ether was thought to exist and to be the medium through which light propagated. This theory was disproven by Michelson-Morley in the late 19th century. He did so by basic scientific experimentation by showing that there was no difference in the speed of light when passing through the assumed ether from various directions, and thus disproving the existence of this element.

Biology of Belief (R7) by Dr. Bruce Lipton provides insights into how the principle of DNA controlling our genes has been debunked with the recent theory of Epigenetics which suggests that our belief systems control our DNA, not our genes.

Reason 4

There are people that think it is not *'cool'* to belong to a religious group, and that they would not be accepted by their circle of friends and society.

Reason 5

Finally, there are the *'dark souls'* that are not attracted to the message of Love. They are not able to see it. This is explained further in later chapters of this book.

Between 2008 and 2009, in response to an evangelical Christian advertising, Ariane Sherine, a comedy writer, proposed an advertising campaign and managed to raise more than £140,000 through donations. The campaign aimed to give voice to atheists and their views. The campaign is known as Atheist Bus Campaign and it run adverts on buses across London with the message *"There's probably no God. Now stop worrying and enjoy your life."*

I can see the point such a campaign was trying to make. However, I believe that money from both campaigns would have been better used for charitable donations.

CHAPTER 4

Reincarnation in Christianity

What is Reincarnation?

For those readers that are not familiar with the term reincarnation, this is a concept that is central to Eastern religions, such as Hinduism, Buddhism, Sikhism and Jainism. Reincarnation literally means *'entering the flesh again'*. To put it simply, the soul passes from one body to another in a repeated cycle of birth, death, and rebirth, for the purpose of learning and clearing karmas (sins) accumulated in previous lives. The cycle of rebirth ends when the individual achieves enlightenment or sainthood (or *'Buddhahood'* as is referenced in Buddhism), and the soul is liberated from the physical body. In the Bhagavad Gita, this process of reincarnation is explained in the following passages:

> *As the soul experiences in this body infancy, youth and old age, so finally it passes into another. The wise have no delusion about this. (Bhagavad Gita 2:13)*

> *My beloved child! There is no destruction for him, either in this world or in the next. No evil fate awaits him who treads the path of righteousness. Having reached the worlds where the righteous dwell, and having remained there for many years, he who has*

*slipped from the path of spirituality will be born again
in the family of the pure, benevolent, and prosperous.
(Bhagavad Gita 6:40-41)*

Krishna says that the soul moves from one body to another for its learnings. The soul is indestructible and eternal. There is no pain or suffering after death, only preparation for the next incarnation.

Reincarnation and Judgement Day

In Christianity, the word *'enlightenment'* is not used. Christians believe that souls that lived an ethical and moral life and followed the ten commandments will enter Heaven, where they will enjoy eternal happiness. Christianity does not accept the concept of reincarnation. There are variations between Christian denominations of what happens after death. Some believe that the spirit world is split between lower and higher spirit sites. The higher spirit side is where souls that have potential to *'reform'* continue their education. Those souls with no hope of reform, stay in the lower site where they wait for Judgement Day, when God decides who will enter Heaven and who will burn in the eternal fires of Hell. Some Christian denominations believe that after death the soul is in some kind of suspended animation waiting for Judgement Day. Others believe that the narrative of Heaven and Hell are metaphorical. These different interpretations of a single aspect of one religion shows that there is no real understanding of what happens after death.

Reincarnation and The Teachings of Jesus

The four New Testament Gospels were written by Matthew and John, who were both disciples of Jesus, and Mark and Luke, who were not. Mark was a young boy when Jesus was teaching, but his mother was a follower of Jesus, and it is thought that he learnt the stories from his mother. Luke was a Greek doctor, and it is thought that he learnt the stories from Saint Paul. Even though the message of Jesus and the description of his teachings are reasonably consistent, it is evident that there are some discrepancies in the details of how they were remembered. It should be noted that the gospels were written some time after Jesus, and it is very likely that memories would have faded. Most of Jesus's disciples were fishermen and simple people, with little or no education; for them understanding complex concepts of life, death and rebirth would have been a challenge. In the below passage, Jesus tried to explain the concept of reincarnation to Nicodemus, and it is clear that Nicodemus did not comprehend what Jesus was saying to him; the principles were too complex for his mind to grasp:

> *There was a man of the Pharisees named Nicodemus, a ruler of the Jews. This man came to Jesus by night and said to Him, "Rabbi (G15), we know that You are a teacher come from God; for no one can do these signs that You do unless God is with him." Jesus answered and said to him, "Most assuredly, I say to you, unless one is **born again**, he cannot see the kingdom of God." Nicodemus said to Him, "How can a man be born when he is old? Can he enter a second time into his mother's womb and be born?" Jesus answered, "Most assuredly, I say to you, unless one is born of water and the Spirit, he cannot enter the kingdom of God. That which is born of the flesh is flesh, and that which is born of the Spirit is spirit. Do not marvel that I said to you, you must be born again. The wind blows where it wishes, and you hear the sound of it, but cannot tell where it comes from and where it goes. So is everyone who is born of the Spirit." Nicodemus answered and said to Him, "How can these things be?" Jesus answered and said to him, "Are you the teacher of Israel, and do not know these things? Most assuredly, I say to you, We speak what*

We know and testify what We have seen, and you do not receive Our witness. If I have told you earthly things and you do not believe, how will you believe if I tell you heavenly things? No one has ascended to heaven but He who came down from heaven, that is, the Son of Man who is in heaven." (John 3:2-13)

In the above passage, Jesus refers to reincarnation. We have to be born again and again, until we are able to enter the *kingdom of God*. The Church interprets this passage as a description of baptism, but when Jesus refers to *'water'* he means the amniotic fluid in the mother's womb.

There are several passages in the New Testament which support the concept of reincarnation. The conversation with Nicodemus above was one such passage; the following is also alluding to the concept of rebirth:

And His disciples asked Him, saying, "Why then do the scribes say that Elijah must come first?" Jesus answered and said to them, "Indeed, Elijah is coming first and will restore all things. But I say to you that Elijah has come already, and they did not know him but did to him whatever they wished. Likewise, the Son of Man is also about to suffer at their hands." Then the disciples understood that He spoke to them of John the Baptist. (Matthew 17:10-13)

Jesus here explains to his disciples that John the Baptist is the reincarnation of Prophet Elijah. Jesus indicates that it is possible for the same soul to return in a different body. Paramhansa Yogananda in his book, *The Second Coming of Christ: The Resurrection Of The Christ Within You* (R8), eloquently describes the relationship between Jesus and John. Yogananda read the Bible, guided by his own Guru (G4), Sri Yukteswar Giri. Yogis understand the metaphysical part of our existence and reading a book such as this provides a different perspective from that of a traditional Christian philosophical text. Even those of us who have limited knowledge of metaphysical principles can see the link between metaphysics and the teachings of Jesus, and that there is much more in His teachings than is traditionally taught. Reading a scripture such as the New Testament without having all the knowledge to comprehend is like studying mathematics without having access to basic equations or a calculator.

The following passages are from the Book of Revelation, the final text of the New Testament:

> *He who overcomes, I will make him a pillar in the temple of My God, and **he shall go out no more**. (Book of Revelations 3:12)*

> *And God will wipe away every tear from their eyes; there **shall be no more death**, no sorrow, nor crying. There shall be no more pain, for the former things have passed away. (Book of Revelations 21:4)*

In these passages, Saint John describes the completion of a soul's learning. Once the soul has *'graduated'* from this earthly school it will not be required to return again in physical form. *"He shall go out no more"* and *"there shall be no more death"*, are explicitly clear.

> *No one puts a piece from a new garment on an old one; otherwise, the new makes a tear, and also the piece that was taken out of the new does not match the old. And no one puts new wine into old wineskins; or else the new wine will burst the wineskins and be spilled, and the wineskins will be ruined. But new wine must be put into new wineskins, and both are preserved. (Luke 5:36-39)*

In the Gospel of Luke above, Jesus explains how important it is for the soul to move into a new body, how our physical body naturally wears out and a new body is required for the soul to continue its learning.

Even though reincarnation has been accepted in the East for thousands of years, well before the beginnings of Christianity, the concept is not new to Europe. The Gnostics, early Christian mystics, believed in reincarnation and for this reason they were persecuted by the Christian Church as heretics.

The Orphic religion of the ancient Greeks, which commenced around the 6th century BCE, believed in reincarnation or metempsychosis (μετεμψύχωσις). Orpheus, its founder, taught that:

> *Soul and body are united by a compact unequally binding on either; the soul is divine, immortal and aspires to freedom, while the body holds it in fetters as a prisoner. Death dissolves this compact, but only to re-imprison the liberated soul after a short time: for the wheel of birth revolves inexorably. Thus, the soul continues its journey, alternating between a separate unrestrained existence and fresh reincarnation, round the wide circle of necessity.*

The above statement is as close as can be to the Eastern belief in reincarnation.

Despite all the evidence that Jesus taught his disciples about reincarnation, the most compelling evidence is in the word *'resurrection'.*

With his death and resurrection, Jesus wanted us to understand that it is possible for the soul to return in the flesh. The New Testament relates the story of Lazarus, who was brought back to life four days after his death. This is a story of *'resurrection'* that stands out in the New Testament, but it is not the only one. In the Gospel of Luke (verse 7:11-17), Jesus and his disciples, while visiting the village of Nain, came across a funeral procession for the only son of a widow. Jesus brought him back to life by simply touching the coffin.

Paramhansa Yogananda, in both his *Autobiography of a Yogi* and *The Second Coming of Christ,* describes the mechanics behind *'miracles'* such as healing and bringing the dead back to life. The average person who does not have an understanding of metaphysics will find these concepts incomprehensible, hence they are considered miracles; however, they are scientific events.

A miracle is something that we cannot scientifically explain, therefore we attribute it to divine intervention. For a believer, miracles do exist, even though he or she doesn't know how to explain them. A non-believer or a scientist may rubbish these as mere superstitions, but miracles are not mere superstitions. They are scientific events that we cannot comprehend. Even if we cannot understand them, it does not mean that they are not real.

Let's first understand what resurrection means. Resurrection is a Latin word meaning *'to rise up'.* This in turn is a translation from the Greek word *'ανάστασης'* (*anastasis*) which also means to *'rise up'.* As previously said, Jesus did not speak Greek, nor English; he taught his disciples in Aramaic. The word used in the Peshitta, a 5th Century Aramaic New Testament, was קימתא (*q'yam'ta*). This word translates to תקומה (*tequmah*) in Hebrew.

Figure 6: Translation of word *resurrection* from Hebrew to English

This word תקומה *(tequmah)* translates as '*rebirth*' (Figure 6). Rebirth is synonymous with reincarnation. Translating this using various dictionaries yielded the same result.

Jesus used the word '*tequmah*' when teaching in Hebrew, and '*q'yam'ta*', when he was using Aramaic. The meaning was understood by Jesus's disciples, but it is unclear why the Greek word '*anastasis*' (*to rise up*) was subsequently used instead of the world '*metempsychosis*' (*reincarnation*). The word had long existed in the Greek language since it had been used by the Greek philosophers. It is highly likely that Jesus's disciples were not familiar with Greek philosophy and religions at the time.

Resurrection or anastasis (and most possibly q'yam'ta) had two meanings. The one was to describe the return of the soul to flesh; the other was a reference to the afterlife or life in Heaven. For example:

> *Now if Christ is preached that He has been raised from the dead, how do some among you say that there is no resurrection of the dead? But if there is no resurrection of the dead, then Christ is not risen. (1 Corinthians 15:12-13)*

Saint Paul argues in 1 Corinthians, if Christ has been raised from the dead, how can it be said that there is no *rebirth*? If there is no such thing as *'rebirth,'* then Jesus would not have risen. In this instance the word *'resurrection'* means rebirth.

> *So when this corruptible has put on incorruption, and this mortal has put on immortality, then shall be brought to pass the saying that is written: "Death is swallowed up in victory." "O Death, where is your sting? O Hades, where is your victory?" The sting of death is sin, and the strength of sin is the law. But thanks be to God, who gives us the victory through our Lord Jesus Christ. Therefore, my beloved brethren, be steadfast, immovable, always abounding in the work of the Lord, knowing that your labour is not in vain in the Lord." (1 Corinthians 15:54-58)*

In this Epistle, Saint Paul talks about abolition of death. Once the soul returns to its original state, there will be no need for physical bodies, but only imperishable spiritual bodies. While the soul is in the physical body, in the cycle of reincarnation, it is not possible to inherit the Kingdom of God. Here Saint Paul is quoting from the Old Testament (Hosea 13:14): *"I will ransom them from the power of the grave; I will redeem them from death. O Death, I will be your plagues! O Grave, I will be your destruction! Pity is hidden from My eyes."*

In the following New Testament passage, there is discussion and clear explanation of resurrection:

> *The same day the Sadducees (G17), who say there is no resurrection, came to Him and asked Him, saying: "Teacher, Moses said that if a man dies, having no children, his brother shall marry his wife and raise up offspring for his brother. Now there were with us seven brothers. The first died after he had married,*

and having no offspring, left his wife to his brother.
Likewise the second also, and the third, even to the
seventh. Last of all the woman died also. Therefore,
in the resurrection, whose wife of the seven will she
be? For they all had her." Jesus answered and said to
them, "You are mistaken, not knowing the Scriptures
nor the power of God. For in the resurrection, they
neither marry nor are given in marriage, but are like
angels of God in heaven." (Matthew 22:23-30)

In this passage, the Sadducees interpreted *'resurrection'* as the rebirth of the physical body, whereas Jesus was referring to the spirit's life in Heaven. When the Sadducees asked Jesus about the woman and to whom she would be married when she rose from the dead, Jesus replied that she would not be anyone's wife, because in Heaven there is no concept of marriage; she would not be a physical form but a spirit like the angels.

This story reminds me of a conversation I had with my Higher Self. I asked what happens to persons who are living their final lives and who have completed their learnings. Where do the souls go? My Higher Self replied: *"They evolve into different types of beings; they becomes an angel."*

This is what Jesus says in the above passage. When souls complete their learnings, they evolve into angels.

The subject of reincarnation, rebirth of the soul returning to flesh, can also be found in a number of passages in the Old Testament. Prophet Elijah raised a boy who had died (1 Kings 17:17-24). Elisha raised the son of a Shunammite woman (2 Kings 4:32-37), and in another passage (2 Kings 13:21), a man came back from the dead after his body had been placed next to Elisha's relics (G16).

My research into reincarnation led me to the life and teachings of Origen Adamantius, also known as Origen of Alexandria. Origen was an early Christian scholar, theologian and ascetic, who lived in the second and third centuries CE. He was educated by his father in Greek and Bible studies and received his theology training from Saint Clement of Alexandria. From an early age, Origen devoted himself to studying the scriptures. He was well educated and went on to become fluent in the Hebrew language to better understand and interpret the scriptures.

Origen was denounced as a heretic by the Emperor Justinian I in 543 CE, almost three centuries after his death, for his unconventional interpretation of the scriptures.

The Church argues that upon the Second Coming (G19) of Jesus, the dead will be resurrected (ἀνάστασις νεκρῶν in the Greek language). Origen argued that this is not possible because the physical body is in a continuous state of transformation. We eat food, which is absorbed by the body and turned into tissue, and when the body dies all elements of the physical body return to nature. Therefore, he argued, it is not possible for the dead body to come back to life.

> *Just as the food which we eat is assimilated into our body and changes its characteristics, so also our bodies are transformed in carnivorous birds and beasts and become parts of their bodies; and again, when their bodies are eaten by men or by other animals, they are changed back again and become the bodies of men or of other animals. (Origen, Fr. Tadros Y. Malaty, R17)*

This point of view is shared by Hindus and Buddhists. The Eastern religions are very clear about the concept of the physical body. It is transient and is merely a *'vehicle'* for the soul to experience and learn in a particular lifetime. Nothing more.

Our physical bodies are made of the following elements, none of which are purely '*human*' (Figure 7). All the elements that make up the human body exist in the environment. When the body dies and is buried, it decomposes and is converted back into solids, liquids, and gases. There is no energy loss in this process. It is converted but the total energy remains the same, in line with the scientific principle of the conservation of energy. Similarly, when the physical body is cremated, energy is conserved and not lost, but converted to solids and gas.

ELEMENT	SYMBOL	PERCENTAGE IN BODY
OXYGEN	O	65.0
CARBON	C	18.5
HYDROGEN	H	9.5
NITROGEN	N	3.2
CALCIUM	Ca	1.5
PHOSPHORUS	P	1.0
POTASSIUM	K	0.4
SULFUR	S	0.3
SODIUM	Na	0.2
CHLORINE	Cl	0.2
MAGNESIUM	Mg	0.1
TRACE ELEMENTS INCLUDE : BORON (B), CHROMIUM (Cr), COBALT (Co), COPPER (Cu), FLUORINE (F), IODINE (I), IRON (Fe), MANGANESE (Mn), MOLYBDENUM (Mo), SELENIUM (Se), SILICONE (Si), TIN (Sn), VANADIUM (V), ZINC (Zn)		LESS THAN 1.0

Figure 7: Physical Body Elements

Origen further argued that the union with the body provides the opportunity for the soul to progress its learning through struggle and victory, and to achieve its ultimate aim of permanently returning to its original state.

The Eastern religions believe that the ultimate aim is to return to The Source or Nirvana (comparable to *'Heaven'* in Christianity). The soul breaks free from the physical body when it returns to its original state. Origen's teachings closely mirrored these concepts, but he was denounced by the Church because his teachings were not in line with the established dogma. The Church went in a different direction with its interpretation of the resurrection.

CHAPTER 5

Karma

Karma v Sin

The word 'karma' is used very loosely in the western world. "It's karma, what goes around, comes around" is a more casual way of saying that people will pay for the harm or injustice they have caused. However, karma is not about punishment or payment, it is about learning. In Christianity, the word 'sin' has the same meaning.

Karma in Hinduism

Karma is a Sanskrit word (कर्म) which means *'action'*. This is the Law of Cause and Effect. This law states that for every cause there is an effect just as for every effect there is a cause. Our thoughts, bahaviours and actions influence our future, either in this life or another. Good deeds contribute to good karma, and bad deeds contribute to bad karma. These learnings are encrypted in the energy body. Bad karma contaminates the soul and it dims the brightness of its light. Good karma contributes to clearing the soul's karmas and restores the soul to its original state. When the soul is restored to its original crystal-clear light state, then it becomes liberated from the body and returns to The Source, Heaven, Nirvana, or whatever it is called depending on the religion.

My beloved child! There is no destruction for him, either in this world or in the next. No evil fate awaits him who treads the path of righteousness. Having reached the worlds where the righteous dwell, and having remained there for many years, he who has slipped from the path of spirituality will be born again in the family of the pure, benevolent, and prosperous. (Bhagavad Gita 6:40-41)

In the above text, Krishna explains the impact of karma and the cycle of reincarnations. He also explains that there is no 'evil fate', which in Christianity is referred to as eternal punishment or Hell.

Karma in Christianity

Jesus was clear about the impact of karma or sin.

But Jesus said to him, "Put your sword in its place, for all who take the sword will perish by the sword". (Matthew 26:52)

Jesus advocates peace and humility. When Jesus says, *"all who take the sword will perish by the sword",* he is referring to the karmic impact of cause and effect. We will experience the pain we cause to other people, either in this life or another; this is part of our learning process. An analogy for comparison is taking an exam; if one fails, then he or she has to go through the pain of studying and taking the exam again until he or she passes.

The Bible has several references referring to karma.

But this I say: He who sows sparingly will also reap sparingly, and he who sows bountifully will also reap bountifully. (2 Corinthians 9:6)

Do not be deceived, God is not mocked; for whatever
a man sows, that he will also reap. For he who sows to
his flesh will of the flesh reap corruption, but he who
sows to the Spirit will of the Spirit reap everlasting
life. And let us not grow weary while doing good, for
in due season we shall reap if we do not lose heart.
(Galatians 6:7-9)

In the above Epistles, Saint Paul affirms that there will be consequences to our actions.

In the Old Testament, the word *'sin'* appears hundreds of times, and is predominantly associated with harsh punishment. Where sin and accompanying punishment are described, the text portrays a God who is cruel and vengeful.

In Genesis 19, we read about God's punishment towards sinners in the destruction of Sodom and Gomorrah.

Then the LORD rained brimstone and fire on Sodom
and Gomorrah, from the LORD out of the heavens.
(Genesis 19:24)

Sin in Christianity

The word *'sin'* derives from the old English *'synn'*, which in turn may be related to the Latin word *'sons'* meaning *'offence'*. Therefore, in a religious context *'sin'* is a transgression against divine law.

The New Testament has a different stance on sin from that of the Old Testament. Jesus refers to sin in the context of forgiveness and repentance, not punishment. The following passages highlight this, as Jesus urges people to ask for forgiveness and they will be forgiven:

Then behold, they brought to Him a paralytic lying on a bed. When Jesus saw their faith, He said to the paralytic, "Son, be of good cheer; your sins are forgiven." (Matthew 9:2)

Our sins are easily forgiven if we show true remorse for our wrongdoings.

And when the Pharisees saw it, they said to His disciples, "Why does your Teacher eat with tax collectors and sinners?" When Jesus heard that, He said to them, "Those who are well have no need of a physician, but those who are sick. But go and learn what this means. I desire mercy and not sacrifice. For I did not come to call the righteous, but sinners, to repentance." (Matthew 9:11-13)

A doctor does not need to heal a healthy person. This is what Jesus says metaphorically in the above passage. He has not come to help people who have already progressed spiritually, but to help those that are struggling with their spiritual development. His mission was to show people the way through darkness and into the light.

Then Peter came to Him and said, "Lord, how often shall my brother sin against me, and I forgive him? Up to seven times?" Jesus said to him, "I do not say to you, up to seven times, but up to seventy times seven." (Matthew 18:21-2)

In the above passage, Jesus is teaching us that there is no limit to how many times we should forgive. We should forgive as many times as necessary to help the person understand his errors. It does not matter how many times we make the same mistake; God will forgive us regardless, until we learn from our mistakes.

> *And when they could not find how they might bring him in, because of the crowd, they went up on the housetop and let him down with his bed through the tiling into the midst before Jesus. When He saw their faith, He said to him, "Man, your sins are forgiven." (Luke 5:19-20)*

Jesus knew that the sins of this person were forgiven. He saw the true remorse and faith in his eyes.

> *Therefore I say to you, her sins, which are many, are forgiven, for she loved much. But to whom little is forgiven, the same loves little. (Luke 7:47)*

In the above passage, Jesus reiterates the power of Love. A person who has sinned but has shown love and compassion to others is able to clear his/her sins.

> *Likewise, I say to you, there is joy in the presence of the angels of God over one sinner who repents. (Luke 15:10)*

In the above passage, Jesus explains that angels celebrate when a person shows remorse.

There are some translation and interpretation differences between the Greek and English versions of the Old and New Testaments, which are important in the analysis of the texts.

For example, in the English and Greek versions of the Old Testament text below, which references Hell:

> *For a fire is kindled in My anger, and shall burn to the lowest **hell**; it shall consume the earth with her increase, and set on fire the foundations of the mountains. (Deuteronomy 32:22)*

Οτι πυρ εκκεκαυται εκ του θυμου μου καυθησεται εως
αδου *κατω καταφαγεται γην και τα γενηματα αυτης*
φλεξει θεμελια ορεων. (Deuteronomy 32:22)

In the above Old Testament example, *'lowest hell'* in the English version is associated with the Greek word **Ἅδης or Hades** in the Greek text. Hades was the Greek God of death, the king of the underworld. In this case, the old testament's references appear to be influenced by Greek mythology.

> *If your right eye causes you to sin, pluck it out and cast it from you; for it is more profitable for you that one of your members perish, than for your whole body to be cast into hell. And if your right hand causes you to sin, cut it off and cast it from you; for it is more profitable for you that one of your members perish, than for your whole body to be cast into **hell**. (Matthew 5:29-30)*

> *Εἰ δὲ ὁ ὀφθαλμός σου ὁ δεξιὸς σκανδαλίζει σε, ἔξελε αὐτὸν καὶ βάλε ἀπὸ σοῦ· συμφέρει γάρ σοι ἵνα ἀπόληται ἓν τῶν μελῶν σου καὶ μὴ ὅλον τὸ σῶμά σου βληθῇ εἰς γέενναν. Καὶ εἰ ἡ δεξιά σου χείρ σκανδαλίζει σε, ἔκκοψον αὐτὴν καὶ βάλε ἀπὸ σοῦ· συμφέρει γάρ σοι ἵνα ἀπόληται ἓν τῶν μελῶν σου καὶ μὴ ὅλον τὸ σῶμά σου εἰς **γέενναν** ἀπέλθη. (Matthew 5:29-30)*

In this above passage in the Gospel of Matthew, Jesus is speaking metaphorically and is not encouraging self-mutilation. His meaning is related to behaviours: if anything is causing one to behave badly, then he/she needs to change that which is causing the behaviour. For example, if the cause is the company one is keeping, then the action should be to stop socialising with these individuals. If one is employed by a company that exhibits unethical behaviours, the easy option is to continue working with this company, directly or indirectly condoning its culture and behaviours; the correct option is to resign and walk away.

You will notice that both the English and Greek Bible translations have been provided for this text. The equivalent word for 'hell' in Greek is *'κόλασις'* (*kolasis*), which means *'torment'* or *'suffering'*. The same passage in the Greek New Testament, however, says γέενναν (*Geennan*). This comes from the Hebrew Gehenna, which is a real place, outside the city walls of Jerusalem, where child sacrifices took place, and bodies of executed criminals and garbage were disposed of by burning. Consequently, Gehenna was associated with horror or burning flesh. *'Hell'* is not a spiritual dimension where souls are tormented for eternity. It is a metaphorical reference to *'mental torment'* or learning the soul will have to experience to compensate for its karmas.

Another concept that is greatly misunderstood, is the use of the word *'eternal'*.

> *And these will go away into* **everlasting** *punishment,*
> *but the righteous into* **eternal** *life. (Matthew 25:46)*

> *"καὶ ἀπελεύσονται οὗτοι εἰς κόλασιν* **αἰώνιον***, οἱ δὲ*
> *δίκαιοι εἰς ζωὴν* **αἰώνιον***." (Matthew 25:46)*

The literal English translation from the ancient Greek version is:

> *And they will go away into a long-lasting torment,*
> *and the righteous, into long-lasting (or everlasting)*
> *life. (Matthew 25:46)*

In the above passage from the New Testament, the English version refers to *'everlasting'* or *'eternal'* punishment. The word used in Greek is **'αἰώνιον'** (*eonion*). *Ἀιώνας'* (*eonas*) literally means a century or 100 years. This is also the root for the English word *'eons'* which means *'for a very long time'*. Greek words often have more than one meaning. In this case, *Ἀιώνιος'* (*eonios*) could mean a very long period of time as well as eternal. Therefore, the English translation has been taken out of context. Literally translated, **κόλασιν αἰώνιον** (*kolasin eonion*), means *'torment or suffering for a very long time'*. This refers to the mental torment the soul repeatedly goes through in the physical form, trying to atone for its karmas. The use of the word *'everlasting'* implies punishment forever with no hope of redemption. This is not the case; when the lessons have been learnt and the karmas erased the soul will experience the eternal peace of Heaven/Nirvana/The Source.

To conclude, Hell is a manmade concept based on misinterpretation of the scriptures.

The Bible refers to Judgement Day and Final Judgement Day. This is interpreted differently from one Christian denomination to another. If we take the interpretation of the Eastern Orthodox Church, it is believed that the first judgement happens when the soul returns to the spirit side, where it will wait for the Final Judgement Day, after Jesus's second coming. God will decide on Final Judgement Day if the person will pass into Heaven for eternal life, or to Hell for eternal torment.

Indeed, there is a judgement each time the soul moves to the spirit side, to decide upon the required learnings in the next life. These learnings will become the *'blueprint'* for that life. I have seen this in my hypnotherapy sessions. During hypnosis, after completing a past life regression, the individual is guided to the spirit side, where he/she recounts communicating with a *'council'* and reviewing the learnings of the last life and residual learnings that need to be carried over into the next life.

In her book *Between Death and Life* (R9), Dolores Cannon describes several cases from her hypnosis sessions, of clients she guided to the spirit side who gave detailed accounts of their experiences. This is an excellent reference for those who want to learn more about life after death.

Dr. Michael Newton, the author of *'Journey of Souls'* (R18), also recorded hundreds of hypnotherapy cases while performing 'Life Between Lives' Hypnotherapy sessions. Each regressed person described a discussion with the Council of Elders, where they were given details of their learnings.

> *But I say to you that whoever is angry with his brother*
> *without a cause shall be in danger of the judgement.*
> *And whoever says to his brother, 'Raca!' shall be in*
> *danger of the council. (Matthew 5:22)*

In the above passage, Jesus says that when we behave badly towards another person, we will be judged by the *'council'*. This *'judgement'* refers to the spirit side council after this life has ended. *'Raca'* most probably means *'fool'* from the Aramaic word *'reca'*.

Karma in Buddhism

Buddhism does not believe in the concept of the soul, unlike both Christianity and Hinduism. Buddhism believes in the concept of *'impermanence'* or *'anicca'*. Nothing is permanent; everything changes. This means that an eternal soul, or *'anatta'* cannot exist. However, Buddhists believe that the energy body of the person is being reborn.

According to Buddhism, life is a cycle of death and rebirth called *'samsara'*. When a person dies, his/her energy passes into another form or body.

As in Hinduism, Buddhism teaches that karma is the consequence of our actions. These lead to a cycle of death and rebirth until all the lessons have been learnt, and the subtle or energy body is liberated and moves to Nirvana.

• CHAPTER 6 •

Sainthood

Introduction to Sainthood

The following is a transcript from one of my conversations with my Higher Self. The first part of this conversation has already been included earlier in the book but is repeated for its relevance in this discussion.

D: I have been having problems with my legs for a long time and this is making me anxious. I can't sleep well at night. What is causing this?

HS: Past life trauma.

D: Do you mean the way I died in a previous life?

HS: Correct.

D: How did I die?

HS: You were tortured.

D: That sounds terrible. Was I a man or a woman?

HS: A man.

D: What was my name?

HS: Artemis. I see you are wearing something shining on your chest. I can't find a word for it (My Higher Self is looking for words in Jane's vocabulary)

D: Which year was it?

HS: I can't see the year in physical time, but it was a very long time ago.

D: Okay. Now that I am aware of this, will these problems with my legs go away? I am really suffering from this.

HS: But you are already feeling better!

D: I am, but not completely well. Can you tell me how I can get completely cured?

HS: It will go away in good time.

It is necessary to explain some key concepts at this point to allow a better understanding of this conversation. In our work as Clinical Hypnotherapists, we find that several unexplained, non-hereditary conditions are a result of painful experiences or deaths in other lives. People that drowned or died in fires in other lives might be born with or develop asthma or other respiratory conditions. In my case, as described in the above conversation, the torture in an earlier life resulted in pain in my legs in this one. Several years of suffering and frequent visits to doctors did not identify the root cause of the problem. However, over the past few months, prior to making contact (channelling) with my Higher Self, I was feeling better.

I become overwhelmed and very emotional after each session with my Higher Self and sometimes forget what I needed to ask. After some time, I learnt to prepare for my next channelling and have my questions ready. After one such session, as I was listening to the recording to *'digest'* the outcomes of the discussions, I remembered a dream that I had a couple of months ago.

A few months earlier we had celebrated my mother's ninetieth birthday, a memorable family event. She was very happy to be surrounded by all her children, grandchildren, great-grandchildren, and other members of her extended family. She was not aware that a couple of weeks earlier she had been diagnosed with breast cancer.

My siblings and I had decided to keep it from her while thinking about how to handle it, because she was too fragile to deal with such stressful news. I was sad but also angry. I asked God *"Why now? She is 90. Why does she have to suffer? She has never harmed anyone. She is a person that lives a very simple life and is satisfied with very little. What has she done to deserve this?"*.

"Why not?" you may say. So many other people die every year from cancer, why not her? And you would be right. But when such news hits so close to home, one becomes self-centred and only considers their own situation.

One evening I had a very vivid dream which involved Saint Therapon. In one scene, I saw a box with his relics, and in another scene, my mother, two of my sisters and myself were having a casual conversation about the Saint. Then I woke up, puzzled by the dream and its meaning.

In Christianity, we have many saints. In many Christian sects, including my own Greek Orthodox branch, we name our children after them, and churches are dedicated to particular saints. We celebrate the date of their death once a year, which becomes the Name Day for people that carry the same name. Therapon is not a common name, and in Cyprus we have very few churches dedicated to his memory. As soon as I woke up the next morning, I immediately went on the internet to find out about this Saint.

Precise details of Therapon's life are limited and there are two distinct versions and timelines of his life. One from the 3rd Century CE, when he was martyred during the Christian persecutions by either the Emperor Valerian or Diocletian. The other from 7th Century CE when he was killed during the first Arab invasions of Cyprus. However, there are common themes between the two versions. Therapon was a monastic who travelled to Cyprus where he was eventually martyred, either by the Romans or the Arab invaders. It is also probable that

Therapon was not his real name. Therapon literally means *'healer'*; it was the name given to him by the Church after his death, in recognition of his healing abilities. His original name is not known.

While listening to the recording of the very first conversation I had with my Higher Self, I remembered my dream of Saint Therapon. Our conversation about one of my earlier lives referred to similarities with the life of Saint Therapon. I was told that I was a healer in all my lives. I was also tortured and martyred in this particular life. My Higher Self said I was wearing something shiny on my chest. Could it be the cross that monastics or bishops wear around their necks (Saint Therapon was appointed as a Bishop)? I was very confused about all of this and made a note to ask more details from my Higher Self the next time we spoke. The second conversation went as follows:

D: Last time you told me that in one life I was called Artemis, is that correct?

HS: Yes.

D: You said I was tortured to death?

HS: Correct.

D: After my death, was I declared a Saint by the Church?

HS: Yes.

D: Did they change my name after my death?

HS: No.

D: So, Artemis kept his name?

HS: Correct.

D: Okay thanks. Do you know why I had that dream of Saint Therapon a few months ago?

HS: You were Saint Therapon's mother in one of your lives. A mother is a mother no matter how many lives have passed.

D: I saw his relics in my dream. Do you think he was trying to pass me a message?

HS: (Pauses for a few seconds while searching for information). I don't know.

D: OK, but do you think I can connect with him the same way I am connecting with you?

HS: (Another pause) No, it's not possible

D: Why not?

HS: The bridge to God is sainthood.

D: What does that mean?

HS: He is more enlightened than you.

D: Do you mean that he has reached Heaven?

HS: Yes, his vibrations are different than yours.

D: I do understand now. You are saying that because our vibrations are different, it is not possible to contact me.

HS: Correct ... But when you find his relics and touch the box that contains them, he will make contact with you.

D: Thanks. Can you tell me how many lives I have lived on earth?

HS: Six. You reached the fifth level. Two more levels to go.

D: Oh ... that's good to know. How many more lives do I have before I 'graduate' from this level?

HS: Two more.

D: So, this one and two more?

HS: No, this one and one more. You will live a total of 9 lives. Your remaining lives will be easier than the ones you had. (My Higher Self explained that the last two lives will be in the sixth level. Level 7 is what we call *'Heaven'*.)

This was, to say the least, a shocking discovery. This needs to be explained in the overall context of sainthood.

When souls achieve enlightenment or sainthood, *'the bridge to God'*, move to a different dimension, where they don't need to be reborn again. They evolve into a different type of being; they become angels.

Saint Therapon has already achieved this goal but Artemis (me in a previous life), is still working on his karmas. In the above conversation with my Higher Self, I was told that most likely I only needed three more lives to clear these karmas and achieve my enlightenment.

Finding details of Artemis's life was easier. Although Therapon was also canonised (G3), Artemis was a well-known historical figure, and his life is well recorded, unlike Therapon's. During one of my discussions with my Higher Self, more details about Artemis were revealed to me.

The *'shining thing'* on my chest was most probably body armour. Artemis was born in Egypt and converted to Christianity before becoming a general under the Emperor Constantine the Great, who reigned between 306 CE to 337 CE. Artemis was a successful commander and Constantine was pleased with him and promoted him Viceroy or Governor of Egypt. Egypt was part of the Roman Empire.

Artemis also served under Constantine II, the son of Constantine the Great, who succeeded his father. Constantine II in turn was succeeded by Julian the Apostate, who was determined to restore paganism (G12) in the Empire and ordered the persecution of the Christians. Artemis, a loyal friend to Constantine the Great and his son Constantine II, denounced Julian's actions, and was arrested and tortured to death. It is believed that Artemis was given the option to denounce Christianity in exchange for his life. He refused and as a result was executed. He was declared a martyr (G10) and became Saint Artemius of Antioch. The Church also proclaimed him a miracle healer.

Even though Artemis may have been a good man, he had committed *'group karmas'* in carrying out his military and viceroy duties. War is brutal and results in atrocities, and positions of authority frequently result in unjust and immoral actions and decisions. This is why subsequent lives were required to clear the karmas, even though Artemis was canonised. A declaration of sainthood by humans does not clear the sins. They can only be cleared by the appropriate experiences and learnings.

Miracles

So, what are miracles? A miracle is simply something that cannot be explained by science and is therefore attributed to divine intervention.

Are miracles real? We are glued to our television sets when we watch movies where average looking people have supernatural abilities - The Fantastic Four, X-Men, Spiderman, Superman and many more. We don't ask, *"how can this be possible?"*. It's just entertainment. We also see superheroes and villains alike getting their dismembered limbs magically reattached and their bullet wounds healed with a magical touch or some kind of special liquid. And while we see the wound healing, we imagine all those cells reproducing and spontaneously healing. We don't take this seriously and treat these movies as fiction and fun to watch.

However, there are many examples of miracles in the scriptures. The Gospels describe several healing incidents. The paralysed man who was cured:

Rise, take up your bed and walk." (John 5:8)

And the healing of the blind and mute man.

Then one was brought to Him who was demon-possessed, blind and mute; and He healed him, so that the blind and mute man both spoke and saw. (Matthew 12:22)

Jesus raised Lazarus who had died four days earlier. He also walked on water, turned water into wine, and fed five thousand people with five loaves of bread and two pieces of fish. These are a few examples of the miracles that Jesus carried out during his lifetime. How was this possible? Sceptics would say that these are only stories and such acts are not possible. However, what Jesus achieved were not miracles but were based on scientific principles. Such powers were not limited to Jesus and the Christian Saints; there are similar examples from other religions.

Jesus was not an average human, despite his young age and his humble upbringing. Paramhansa Yogananda explains Jesus's *'miracles'* in the *Second Coming of Christ*.

> *To Jesus wine was not wine. It was a specific vibration of electrical energy, manipulatable by knowledge of definite superphysical laws. All of God's creation operates according to this law. Events and processes governed by already discovered 'natural' laws are no longer considered miraculous; but when the law of cause and effect operates too subtly for man to discern how something comes to pass, he calls it a miracle.*

Paramhansa Yogananda explains most of Jesus's *'miracles'* by applying the metaphysical and superphysical laws that most of us are not familiar with. Science is concerned with the physical nature of things, matter. Therefore, scientists are not able to explain such *'miracles'*, which are not related to matter but to energy and its vibrational frequency. Jesus had access to cosmic energy and that is why he was able to carry out his *'miracles'*. He had direct communication with the Source and was able to instruct souls to return back to a physical body. Numerous incidents of healing have been reported over the centuries, performed by both living and dead saints. Living saints are those enlightened souls that are living their last life on the physical plane, or those souls that are reborn for a mission, as Jesus was. Instances of prayers to dead saints leading to healing have also been recorded.

Similar to Jesus, the Buddhist scriptures record that the Buddha also walked on water.

The average person has the ability to perform healing if he or she receives the appropriate training. Everyone can be trained in a healing modality such as hypnosis, reiki, sound healing, theta healing and many other such healing techniques. This kind of healing is *'energy medicine'* and the modalities are trainable. As in every profession, some people have natural abilities and require little training while others require more effort and hard work to learn the required skills.

Persons with such healing abilities were persecuted by the Church in the Middle Ages, and were accused of witchcraft and tortured and burnt alive by the Inquisition. Metaphysics provides a clear scientific explanation for these abilities; they are neither miracles nor witchcraft.

Recently I became engrossed in a programme which is available on YouTube called *It's a Miracle*, a US television series aired between 1998 and 2004. On this show, people share real-life experiences that can only be explained by divine intervention.

In one of the episodes, *Dinner with an Angel,* a single mother of two boys tells her story. One Thanksgiving Day she had nothing to feed her kids other than three hotdogs, which she packed into a basket before taking the boys to the park. On their way back home, the mother was extremely sad when the boys said that they were still hungry, because she had nothing else to give them to eat. When they arrived back at their apartment block, an old lady who they did not know, invited them to her apartment for dinner. The mother politely refused but the stranger insisted and the boys wanted to go, so the mother eventually accepted the invitation. The old lady had already set the table for four and seemed to know a lot about them. They had a very nice dinner, and the old lady packed the leftovers to take with them. A couple of days later the mother returned to the old lady's apartment with the empty containers only to find the property completely deserted. When she asked the manager of the complex about the old lady, he told her that the apartment she was referring to had been empty for a long time and he did not know of any old lady ever living there.

God listens to our prayers and sends help when we need it. This experience was an example of divine intervention.

The conversations with my Higher Self have given me much to think about. Sainthood and enlightenment are one and the same; saints are those souls that have achieved liberation from their physical bodies by clearing their karmas and finally *'graduating'*, having completed the required cycles of death and rebirth. Sainthood is not a Christian privilege; people from all faiths can achieve enlightenment. Sainthood is not a promotion or an award that the Church or any other religious institution can offer. The soul naturally evolves into a different type of being and resides in a different dimension.

Sainthood exists in most religions, for example, Hindus call them Rishis and Buddhists call them Tzadik. Christianity is the only religion to canonise saints.

> *He who is spiritual, who is pure, who has overcome his senses and his personal self, who has realised his highest Self as the Self of all, such a one, even though he acts, is not bound by his acts. Though the saint sees, hears, touches, smells, eats, moves, sleeps and breathes, yet he knows the Truth, and he knows that it is not he who acts. (Bhagavad Gita 5:7-8)*

In the above passage, Krishna describes sainthood. He explains the power of selflessness, what Jesus describes as Love. The soul is liberated when the seeker is not driven by physical senses and detaches from physical needs.

Saint Therapon, my son in another life, was canonised by the Church. In this instance, the Church was right to recognise him for his pure life, his healing abilities, and his unconditional and selfless love for people. It has been confirmed to me that Saint Therapon has already crossed '*the bridge to God*'. '*Saint*' Artemis however (an incarnation of myself in another life), is still going through the cycle of death and rebirth trying to clear the karmas created from the wars he was involved in, and the bloodshed and deaths he was responsible for. This discovery I found ironic and sad. Ironic that parents have named their children after Artemis because of his declared sainthood, and sad that many people pray and ask for help from a spirit that is still trying to fulfil the requirements for sainthood.

Artemis's leader, Constantine the Great, has also been declared a saint by the Eastern Church. Constantine may have been the person that recognised Christianity in the Roman Empire, but that alone does not mean that he has cleared all his karmas and crossed the '*bridge to God*'. How could he have done, with all the wars and resulting death and destruction? And yet, Constantine is a well-known Saint, with Churches erected everywhere in his name, and people pray for him to carry out miracles and heal them. The point is that sainthood should not be a corporate process. There is no way for the Church to know who has achieved true sainthood and who is still clearing karmas and still on the path to enlightenment.

'*Saint*' Artemis was not the only military man who was recognised as a Saint. Saint Demetrius, Saint George and Saint Minas, among others, were all military men. I cannot say if they have achieved sainthood or not. I have not asked.

In the early days of Christianity, Christians were persecuted for their faith and were forced to renounce their religion. Those who refused were tortured and executed, and the Church declared them saints. Saint Therapon is also *'Hieromartyr'*, a title given by the Church to those who were clerics at the time of their execution.

The word martyr comes from the Greek work *'μάρτυς'* (*martys*), meaning *'witness'* or *'witness of the truth'*. This term was purely used for those who died protecting their faith. Nowadays, it is loosely used for those who die in wars.

> *And though I bestow all my goods to feed the poor,*
> *and though I give my body to be burned, but have not*
> *love, it profits me nothing. (1 Corinthians 13:3)*

Not everyone who dies, or is martyred for their faith, attains true sainthood. Saint Paul explains in the passage above that, even though you feed the poor and your body is *'burned'* you are not enlightened and do not attain sainthood unless you reach the spiritual level of Divine Love.

Canonisation

The early Christian Church enjoyed some autonomy; however, Constantine changed that by ensuring that the Church was controlled by the emperors. Popes were selected by the Emperor to help them achieve their political agendas. Canonisation also became a corporate process controlled by the Emperors in order to achieve certain political goals, such as glorifying war through religion.

Canonisation is the process by which the Church posthumously bestows sainthood on an individual. In the first millennium of the Christian Church, in the absence of a defined process, bishops informally canonised men and women within their communities. After the first millennium, the Catholic Church created a formal canonisation process, with the Pope making the ultimate decision and declaration of sainthood.

The process of canonisation has various phases. Strict adherence to the process would require a minimum period of five years after death to elapse before the process is started. This rule has not been followed in recent years. For example, Pope Benedict XVI canonised Pope John Paul II before completion of the five years, and Pope John Paul II himself also canonised Mother Teresa before the required five year period had elapsed.

The canonisation process is summarised below:

- After the five-year period has passed the diocese where the person died must open an investigation into his/her life to find sufficient evidence of suitability for canonisation. The formal process requires evidence of miracles which are corroborated by witness testimonies.
- The bishop of the diocese sends all evidence to the *Congregation for the Causes of Saints* for review.
- Once the *Congregation for the Causes of Saints* reviews and approves the application, it is then forwarded to the Pope.
- Upon approval by the Pope, the individual is declared a *'Servant of God'*.
- The next stage requires a posthumous miracle to be directly attributed to the individual.
- The relevant committee reviews evidence of the miracle and confirms its validity, or otherwise.
- The last stage is canonisation, and the declaration of sainthood.

This can be compared to a corporate process in any large business, but it does not take into account the real qualities and behaviours that would truly make someone qualify for sainthood. The following section expands on this theme.

Of the 266 Popes that have served to date, 83 have been recognised as saints by the Catholic Church. Furthermore, 52 of the first 54 Popes were recognised as saints, 31 of whom were martyred. We do not know how many of those reached true sainthood, but history tells us that some popes committed horrible crimes against humanity. They authorised the inquisitions which carried out persecutions, torture and executions towards those whom they considered heretics or practitioners of *'witchcraft'*. Popes Sixtus IV, Innocent VIII and Leo X, amongst others, were responsible for gross acts of violence against those that did not fully adhere to the rigid doctrines of the Church. One wonders how leaders of a faith that was built on a foundation of love and forgiveness can behave so violently and fanatically.

Pope Francis has canonised over 1200 individuals since his election in 2013, while Pope John Paul II canonised 482 saints during his time as a Pope.

In the book *Witness of Hope*, the biography of Pope John Paul II (R10), George Weigel writes:

> *The Christian ideal, for John Paul II, is the martyr: the witness whose life completely coincides with the truth by being completely given to that truth in self-sacrificing love. The Pope has regularly reminded the world that the twentieth century is the greatest century of martyrdom—faithful witness unto death—in Christian history. And no martyr of the twentieth century has been, for John Paul, a more luminous icon of the call to holiness through radical, self-giving love than Maximilian Kolbe. Kolbe was the "saint of the abyss"—the man who looked straight into the modern heart of darkness and remained faithful to Christ by sacrificing his life for another in the Auschwitz starvation bunker while helping his cellmates die with dignity and hope.*

The above passage provides confirmation of Pope John Paul's belief that martyrdom was the ultimate sign of love. In 1987, Edith Stein, a Catholic nun who died in the Auschwitz concentration camp, was declared a Saint without a confirmed miracle. This was a controversial move since the formal canonisation process requires evidence of a miracle for the individual to be considered as eligible for sainthood. Pope John Paul II considered her death in a concentration camp as martyrdom.

The existence of saints is not being questioned, but the principle of who should be declared a saint and what qualities they should have exhibited can be controversial. Who truly knows whether the individuals declared as saints have completed their spiritual evolution?

The Power of True Sainthood

We have mentioned the ability of saints to control nature's powers, raise the dead and cure diseases. Saints also possess physical powers that have been recorded over the centuries.

Incorruptibility

There are examples of saints' bodies that have not decomposed, hundreds of years after their deaths. The bodies of these saints are on display in various churches for all to see. Examples, among others, include Saint Bernadette of Lourdes, Saint Zita, Saint Francis, and Saint Catherine of Laboure. Why have their bodies not decomposed? In the absence of any physical reason the only alternative explanation would be some form of divine intervention.

When Paramhansa Yogananda died on March 7, 1952, his body was displayed for twenty days. Harry Rowe, the Mortuary Director of Forest Lawn Memorial-Park Association, wrote in a letter:

The physical appearance of Yogananda on March 27th, just before the bronze cover of the casket was put into position, was the same as it had been on March 7th. He looked on March 27th as fresh and as unravaged by decay as he had looked on the night of his death. On March 27th there was no reason to say that his body had suffered any visible physical disintegration at all. For these reasons we state again that the case of Paramhansa Yogananda is unique in our experience.

Yogananda's body was placed in a casket which occupies a crypt in Forest Lawn Memorial-Park Association in California.

Stigmata

Some people were reported displaying prominent and painful wounds and scars on their hands and legs, comparable to Jesus's crucifixion wounds. The wounds had the fragrance of perfume and would not heal. This phenomenon is called '*stigmata*'. Saint Francis of Azizi was the first recorded instance of stigmata, but the medical community have rubbished the claim; seven hundred years after Saint Francis's death, doctors and scientists have attributed his stigmata to diseases such as leprosy. However, Saint Francis was not the only case reported; there were more, with the most recent case being Padre Pio, or Saint Pio of Pietrelcina. In a 1911 letter to his spiritual advisor, Padre Benedetto, Padre Pio wrote:

Then last night something happened which I can neither explain nor understand. In the middle of the palms of my hands a red mark appeared, about the size of a penny, accompanied by acute pain in the middle of the red marks. The pain was more pronounced in

the middle of the left hand, so much so that I can still
feel it. Also, under my feet I can feel some pain.

The Vatican imposed restrictions on him performing mass, blessing people, and showing his stigmata. The Church also tried to remove him from his position, without success as the people in his community resisted and threatened to riot.

In 1919, the Church authorised a pathologist to examine Padre Pio's wounds. The first physician concluded that the wound was caused by the use of chemicals, but a second doctor examined the wounds and could not explain their origin. He also confirmed the presence of a pleasant fragrance.

In 1947, Father Karol Josef Wojtyla, the future Pope John Paul II, visited Padre Pio, who prophesied to him that one day he would become the head of the Catholic Church.

Padre Pio died at the age of 81, exactly 50 years to the day after developing his stigmata. In 2002, Pope John Paul II declared Padre Pio a Saint. His remains were exhumed, approximately 40 years after his death, and it was declared that his body was in *'fair condition'*. His scalp was skeletal but the remainder of his body was well preserved. Padre Pio had not only developed stigmata, but his body had not decomposed. Padre Pio's body is now displayed in a glass casket at San Giovanni Rotondo in the Apulia region in southern Italy.

No need of food consumption

Therese Neumann was a German mystic. She carried the stigmata and, as in the case of Padre Pio, was also discredited by the medical and scientific community. From 1923 to her death in 1962 she consumed no drink or food. She was watched closely by a medical committee, but without any conclusions being drawn.

Paramhansa Yogananda eloquently explains this phenomenon after visiting Therese in Bavaria in 1935.

> *Therese Neumann's life demonstrates in this age the teaching of Jesus that the body does not live by "bread alone." As she expressed it to me, "I live by God's light." The saintly stigmatist lives by her will drawing on Cosmic Energy from the ether, sun, and air; and by the Cosmic Consciousness of Christ.*

Spiritually advanced people, those living their last life on this plane, have supernatural abilities. They have access to cosmic energy, and do not require food and drink to survive. Energy for the physical body is provided by food and drink. However, some people have direct access to cosmic energy, and their physical body is *'charged'* through their energy body.

Therese Neumann was never declared a Saint by the Catholic Church.

Several other cases have been recorded around the world. Giri Bala, a Bengali, lived without eating for more than 56 years. A more recent example is Prahlad Jani, an Indian Yogi who had not eaten for 70 years. Prahlad died in May 2020 at the age of 90.

Prahlad's case was investigated by the scientific community but no conclusions were reached. Scientists have difficulty in accepting something as fundamentally opposed to current scientific thinking as a physical body being able to survive without food, or the ability of a person to carry non-self-inflicted wounds for many years.

Levitation

Several saints and holy people were reported as *'levitating'* or having the ability to hover in the air. In Christianity, Saint Francis of Assisi was recorded as having been *'suspended above the earth'*.

Levitation is also discussed by Yogananda in his *Autobiography of a Yogi*, in which he discusses the case of the Indian Saint Nagendranath Bhaduri, who was seen levitating by witnesses.

Bilocation

Most of us have at some time watched sci-fi movies, such as *Star Trek* and *Star Wars*. We are fascinated by the thought of people being instantly transported from one place to another by a machine that dematerialises their physical bodies in one location and rematerialises it somewhere else. Many of us secretly wish that such technology existed, but our technology is currently too primitive to accomplish this. The spirit world is much more sophisticated and dematerialisation/rematerialisation is possible for enlightened souls.

Bilocation is when a person can be in two places or more at the same time. This concept was used in ancient times by Greek philosophers in their intellectual discussions. Several cases of saints and monks bilocating were recorded in Hinduism and Christianity.

Paramhansa Yogananda in his *Autobiography of a Yogi* describes his personal encounter with such a phenomenon. At the age of 12, he was asked by his father to deliver a letter to someone living in the house of Swami (G22) Pranabananda. Upon arriving at the Swami's house, the person he was seeking was absent, and he found Swami in a state of meditation. He was told to wait for 30 minutes and the person he was seeking would come. After exactly 30 minutes, the person he was seeking arrived, telling him that the Swami had come to him 30 minutes earlier to inform him that Yogananda was waiting for him. Yogananda was shocked. The Swami had never left the house. He was there in front of him in a state of meditation. How did he appear to another person in a different place at the same time? Holy people can break the barriers of time and space. They can astral travel and materialise and dematerialise their bodies.

Ascension

Ascension is the ability of a saint at the highest spiritual level to dematerialise their body and live on this plane without experiencing death. Ascended masters have also been recorded to have been seen in the physical form. Saint Francis of Assisi reported seeing Jesus in *'flesh and blood'*. The passage below describes the moment Jesus was lifted to Heaven in the presence of his disciples.

> *Then their eyes were opened, and they knew Him; and He vanished from their sight. (Luke 24:31)*

> *Now it came to pass, while He blessed them, that He was parted from them and carried up into heaven. (Luke 24:51)*

There are many examples from multiple religions of physical form ascensions. One of the most important figures in Hinduism, Mahavatar Babaji, and another from the Zoroastrian religion, Peshotanu, were both reported to have ascended into Heaven. Prophet Elijah is also mentioned in the Old Testament as having ascended into Heaven.

Ability to detach from the physical body

Enlightened Yogis, having trained for 20-30 years, are able to choose when they want to depart from this world. Their soul is already liberated; therefore, they can choose how to detach it from the body and move to the spirit side.

Paramhansa Yogananda describes how a strong and healthy guru, Sri Yukteswar, a few days before his death, informed him that his time has come to move to the spirit side. A couple of days prior to his departure, he said: "My task on earth is now finished; you must carry on".

When enlightened souls like Sri Yukteswar complete their mission on this plane, they can voluntarily detach their souls and move to the spirit side. This is quite common among advanced yogis.

Similarly, a few days prior to his death, Yogananda hinted to his disciples that his time was close. On March 7, 1952, after making a brief speech and reciting a poem at an official dinner in honour of the visiting Indian Ambassador to the US, he lifted his eyes to his *'Kutastha'* (G8), and his body slumped on the ground. His spirit had separated from his body. Yogananda was on a mission to take Kriya Yoga to the west. His task completed, he had no further reason to remain in the physical world.

This is a much debated subject amongst scholars and theologists, some of whom argue that this is 'spiritual suicide'.

The Fragrance of Relics

Saint Andrew recorded the presence of a strong and pleasant fragrance during the transportation of Saint Therapon's relics to Constantinople in the early 800s. The fragrance was strong enough to have been noticed by all the travellers in the boat and caused some commotion and amazement.

This phenomenon has been reported on several occasions. Saint Teresa of Avila and Saint Maravillas of Jesus, both from Spain, and Saint Therese de Lisieux, are some examples.

Conclusion

Sainthood or enlightenment is more than the ability to perform miracles. Spiritually advanced souls have supernatural powers that current scientific knowledge is too primitive to explain, and for this reason, such phenomena are dismissed as mere superstitions.

Sainthood is not an award that can be arbitrarily bestowed by any person on this earthly plane, as we have no way of knowing if the soul has reached enlightenment and true sainthood. It is understandable that the Church wants to recognise those individuals who have been shining examples of unconditional love and sacrifice so that people can follow their example. However, canonisation is not the appropriate means to achieve this; people cannot decide who is eligible for entry into Heaven, Nirvana or the Source; this is decided on the spirit plane.

CHAPTER 7

The Soul

The journey in the physical plane is one of learning, not of punishment. Karma is the mechanism of cause and effect. If in one life we cause pain (the cause), during the same life or the next life we will experience the same pain we caused (the effect). This is how we learn. This is analogous to what trainers would call *'experiential training'!*

This process is complex, but simply put, our soul (our spiritual body) is entrapped in our physical body. A soul can only be liberated when it returns back to its original state. Over many lives, the soul gets contaminated with negative energy or karmic debris. The soul goes through repeated cycles of death and rebirth until it finds liberation.

Sri Yukteswar in his book *Holy Science* explains this in a very scientific way. My Higher Self has given me a simpler explanation:

D: How does the soul get liberated?

HS: When the soul becomes crystal clear.

D: Last time you said that the soul is energy of pure Love, pure Bliss, right?

HS: In its original state, yes. But it also contains the negative energies from all our lifetimes.

D: So, you mean the soul gets contaminated?

HS: Yes. It absorbs all the negative energies.

D: Do you mean from energies such as hatred, negativity, jealousy?

HS: Correct.

D: So, it becomes dim?

HS: Darkness is the absence of light.

My Higher Self meant that the bright energy of Love absorbs the negative energies and becomes dimmer. In physics an object becomes darker when it absorbs photons; this is the same concept.

I remember one time I asked my client to locate the bright light of her Higher Self and she said, *"yes I can see it, but it's not bright. It's dim"*. I was a little embarrassed, but it was a valuable lesson for me. This particular client had a lot of *'karmic debris'* but her energy has now become much clearer with her learning progression. In a recent regression, she reported that her energy is now *"amber"* in colour.

Life and Death

In order to understand the soul, you must first understand the meaning of Life and Death. According to Vine's Expository Dictionary (R11):

> **Life** *is a Conscious existence in communion with God.*

> **Death** *is a Conscious existence in separation from God.*

That means that the concept of death is simply a delusion. Life refers to eternal life once the soul reaches enlightenment. Death refers to the cycle of death and rebirth that the soul goes through for several lives in order to reach enlightenment. Christianity refers to this state of enlightenment as Heaven.

Most assuredly, I say to you, he who hears My word and believes in Him who sent Me has everlasting life, and shall not come into judgement, but has passed from death into life. (John 5:24)

"Most assuredly, I say to you, if anyone keeps My word he shall never see death." Then the Jews said to Him, "Now we know that You have a demon! Abraham is dead, and the prophets; and You say, if anyone keeps My word he shall never taste death." (John 8:51-52)

Repeatedly Jesus said that he is the *'light'* that will show us the way through darkness and into liberation. This is literal. Our soul becomes dark from the negative energies, and the teachings of Jesus are the *'light'* to show us the way out of darkness. In the above passages from the Gospel of John, Jesus says that whoever understands his teachings will not have to experience death anymore. With statements such as *"shall never taste death"*, *"will have an everlasting life"*, Jesus is explaining the concept of reincarnation. His fellow Jews, not understanding his teachings, accused him of being a *'demon'*, referring to the evil of Satan. They referred to Abraham's death and questioned how Jesus could say that whoever followed his word would not die? It made no sense to them.

Do you not know that to whom you present yourselves slaves to obey, you are that one's slaves whom you obey, whether of sin leading to death, or of obedience leading to righteousness? (Romans 6:16)

For the wages of sin is death, but the gift of God is eternal life in Christ Jesus our Lord. (Romans 6:23)

For when we were in the flesh, the sinful passions which
were aroused by the law were at work in our members
to bear fruit to death. (Romans 7:5)

In the passages above, Saint Paul explains that sin leads to death, the cycle of death and rebirth, or reincarnation. Virtuous life leads to righteousness, enlightenment, or eternal life with God in Heaven.

What is the Soul?

Most religions, including Christianity, believe that the soul is the eternal, immortal part of the human being. The soul or psyche (from the Greek word 'ψυχή') is also the root of such words such as Psychiatry or Psychology.

The ancient Greek philosophers, such as Aristotle, Socrates and Plato, acknowledged the ψυχή or soul as the immaterial, eternal part of the human being. There is evidence that the ancient Egyptians also believed in the concept of the soul. In one way or another, most of the world's religions, past and present, have believed in the existence of the soul

The soul is a speck of God, pure Love energy. The Eastern religions believe that the soul enters the body when the foetus is approximately 49 days old and only leaves the body upon death.

It is heart breaking when a woman has a miscarriage; I know first-hand how it feels, because it happened to me. I was secretly mourning for a very long time. I now know that the soul that chose me to be the vehicle to enter into the physical world, waited patiently for another pregnancy. Later, when I realised that the foetus had gone, but the same soul returned to me through a different pregnancy, I felt relieved and let go of all my sorrow.

Below are the details of another conversation with my Higher Self about the soul.

D: Does the soul reside in the pineal gland?

HS: No.

D: Ah … I thought that the soul resides in the pineal gland.

HS: It's in the centre of the heart.

D: This is confusing. When people have an out of body experience, I thought that the soul exits the body. Somewhere I also read that the soul gets bored at night and leaves the body!

HS: The soul never leaves the body. How would you have vivid dreams otherwise? The soul only leaves at death.

D: So, what leaves the body when people have out of body experiences? I understood that the energy that travels from the spine pushes the soul from the pineal gland out of the body.

HS: This is not correct. The pineal gland only has hormones. What you are describing is astral travel.

D: So, you are saying that the energy body does not have to leave the body to experience an out of body experience.

HS: Correct.

D: So, where does the soul go after death? And what happens to the energy body?

HS: They are one. They cannot exist without each other. The soul experiences through the energy body when outside the physical body. It moves back to the community after death.

D: This is what we call the spirit side?

HS: Correct. It prepares for the next incarnation. Souls make contracts with other souls before they return.

D: How about when the soul 'graduates'? Where does it go?

HS: It evolves into a different type of being. It becomes an angel.

D: And it moves to what we call 'Heaven', a different plane of existence?

HS: Correct.

The soul requires a *'body'* to experience and learn. In the physical world, it uses the physical body to learn and experience. On the spirit side, it uses the energy body to continue its learning. When a person has an out of body experience, the energy that travels through the spinal cord and ends in the pineal gland causes a chemical reaction of the hormones in the pineal gland that forces the physical senses to *'switch off'*. The person thus experiences the senses through the energy body, while they are still conscious. The energy body is a duplicate of our physical body; it hears, it sees, and it smells. This is different from sleep. When we sleep, our senses switch off but at the same time we become unconscious. My Higher Self told me that we become *'semi-dead'*.

People who have had near-death experiences describe their experiences in very similar ways. They describe how they are hearing and seeing through their energy body. One illuminating example is Anita Moorjani, who described her near-death experience and miraculous recovery from the last stages of cancer in *Dying to Be Me* (R12), a wonderful and essential book for those who want to learn more about this subject.

The Soul in Christianity

In various passages in the New Testament, Jesus says that those who achieve the highest level of spirituality will enter Heaven and will be called Sons of God. When the soul is liberated from the physical body, the essence of the soul is the same as the soul of the Father or God. This is also the meaning behind the declaration that God made man *"in his own image" (Genesis 1:27)*.

The Soul is a speck of God - pure Love, pure Bliss.

*And we have known and believed the love that God
has for us. **God is love**, and he who abides in love
abides in God, and God in him. (1 John 4:16)*

Saint Paul, in the Epistle to Saint John, says *God is Love*. He
understood the true nature of the soul. He knew that the path back to
God was through Love.

The Soul in Hinduism

Krishna in the Bhagavad Gita describes in the following verse what
the soul is:

*The Spirit, which pervades all that we see, is
imperishable. Nothing can destroy the Spirit.*

*The material bodies which this Eternal, Indestructible,
Immeasurable Spirit inhabits are all finite. Therefore
fight, O Valiant Man!*

*He who thinks that the Spirit kills, and he who thinks
of It as killed, are both ignorant. The Spirit kills not,
nor is It killed.*

*It was not born; It will never die, nor once having
been, can It cease to be. Unborn, Eternal, Ever
enduring, yet Most Ancient, the Spirit dies not when
the body is dead.*

*He who knows the Spirit as Indestructible, Immortal,
Unborn, Always-the-Same, how should he kill or
cause to be killed?*

As a man discards his threadbare robes and puts on new, so the Spirit throws off Its worn- out bodies and takes fresh ones. (Bhagavad Gita 2:17-22)

This verse is crystal clear and requires no explanation. Hindus have been aware of the mechanics and science behind the journey of the soul for some five thousand years. They understood the principle of karma and the metaphysical nature of the human being. The soul becomes liberated once it completes its learnings, and it then returns to its original state.

The Soul in Buddhism

Buddhism has a different view of the soul, and this is one of the fundamental differences between Buddhism and Hinduism/ Christianity. The term *'Anatta'* means *'an'* (without) and *'atta'* (soul). In Buddhism, there is no permanent substance that can be called a soul.

Buddhism believes that the actions of the person lead to death and rebirth, the cycle which is called *'samsara'*, or reincarnation. This cycle continues until liberation from *'dukkha'*, the desires which bring suffering and keep us on the physical plane. The subtle body or energy body moves from one body to another until it finds liberation from suffering.

Buddhists also do not believe that there is an eternal creator or God, contrary to the beliefs of Christianity and Hinduism.

The information given to me by my Higher Self confirms the existence of the soul and its path of liberation, which will be described in the coming pages. However, the concept of Desires and Suffering is also prominent in what was provided to me.

It really does not matter if Buddhists believe in the existence of the soul or God or not. We must see the big picture and the similarities between the three religions, rather than the areas of disagreement.

How Does the Soul Become Liberated?

Our soul is a speck of God, pure Love energy. Physical desires trigger negative behaviours. *Desires* and *Emotions* are not the same thing. Emotions have a purpose; for example, the emotion of fear protects. If there was no sense of fear, how would one be able to identify a dangerous situation that might endanger one's life? A *desire* such as jealousy, on the other hand, has no purpose other than derailing spiritual growth. Psychologists and psychiatrists might disagree with this difference between the two, but this is a fundamental principal of understanding the soul and the cycles of reincarnation. For the purpose of our spiritual development, *desire* is what drives negative behaviours, which contaminate the soul with karmic debris. While moving from one life to another, the soul becomes clearer if it is learning, or darker if it is not. Once a lesson is learnt, it cannot be unlearnt. When a child learns to walk, he/she cannot unlearn and return to crawling. However, if there is a lesson that has not been learnt, it is possible that the end result is worse than before. For example, a soul which has been hateful life after life cannot go back to this desire if it finally learns compassion. Lessons cannot be unlearnt, but a soul exhibiting hate can become darker and more hateful if it is unable to learn. It falls deeper into a dark bottomless pit.

A person operating purely through his/her physical body, without any interaction with his spirit, will reinforce his/her darker side. Everyone, other than those souls that achieve enlightenment and are living their final life, have some level of contamination. The clarity of the soul depends on the level of enlightenment.

The dark to light scale shown in Figure 8 illustrates how our souls become contaminated by negative energies, and how they gradually become clearer as we learn and clear our karmas. The crystal-clear state of the soul leads to enlightenment. Those behaviours are called Divine Love. This type of Love is a behaviour, not a desire, and results in spiritual growth. Divine Love is not the same as the emotional love we feel for each other as physical entities.

Figure 8 illustrates the two polar opposites. On the left we have the path taught by the Buddha. He said that Desire leads to suffering, and that unless we detach ourselves from Desire we will not be liberated. Jesus said that unless we engage in Divine Love, we cannot be liberated. They are saying the same thing, from a different angle. The Buddha gave us the path to enlightenment through eliminating Desire, and Jesus taught us the path of Love. Achieving enlightenment, the Buddhist way, requires the person to detach completely from physical and mental desires that bring suffering. The polar opposite of each desire is the behaviour of Divine Love which is Jesus's path to enlightenment.

Hinduism is very much aligned with these concepts. Hinduism is not only about yoga. Yoga is the scientific way of accelerating enlightenment; however, Krishna clearly said that yoga is not the only path to enlightenment. Yoga is the *'accelerated programme'* that requires the seeker to lead a monastic life, detached from desires and physical needs. Detachment from physical desires is a must for all three religions. Enlightenment is a gradual process and complete detachment happens during the last life of the seeker on this earthly plane. Krishna also taught that leading an ethical life, the path that has been taught to us by both Jesus and the Buddha, is another way to enlightenment.

> *Desire, aversion, pleasure, pain, sympathy, vitality*
> *and the persistent clinging to life, these are in brief the*
> *constituents of changing Matter. Humility, sincerity,*

harmlessness, forgiveness, rectitude, service of the Master, purity, steadfastness, self-control; Renunciation of the delights of sense, absence of pride, right understanding of the painful problem of birth and death, of age and sickness; Indifference, non-attachment to sex, progeny or home, equanimity in good fortune and in bad. (Bhagavad Gita 13:7-10)

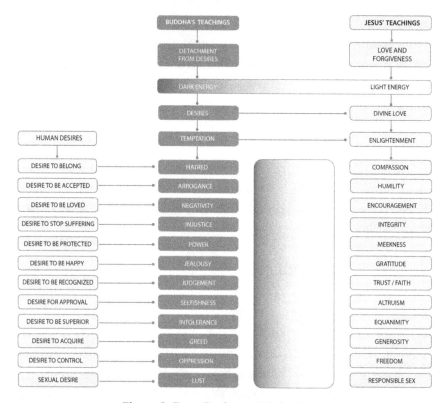

Figure 8: From Desires to Divine Love

From Darkness to Enlightenment

In describing negative energies, I will be referring to the extreme example of *'dark energy'*.

While working with clients, after visiting a past life, I would regularly talk with my clients' Higher Selves. I always ask about my client's learning and how he/she can clear their karmas. The responses to these questions indicate a pattern of learning needs: *"She is negative", "He has caused injustice", "She was arrogant"*, and so on. In the beginning, I was not able to understand the exact mechanism of karma, but conversations with my Higher Self helped me to close the gaps in my knowledge.

Of course, the science of karma is much more complex, but for the purpose of this book we will provide a simplified explanation.

When a person reaches a certain threshold (Figure 9), their behaviours will change, depending on whether they are leaning towards the lighter or darker ends of the spectrum. For example, people that live their lives in hatred will generate dark energy, irrespective of their actions and achievements. The person is unable to experience compassion because the energy of love has been absorbed by the energy of hatred. So how does a person then learn and progress along the path to enlightenment?

THE MIDDLE LINE THRESHOLD

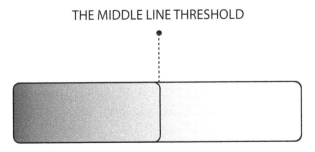

Figure 9: The Darkness Threshold

The soul's contamination can be carried over into several lives. Personality is not inherited, but due to the contamination of the soul, a baby is born with a disposition or tendency towards certain behaviours, from the impact of their past lives' behaviours and learnings. Twins that are born with identical genetic makeups, raised in the same family, and having received the same amount of love, can be completely different personalities. There are three main reasons for this:

The level of soul clarity: Souls leaning towards the lighter end of the spectrum will be easier to raise or be *'moulded'* by their parents. Souls that lean towards the darker end will be more of a challenge and will require more effort from the parents. If such a person, who is already leaning towards the dark end, is born into a dysfunctional family, with say alcoholic or abusive parents, he or she can easily be tempted into a life of drugs, crime etc.

Depending on the learnings of the soul, the individual will also come with a blueprint of needs and goals, which will drive him/her towards the required learnings. This blueprint will provide the guidance for the selection of profession, lifestyle and other life choices that will support the person to reach their ideal learning goal. Again, learning will depend on the level of the soul's clarity and the influence and impact of their family, friends, and community support systems.

Belief Systems

Irrespective of the soul's clarity and the blueprints, we start *'programming'* our minds from the day that we are born. Our minds are programmed in the way that a computer is when it is provided with applications such as Microsoft Windows, Word etc. Our minds are continually learning by absorbing information from all our senses. This information creates a thought which leads to an emotion, negative or positive, and then *'saves'* this information as negative or positive, depending on the emotion we felt at the time. Each time we receive the same signal in the future, we search our minds for information, which then drives our behaviours.

To illustrate this, I will provide an example from my own life experience. When I was six years old, my teacher, a gentle, caring person, told me that because I had a soft voice, she did not feel that it was a good idea for me to take the lead part in the end of year play. She said this in a gentle manner and did not intend to hurt me, nor did she think about the impact this would have on my confidence. However, what she said registered in my mind that there was something wrong with my voice. This had a negative impact on my personality, and I become shy and introverted. It also became an issue for me when I started working in the corporate world, and I found it hard to talk in public. So, a simple throwaway comment said without any intended anger or spite created fundamental issues for me over a long period of time. It was during a much later hypnosis session that I discovered the root cause of the problem, and the hypnosis helped me to get over the self-doubt and phobia of public speaking.

Someone who has been bitten by a dog will naturally have a fear of dogs, and someone else who only had pleasant experiences with dogs will love them. Everyone operates like this; our behaviours, likes and dislikes, fears, and insecurities, are generated by the programming we have created.

Therefore, we do not start with a 'clean slate' when we are born. There is nothing called bad 'taste' in fashion, food, and other life choices. Our preferences are shaped daily by our experiences, and our beliefs are shaped by our family, our education, our society, and our religion. This is particularly so in our early, formative years.

People identify themselves with what they wear and how they look, in order to fit in with a certain group. I once asked someone, *"Why is it so important for you to wear designer clothes"*. He said, *"It's not about designer clothes, it's about the social status"*. This person identified designer clothes with the 'right' level of society. To fit into this level, he had to wear designer clothes. Similarly, all our preferences, for example how we furnish our homes, what cars we drive, how we entertain ourselves, and many other such aspects of our lives, are all generated from our programming. There is no such thing as good or bad taste. There are personal preferences based on our belief system, our programming.

This same programming causes blockages in our lives. For example, if your parents told you at an early age that *"money does not grow on trees"*, you have already created a belief system that says *"money does not come easily"*. If a husband is abusive to his wife, the daughter may develop a limiting belief that *"men are not to be trusted"*.

Our beliefs are encoded, just like a computer programme: *"I am not worth it"*, *"I am not good enough"*, *"I am not pretty"*, *"I am not smart"*.

The mind is like a broadcasting station that sends a signal out into the universe, and we receive what we send out. We get people and events in our lives to validate those beliefs. And then we say, *"I knew it, I was not worth it"*.

So, our soul's clarity, our blueprint and our beliefs are influencing our decisions, choices and emotions, and these emotions then drive our behaviours.

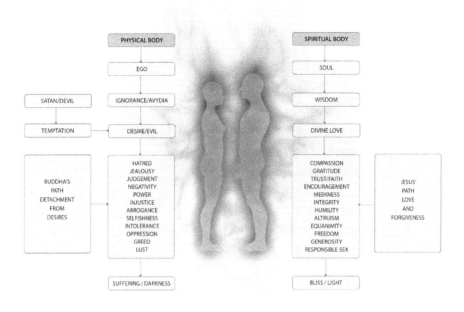

Figure 10: Physical Body and Spiritual Body

We need to understand this *'substance'* that contaminates our soul. What is it? It is energy, but it is not the same energy as our emotions. Let's look at this from a religious perspective.

Our physical body is driven by our Ego and operates with Ignorance of our True Self. Due to this ignorance, and not understanding that it is only a temporary vehicle for our soul to experience and learn in the physical world, the body is driven by desires, which lead to contamination, suffering and darkness of the soul.

Our spiritual body, the soul, operates with wisdom and is driven by Divine Love. This path leads to liberation of the soul, and a state of pure bliss, enlightenment, or sainthood. This is illustrated in Figure 10.

Evil

The word *'evil'* that is referenced in multiple passages in the Bible refers to immoral, unethical behaviour.

> *And this is the condemnation, that the light has come into the world, and men loved darkness rather than light, because their deeds were evil. For everyone practising evil hates the light and does not come to the light, lest his deeds should be exposed. (John 3:19-20)*

Saint John explains that evil is dark energy that contaminates the pure light of the soul. The soul absorbs the dark energy, it loses its glow and becomes dim. *"Darkness is the absence of light"*, my Higher Self told me.

> *A good man out of the good treasure of his heart brings forth good; and an evil man out of the evil treasure of his heart brings forth evil. For out of the abundance of the heart his mouth speaks. (Luke 6:45)*

In the above passage, Saint Luke says that a good man can only produce good energy for his soul. This is how a soul clears its karmas and progresses spiritually, life after life, closer to liberation. Good deeds produce good, positive energy. Bad deeds produce negative energy that contaminates the soul and slows the progress of the soul towards enlightenment.

Satan and Temptation

Satan, or the Devil, is not a supernatural being. To put it very simply, Satan is temptation and contributes to the concept of polarities. Physical existence is not possible without polarities - good and bad, north and south, masculine and feminine, dark and light, and so on.

Without the existence of Satan, temptation, our learning would be very easy. It's like taking an open book exam!

The concept of polarities is very prominent in ancient Chinese philosophy. A fundamental Chinese concept, Yin and Yang (陰陽), represents dark-bright or negative-positive. This philosophy describes how opposite forces complement and balance each other. In fact, according to this philosophy, nothing is really one or the other. This is why we see the dots on both sides of the Yin Yang symbol (Figure 11). For example, if the moon is not visible, the stars provide some light. In the case of the soul, it will have some contamination while in a physical body. When the soul is completely clear, it becomes liberated and moves to Heaven, Nirvana, or the Source.

Figure 11: Yin & Yang Symbol

In the Old Testament, the purely metaphorical narrative in Genesis describing the fall of Adam and Eve, describes the concept of Satan (temptation), and how temptation lured Adam and Eve to eat from the forbidden tree (sin), which in turn led to the commencement of their cycles of death and rebirth. Even though this is a key passage in the Old Testament, It is important to understand that this is a representation of a concept and not an actual event.

> Now the **serpent** was more cunning than any beast of
> the field which the LORD God had made. And he said
> to the woman, "Has God indeed said, you shall not eat
> of every tree of the garden'?" And the woman said to
> the serpent, "We may eat the fruit of the trees of the

garden; but of the fruit of the tree which is in the midst of the garden, God has said, 'You shall not eat it, nor shall you touch it, lest you die'". Then the serpent said to the woman, "you will not surely die. For God knows that in the day you eat of it your eyes will be opened, and you will be like God, knowing good and evil". So when the woman saw that the tree was good for food, that it was pleasant to the eyes, and a tree desirable to make one wise, she took of its fruit and ate. She also gave to her husband with her, and he ate. Then the eyes of both of them were opened, and they knew that they were naked; and they sewed fig leaves together and made themselves coverings. And they heard the sound of the LORD God walking in the garden in the cool of the day, and Adam and his wife hid themselves from the presence of the LORD God among the trees of the garden. Then the LORD God called to Adam and said to him, "Where are you?" So he said, "I heard Your voice in the garden, and I was afraid because I was naked; and I hid myself." And He said, "Who told you that you were naked? Have you eaten from the tree of which I commanded you that you should not eat?" Then the man said, "The woman whom You gave to be with me, she gave me of the tree, and I ate." And the LORD God said to the woman, "What is this you have done?" The woman said, "The serpent deceived me, and I ate." So the LORD God said to the serpent: "Because you have done this, You are cursed more than all cattle, And more than every beast of the field; On your belly you shall go, And you shall eat dust All the days of your life". (Genesis 3:1-24)

In this metaphorical narrative, the serpent represents temptation, and depicts how people are lured into temptation by negative cosmic energy, which leads to karma and contamination of the soul. This passage has a very powerful hidden message with respect to the gift of free will. When we exercise our free will, we make good or bad (evil) choices; the evil actions consequently lead us to karma or sin, and the cycle of death and rebirth.

> *Then Jesus was led up by the Spirit into the wilderness*
> *to be tempted by the devil. (Matthew 4:1)*

In the above passage, Jesus was tempted by dark cosmic energy, while fasting and praying for forty days and nights. Further passages describe how Jesus overcame the temptation. Jesus's soul, although enlightened, was in a physical body, and thus exposed to temptation.

Yogananda describes how the Buddha was confronted by Mara. Mara is the equivalent of Satan in the Buddhist religion. Mara appeared to him in the shape of dancing girls, tempting him to exchange his divine bliss for sensual pleasure. The Buddha remained untempted.

In *The Holy Science,* Swami Sri Yukteswar Giri, writes the following to explain how we are tempted into darkness.

> *When man understands even by way of inference the*
> *true nature of this creation, the true relation existing*
> *between this creation and himself; and when he*
> *further understands that he is completely blinded by*
> *the influence of Darkness, Maya, and that it is the*
> *bondage of Darkness alone which makes him forget*
> *his real Self and brings about all his sufferings, he*
> *naturally wishes to be relieved from all these evils.*
> *This relief from evil, or liberation from the bondage*
> *of Maya, becomes the prime object of his life.*

Maya is equivalent to the Christian Devil or Satan. Maya, or Satan, is nothing but the energy of temptation that leads us down the wrong path and delays our spiritual progress. Maya is not some kind of supernatural evil force or spirit. Evil actions are nothing but the desires that lead us into darkness. This is not metaphorical; literally, our soul's energy is stained by such energies as hatred, jealousy, and judgement.

While in the physical state, and in complete oblivion of his/her real self, the person acts from *ignorance*. In this state, we are ignorant of our true self, our spirit, and we are unable to see beyond our physical body and understand our true self, our immortal soul. Hindus call this *Avidya*. While the person is developing spiritually, from *ignorance* he/she gradually moves towards *wisdom*. The soul eventually finds liberation, and death and rebirth are no longer necessary.

Demons

Demons are different from Satan. References to demons in the Bible are lost spirits that may get attached to living people, and can be released through exorcism. In my work I have found such cases, and such attachments can be released with hypnosis and other spiritual methods. When the spirit attachments are benign, the host is not significantly impacted. However, if the spirit is aggressive, the person will exhibit irrational, intimidating, schizophrenic or a number of other negative behaviours. Jesus performed several exorcisms which are recorded in the New Testament.

> *Then His fame went throughout all Syria; and they brought to Him all sick people who were afflicted with various diseases and torments, and those who were* **demon-possessed***, epileptics, and paralytics; and He healed them. (Matthew 4:24)*

In ancient Greek, the word '*demon*' simply means *spirit*.

The main philosophy of Buddhism is around desire. Desire is the Christian *evil*; the relationship between the two is illustrated in Figure 10.

CHAPTER 8

Managing Desires, and Soul Liberation

When we operate purely through our physical nature, using our intellect, we are operating in a state of *ignorance*. We are not our bodies; we are our souls. The soul is the true nature of each of us and it is entrapped in the physical body waiting for its liberation. Liberation can only happen when the soul returns to its crystal-clear state. An enlightened person operates from his/her soul or spirit, using wisdom as the driving force. Ignorance understands Desires, which in turn drive us to temptation, releasing the dark energy. Wisdom understands Divine Love, the crystal-clear energy. An average person will operate in between, maybe leaning towards the lighter side; however, there are souls that are darker and unable the see the truth. We all have some level of contamination; the goal is to get closer to liberation with each of our lives.

There are different ways to liberate and heal the soul, but this depends on the level of contamination. Even highly contaminated souls, for example people who have committed serious crimes, have the chance of quick progression and reform which will enable them to avoid repeating the same lessons in the cycle of death and rebirth.

The Desires which lead us to temptation have many causes, some (but not all) of which are listed below:

- Rejection
- Lack of love
- Insecurities
- Fears
- Physical and mental abuse
- Loneliness
- Betrayal
- Anger
- Bitterness
- Low self-esteem
- Low confidence

There are reasons why a person turns to the *'dark side'*. It's not their natural personality to be *'evil'*, nor is it their genes that drive them to a life of crime. It's their environment and circumstances, life after life.

We tend to label people like that as *'evil'* and reject them. We call others *'toxic'* and we avoid them. We throw them deeper and deeper into their darkness by repelling them. These people require love, compassion and acceptance in order to come out of the *'darkness'*.

Once a person identifies their required area of learning, they can practice the polar opposite of their learning. For example, if someone is aware of jealousy towards others, he/she can practice daily gratitude for what they already have. This is called experiential learning. Forgiveness is a key to clearing the soul and will be discussed separately.

Hatred – The Desire to Belong

Hatred is the worst of all energies. It suffocates the soul in dark dense energy. So how is hatred linked to Desire? A hateful person is helpless with low self-esteem and insecurities because of their **desire to belong**. Hateful people are aggressive, and they tend to be hostile and unjust. People that choose to associate themselves with hate groups do so because they feel rejected and have a desire to belong and be accepted by others, and also have a sense of identity by being part of a wider group. Very often a person joins a group because he/she feels rejected by a particularly important group (family, school or work colleagues, society, etc). If he/she gains acceptance in the replacement group, this can easily lead to hatred of the original group. At the same time, the already contaminated soul enters a group where hatred is an ideology. The individual becomes influenced and brainwashed and falls deeper into *'darkness'*.

You only need to turn the television on to see how much hatred there is in the world, against people of a different country, race, religion, sexual orientation, social class, and so on. The list of potential targets is endless.

> *He who is incapable of hatred... is my beloved. (Bhagavad Gita 12:13-14)*

> *Hatred is never appeased by hatred in this world. By non-hatred alone is hatred appeased. This is a law eternal. (The Dhammapada 1:5).*

Krishna in the first passage highlights the importance of being *'incapable'* of hatred in order to progress spiritually. The second quote, by the Buddha from the Dhammapada, teaches us that hatred cannot be healed with hatred. The antidote to hatred is the polar opposite, compassion.

*You have heard that it was said, You shall love your
neighbour and hate your enemy. But I say to you, love
your enemies, bless those who curse you, do good to
those who hate you, and pray for those who spitefully
use you and persecute you. (Matthew 5:43-44)*

In the above passage from the New Testament, Jesus again contradicts
the writings of the Old Testament. Jesus teaches us not to hate anyone,
no matter what they have done to us. Hatred stains the soul.

*Do I not hate them, O LORD, who hate You? And do
I not loathe those who rise up against You? I hate
them with perfect hatred; I count them my enemies.
(Psalms 139:21-22)*

The Old Testament condones hatred in various circumstances. It
makes reference to the word *'hate'* in many passages. The above
passage from the Book of Psalms is one example.

So how can a person with darkness in his soul get back on the right
track? No one is incapable of getting back towards the path of the
pure *'light'*, with the right help and support.

I recently watched the television series *The Story of God,* hosted by
the actor Morgan Freeman. Mr. Freeman was interviewing a former
member of a hate group, who saw the light and disavowed hatred and
left the group to become a model family man. This individual could
see nothing wrong with the group and his membership of it, while he
was involved, but saw it from a totally different perspective once he
managed to disconnect from it. He now deeply regrets his past actions
and the pain he caused. So, what happened to make him see the light?

This man found a woman who loved him unconditionally despite
his shortcomings. When he had a child, the beautiful feeling of
fatherhood solidified his new self. Love and compassion are very

powerful, and light is stronger than darkness. If this man had not found a woman to love him unconditionally, he would perhaps still be associated with that group. This exemplifies a key learning; we don't fight hate with hate, we fight hate with love, kindness and compassion. This is in line with the teachings of Jesus.

In another episode from *The Story of God*, Mr. Freeman visited a serial killer in jail. It was obvious that he was disturbed by the man's unremorseful attitude. A very dark soul does not feel love or remorse when the light of pure Love has been absorbed by all the negative energies of hate, lust, or other such desires. There is hope for reform but only if this man is shown the way of Love, compassion, and kindness. His environment and circumstances, serving a long sentence in an institution where 'dark energy' is dominant, will make any reform difficult, and it is likely that he will not achieve learning progress in this life.

When a person is born, if his or her soul has been contaminated from previous lives, this contamination is still present. However, souls are reborn with a blueprint of their learnings. Souls choose the family, the race, the religion and the country or region, as well as the people that they will come back with, in order to help each other with their learnings. Next time you blame yourself for your parents or your genes, for your looks, health, or misfortunes, remember that you chose them. They were there before you! I have clients who have regressed and experienced past lives in different continents, cultures, and religions. If you are born white in this life, you may choose to be born into a different race in the next life. This is how we learn. If an individual discriminates against a certain race or religion in this life, the probability is that he or she will be born in that race or religion in the next life, to provide the opportunity to complete the necessary learnings, and to progress along the road to enlightenment.

It is common for a person with heavy karmic load to find the path towards the *'light'* when there is strong family support and love.

On the other hand, there is a strong possibility that the same person may turn to a life of crime, if he/she is born into a family where the parents are abusive, violent, fight with each other, or suffer from alcoholism or drug addiction. Even in these circumstances, there are children who find their way towards the light through the support of grandparents or other close relatives, friends, teachers or mentors.

Thus, when we see a person who is hateful, we should avoid responding with hate, and should show compassion. This person requires acceptance, not rejection, and this is an opportunity to help another soul to progress spiritually. *'Light Workers',* those people that help others spiritually, are spiritually progressing themselves; they are collecting *'good karmas'.*

A person like the one in the above story, needs love and compassion. Compassion is the polar opposite of hate (Yin & Yang). It is a common misconception that kindness is the same as compassion. It is not. When you are in a state of compassion, you feel the suffering of the other person and you want to relieve them of their pain. You are empathetic and understand them, despite the behaviour they are projecting.

To be a compassionate person, one must also be kind. A kind person is friendly and generous with everyone, and by nature a gentle person, always courteous and sensitive to other people's feelings. But a kind person might not want to get emotionally involved with a person in suffering.

Hateful people need to be treated with love and compassion, not just kindness. The energy of love and compassion coming from the other person overpowers the hatred and the person starts moving towards the lighter side. Once the person is drawn into the environment of compassion, then he/she is able to clearly see that they exhibited wrong behaviours. The person needs to practice compassion. It won't be easy, but it gets easier with time and perseverance. The person also needs to evaluate their past behaviour, acknowledge who they have hurt, repent, and ask the divine for forgiveness. Another way to accelerate the learning, is to correct past actions by related acts of kindness. For example, if the person by being hateful has been responsible for someone losing his or her job, he or she should help someone else find employment.

People would say that the opposite of hatred is love. This is not correct, because love is much bigger than this. Love is all there is. The opposite of Love is Desire, and Desire is what causes suffering and darkness.

Arrogance – The Desire to Be Accepted

Again, I am going to give an example of an extreme case. Someone on the darker side of the scale. Arrogant people are those people that think that they are better than and superior to others. Arrogance is the behaviour generated by the desire **for acceptance.** An arrogant person will behave in an overconfident manner to gain acceptance and compensate for his/her low esteem and insecurities. Arrogant people are constantly talking about themselves and their achievements. They are loud and have problems developing and maintaining relationships. They don't take criticism well and find it difficult to ask for forgiveness. They view anyone who does not accept their behaviour as their enemy.

> *Assuredly, I say to you, unless you are converted and become as little children, you will by no means enter the kingdom of heaven. Therefore, whoever humbles himself as this little child is the greatest in the kingdom of heaven. (Matthew 18:3-4)*

You have to become as innocent as a little child to enter the Kingdom of Heaven, Jesus said. Young children do not understand arrogance.

An arrogant person is not able to understand what *'humble'* means. This person needs help, and if you know a person like this, it is important to overcome your dislike of this person and avoid being judgmental. Such individuals are insecure and are looking for your acceptance. An arrogant person can easily convert to a humble one with acceptance from others, but unfortunately people tend to label and avoid them, and this develops into a vicious cycle for them. They fall into a dark bottomless pit and cannot get out.

A humble person is always grateful for what they have, is trusting, treats everyone equally, and knows how to forgive. A humble person is patient and has no desire to show off his/her achievements, skills, or possessions. He or she is not interested in material things. Humble people celebrate the success of others; they don't have the need to compete with them.

So how do you deal with arrogant people? The antidote to arrogance is humility. Show them trust and compassion; once they receive trust and acceptance they start moving towards the brighter side of the scale. Then it becomes easier for them to see the mistakes they have made. As with hatred, they have to start practising humility, a step at a time, by repenting and asking the Divine to forgive them for their mistakes and for those they have hurt. Finally, they need to help others. This counts as good karma and helps negate some of their bad karmas.

Judgmentalism – The Desire to Be Recognised

When I was attending classes for my Clinical Hypnotherapy course, while discussing the concept of *'choice'*, the instructor said, *"Everyone makes the right choices"*. I didn't understand at first and asked, *"So, are you saying that criminals make the right decisions? An adult who knows that by killing someone they are depriving someone of a life and going to jail; how can they believe that this was a correct decision?"* She answered by simply asking, *"Despo, are you a judgmental person?"* I was not offended by her question but the answer was not straightforward, and I knew I had to think about it. That night, just before I went to sleep, the answer came to me. I thought I was not a judgmental person, but my course instructor was right; in that instance I had been. This was a valuable lesson. Referring to the example of the *'criminal'*, at the time that the person is committing the crime, despite what the law stipulates, two elements are involved. First, the level of soul contamination, and secondly, the programming of their subconscious mind. In his/her own mind, based on their own values and belief system at the time, they find a reason to justify their actions, and thus reinforce the belief that made the choice. This was difficult to comprehend at first but became clear with time.

> *Judge not, that you be not judged. For with what judgement you judge, you will be judged; and with the measure you use, it will be measured back to you. And why do you look at the speck in your brother's eye, but do not consider the plank in your own eye? Or how can you say to your brother, "let me remove the speck from your eye", and look, a plank is in your own eye? (Matthew 7:1-4)*

Jesus in the above passage from the New Testament taught that we should not judge others, as this is a sin, a karma. No one is perfect, he said. Before we decide to judge others, we should evaluate our own faults.

> *I was in prison and you came to Me. (Matthew 25:36)*

Jesus did not judge those who were in prison. He encouraged people to visit and provide support to those who needed help.

Not judging others is also one of Buddhism's major teachings:

He who does not judge others arbitrarily, but passes judgement impartially according to the truth, that sagacious man is a guardian of law and is called just. (The Dhammapada: 19:257)

The person who judges and rejects another who has been imprisoned will also carry karma. No one should judge another, and a person that judges another person, regardless of what they have done, is no better than them.

Not all prisoners have *'dark'* souls. Some people end up in jail for minor offences, mixing with the wrong people, or being wrongly accused. Such cases often lead to embarrassment and rejection by family and friends. The prison system does not help people to reform, and a person with a *'dark'* soul that has been rejected by family and friends will often commit crimes again when released from prison. The reason they ended up in prison in the first place is largely related to rejection and eagerness to belong. If your own family, friends, and society reject you, what is the likelihood that you will heal and progress?

What leads people to behave judgmentally is a lack of self-confidence and **the desire to be recognised**. Bullying and harassment at a younger age, among other experiences, can cause people to develop low self-confidence and self-esteem which triggers a defence mechanism of projecting their insecurities on others by judging them.

Judgmental people tend to gossip and criticise others, making negative comments and jumping to conclusions without evaluating the facts or attempting to understand the person or the situation.

How do you deal with judgmental people? Do you judge them back? Such people need to be shown the way to trust, by treating them with compassion. A judgmental person may have experienced a sad childhood of bullying or abuse. We need to see things from their side, by putting ourselves in their shoes and questioning what could have caused this person to behave this way. We should not reject their ideas and opinions for the sake of it, and resist taking things personally and reacting. We tend to become defensive when people judge us. This is understandable; however, such a reaction is considered equally negatively when progressing along the spiritual path, and will lead to bad karma for the person reacting as well as to he/she that is judging. Compassion and acceptance are the tools to help such people.

Some people that are judgmental and recognise it but they don't know how to deal with it. Judgmental people lack a sense of trust. Trust always starts from ourselves and a judgmental person must first start trusting and accepting themselves. Trust is an energy that is projected and cannot be received if it is not given. In other words, don't expect others to trust and accept you if you don't trust and accept yourself.

I would like to share another past personal experience, one that made me ashamed of myself. I would first like to clarify that discrimination and prejudice are not the same thing. Discrimination is covered under *injustice.*

Some of you might be aware of a scam from the recent past which originated in Nigeria and consisted of sending letters out with attractive offers which were intended to extort money from innocent people who were fooled into contributing financially. I have received several letters like this in the past, and this subconsciously prejudiced me against Nigerians. My *'small'* mind associated all Nigerians with scams, even though up to that time I had never met anyone in person, nor had I worked with anyone from Nigeria.

About three years ago, while working with a client, I met a number of Nigerians. They are among the funniest, kindest and most fun-loving people I have ever met. They truly stood out as a group and I felt blessed to have met them. My prejudice towards Nigerians immediately disappeared.

My interaction with this group of Nigerians made me deeply embarrassed and ashamed of my prejudice. To make things worse, one lovely lady from the group, called Ruth, invited me to a Nigerian Church event to talk about career progression to the congregation of more than a hundred people. I was honoured to attend. The energy of love and acceptance in that hall was evident and I was so aware of my embarrassment when one churchgoer asked me, *"Do you think that these scams coming out of Nigeria make our chances of finding a job in the UAE more difficult. I think people are prejudiced against Nigerians; don't you agree?"*. I lied to him, right there in the church! I told him that, in my opinion, such prejudices did not exist. How could I stand in the church and tell him that until a month ago, I myself was prejudiced against Nigerians for the same reason?

I am grateful for this lesson and I am grateful to Ruth who thinks she benefited from me when it was actually the other way around.

Prejudice very much exists, and it is common for people to stereotype whole nationalities, groups and races based on ignorant and false perceptions and beliefs, for example all Arabs are terrorists, all Mexicans are lazy, all Nigerians are scammers, and the list goes on. We become victims of a corrupted belief system.

This chapter is dedicated to Ruth with lots of love. Wherever you are, I thank you for this valuable lesson and I hope our paths cross again.

Negativity – The Desire to Be Loved

We use the word *'negative'* so often. But do we really know its meaning from a spiritual perspective?

"The energy in that place was so negative"; "that person is so negative", etc. What do these statements really mean? Negative people always see the worst-case scenario. They are unable to see the possibility of a positive outcome and tend towards disagreeing

136

with others and always adopting sceptical and pessimistic positions. They thrive on conspiracy theories and fake news, and always believe there is an ulterior motive to every situation. In their minds such pessimistic and cynical positions reinforce and validate their beliefs.

Negativity has another dimension. There are people that seem to have a more positive attitude; however, they are not trusting. They are unable to see good intentions in others and they become easily suspicious. So, even though you will not hear them make negative comments about anyone, and they appear to be positive, they are unable to trust or open their hearts. During therapy sessions, there are many instances where the Higher Self tells me that *"He or she has to open his/her heart".* When a Higher Self says this, it is referring to the need for my client to start trusting himself/herself and others, and to receive love as generously as he/she gives it.

Some people are very generous in offering love, but they close off their hearts to protect themselves because they have been hurt in the past. This produces negative energy that contaminates their souls; being closed and not trusting creates karma.

Negative people have typically been hurt many times and have lost faith in people and society. They may have been rejected, bullied, or abused, and are suffering and stuck in their pasts. It's their **desire to be loved** that leads to their negativity.

A deeply negative person considers himself/herself as a realist and everyone else as delusional or irresponsible. They really cannot see the truth through their *'dim'* light and need guidance.

> *Finally, brethren, whatever things are true, whatever*
> *things are noble, whatever things are just, whatever*
> *things are pure, whatever things are lovely, whatever*
> *things are of good report, if there is any virtue and*

*if there is anything praiseworthy, meditate on these
things. (Philippians 4:8)*

Saint Paul very eloquently says in the above passage: Focus on the
true, noble, pure and lovely things; things that matter. Everything
else does not matter.

It's difficult to make a deeply negative person trust you. Trust is the
polar opposite of negativity. Positivity is not the opposite of negativity
and it is not considered a quality in Divine Love, even though it
is very important for our spiritual growth if properly managed.
Over-realistic, or unrealistic positivity, can lead to delusion, which
also brings suffering. This will be discussed further in subsequent
chapters.

Friends or family members who suffer from such negativity traits
need your support. Can you imagine if everyone kept away from
them? They are already suffering as a result of these feelings, and if
they are rejected by those close to them it will throw them deeper and
further towards the far end of the dark side of the scale. Such people
require patience and a positive approach towards them.

Injustice – The Desire to Stop Suffering

Injustice has many levels and meanings.

- The injustice against people who look and behave differently
  from us - race, gender, sexual orientation, religion, age and
  so many other forms of discrimination.
- The injustice we cause to nature and the animal kingdom due
  to our ignorance and selfishness.
- The pain and injustice we cause to others with our lies and
  malicious intent to hurt.
- Unethical behaviour leading to exploitation of the poor and
  other disadvantaged groups.

- Injustice when we support politicians that spread hate and promote extremism and aggression.
- The injustice of knowingly and intentionally cheating and stealing from others.
- The ultimate injustice of terminating someone's life journey before their time.

Jesus said:

> *"Blessed are the peacemakers, for they shall be called sons of God"* (Matthew 5:9).

By *'peacemakers'* Jesus was not only referring to the avoidance of war. He was also referring to any type of injustice. In recent times, he would have been applauding the Martin Luther Kings, the Mahatma Gandhis, the Thich Nhat Hanhs, and the new generation of activists such as the Malala Yousafzais, the Greta Thunbergs, the Emma Gonzalezes, etc, as *'peacemaker'* role models.

Not everyone is born to be an activist, and there is no shame in one admitting this is not something they are comfortable with or enjoy doing. But all of us can become quiet activists in our own homes, in our own universes. This involves us doing whatever is within our abilities and control to protect the environment, spread the word of love, and live our lives without supporting violence or those who advocate it. There is so much each of us can do to make the world a better and more peaceful place; we can each earn an honest living, avoid supporting companies that engage in unethical practices, avoid taking what is not ours, and abstain from spreading gossip and promoting conspiracy theories. The list is endless and each of these actions, small though they may seem when practised individually, make a real difference when acted upon collectively. Question your actions each time you make a decision. Is this the right thing to do? Is my decision going to cause pain or suffering to anyone? Before you open your mouth to say something, ask yourself: how would I feel if someone said that to me? Is it going to hurt the person's feelings? There is a very thin line between being honest and being rude. People that are rude and hurt others do not always understand what impact they are having. They take the position that *"I am being honest"*. If you are going to say something that might hurt someone, perhaps is it best not to say anything at all. If what you are going to say serves no beneficial purpose, then it is better not to say it.

I hear people saying *"I am not recycling, there is no point. I cannot save the world by myself"*. These people are correct when they say that one person cannot save the world. Greta Thunberg cannot save the environment by herself. She needs us all to support her cause, individually the impact is small, but collectively it is massive and game changing.

Abraham Lincoln was a single individual but led from the front to eliminate slavery in the US, even though it cost him his life. Martin Luther King was the catalyst that drove a fundamental change in civil rights worldwide. He was an activist for peace and non-violence. *"I Have a Dream"* he said in his famous speech. His dream was to see a society without social injustice, a society free of discrimination, a society without violence.

Martin Luther King lived and died a true activist. It's because of him that millions of people today enjoy basic civil liberties that we take for granted. Let's not allow his dream to fade away, it's up to us to eliminate discrimination in all its forms.

All souls are equal. In the spirit side, there is no male or female, no skin colour, no young and old, no rich and poor. The only difference between souls is that some are more advanced in their *'education'* that others. The person that does your gardening or cleans your house or serves you coffee with the big smile might be more spiritually advanced than you.

If you know people that are unjust, in one way or another, you shouldn't ridicule them or argue with them. Just tell them your point of view; plant a good seed and one day the seed will bear fruit.

It is important to remember that the person that behaves this way has a sad story to tell. It's their belief system that drives them to behave this way. Understand their point of view and help them, because it's their **desire to stop their own suffering** that causes their behaviour. They believe that one must fight injustice with injustice, and they think this is fair because of the pain and suffering they have suffered.

Murder, suicide and abortion carry karmas. You may be questioning why suicide generates karma. It's because the person, through his/her free will, causes injustice to his/her own soul by cutting its learning journey short. A person that commits suicide is terminating a spiritual contract already made prior to birth, with many other souls and their learning journeys also affected. There are exceptions and allowance that would be made for something beyond the person's control, for example, mental issues such as depression caused by a chemical imbalance; however, karmas are generated for people that take their lives because of financial issues, emotional pressures, work stress, romantic heartache or any other issues that can be worked through to a resolution. Abortion for the wrong reasons also carries karma because this terminates the opportunity of a soul to experience and progress its learning. In some cases, abortion is necessary and does not carry karma, for example when the expectant mother is at risk. The soul will wait patiently for another pregnancy.

In some countries, abortion is forbidden by law and in other countries by religious institutions. From a spiritual perspective, abortion is governed by free will and the laws of cause and effect (karma). It does not mean that a person that has an abortion will not become enlightened. It just means that it will delay their spiritual growth.

Power – The Desire to Be Protected

> *You have heard that it was said, 'An eye for an eye and a tooth for a tooth'. But I tell you not to resist an evil person. But whoever slaps you on your right cheek, turn the other to him also. (Matthew 5:38-39)*

Jesus said, you don't fight power with power. You fight it with meekness.

Very often power is combined with anger. When people are unable to have the power they seek, they throw tantrums and raise their voices. It's a tactic for getting what they want by spreading fear and intimidation. People that are power seekers thrive on other people's fears and insecurities. We often see this fearmongering in political campaigns. Politicians play with people's worst fears and insecurities - a very dirty game to win elections. This is what democracy has come to. I don't think this is what Cleisthenes, the ancient Greek father of Democracy, had in mind.

Power has many forms. We see power in the corporate world. There are good leaders, and not-so-good ones. The good leaders are humble and lead by example. The not-so-good leaders are the ones that spread negativity by flexing their muscles. Power is negative energy. Power seekers will step over *'dead bodies'* to get into power. Their energy is dark, and they neither understand nor have any interest in morals and ethics.

Power seekers project their own insecurities and issues. They project their **desire to be protected.** Behind such bluster and aggression is a weak person in hiding, a person with low self-esteem, a person that feels unloved. By playing the power game, they feel people will respect and love them. By flexing their muscles, they are protecting themselves from getting hurt again, covering up for their insecurities.

Jesus taught that such people can only be approached with meekness, not power, because they are weak and need to be helped through compassion and understanding.

Jealousy – The Desire to Be Happy

Some cultures believe in the so-called *'evil eye'*, and people in these cultures commonly keep glass ornaments in the shape of an eye, or other similar ornaments, around their houses, cars, and on neck chains, to protect them from curses wished upon them by jealous neighbours, friends or even family members. The Christian Church does not accept the concept of the *'evil eye'*. However, I believe that the *'evil eye'* and the damage that this causes to people that are on the receiving end, originates from the negative energy of jealousy.

In Greek mythology, jealousy between gods and goddesses was common. Zeus, the King of the Gods, refused to be monogamous and turned his partner Hera into a jealous wife seeking revenge against her romantic rivals. Zeus in turn had to intervene to resolve jealous rivalries between his lovers.

Jealousy is often associated with a spouse or partner, particularly when one side is possessive and suspicious of the other. However, there are other forms of jealousy - of other people's physical attractiveness, professional success, their relationships, and so on. In the corporate world, we experience the envy and animosity of work colleagues who have ambitions to climb the corporate ladder.

Jealousy comes from someone's **desire to be happy**. Such people associate happiness with whatever they are jealous of. Jealousy is a poison that literally burns the individual from the inside, by causing karmas which manifest as health issues. Jealousy also penetrates the aura of the other person and causes health issues and misfortunes. This is a very dangerous form of *'desire'*. It is difficult to believe that someone's desire to be happy can have such catastrophic outcomes for others. Many people experience jealousy at times, but extreme pathological jealousy can lead to serious crimes and potentially fatal situations.

> *But if you have bitter envy and self-seeking in your hearts, do not boast and lie against the truth. This wisdom does not descend from above, but is earthly, sensual, demonic. For where envy and self-seeking exist, confusion and every evil thing are there. (James 3:14-16)*

> *Love suffers long and is kind; love does not envy; love does not parade itself, is not puffed up. (1 Corinthians 13:4)*

In the first passage above, Jesus explains that envy only brings misery and confusion. The mention of *'evil'* in the first passage is a reference to negative energy and karmic debris. In the second passage, Saint Paul refers to the mutually exclusive relationship between love and jealousy; if someone loves, it is not possible to be jealous. If we are jealous of someone we love, then it is not true love.

> *This city (body) is built of bones, plastered with flesh and blood; within are decay and death, pride and jealousy. (The Dhammapada 11:150)*

The Buddha, in the above passage says that it is our physical body, which is nothing but a *'uniform'* for our soul's experience, that creates negative energies such as jealousy. Our true self knows only Love and is incapable of any *'pride and jealousy'*.

Intolerance – The Desire to Be Superior

Equanimity is what we would today equate with *'emotional intelligence'* - mental calmness and composure no matter what the situation is. On the opposite side of the scale, we have intolerance, which is associated with an individual's difficulty in accepting the values, culture, views, and opinions of others. This invariably leads to short-tempered reactions and frustrations expressed with anger and aggression.

People that are intolerant of others' cultures, values and opinions, behave so because of their **desire to be superior** to others, and this comes from their own insecurities, bitterness and feelings of rejection.

In Buddhism, equanimity, or *'upeksha'*, plays an important role. It is one of the four essential elements of love, alongside kindness, compassion, and joy.

The great Buddhist spiritual leader, Thich Nhat Hanh, said:

> *In a deep relationship, there's no longer a boundary between you and the other person. You are her and she is you. Your suffering is her suffering. Your understanding of your own suffering helps your loved one to suffer less. Suffering and happiness are no longer individual matters. What happens to your loved one happens to you. What happens to you happens to your loved one.*

Thich Nhat Hanh makes the point that a relationship cannot survive without this element being present; otherwise it is not true love. Imagine a relationship where one of the two partners is not able to accept the opinions, values, and views of the other. Not only is he/she unable to listen and understand the other person, but he/she also forcefully expresses views with anger and aggression. If such a relationship lasts, one of the two partners will be unhappy.

In the New Testament, equanimity is equivalent to *patience.*

By your patience possess your souls. (Luke 21:19)

*He who leads into captivity shall go into captivity;
he who kills with the sword must be killed with the
sword. Here is the patience and the faith of the saints.
(Revelation 13:10)*

In the first passage above, Jesus was explaining to his disciples that their lives will be difficult after he has departed from the physical world, *'the patience and endurance will bring joy to your souls'*.

Saint John in the second passage talks about karma: *'If you take someone's life, someone is going to take yours, in this life or another. But the one that has patience and faith, is like a saint.'*

Equanimity plays an important role in Hinduism too. In Chapter 2 of Bhagavad Gita, Krishna says:

*The hero whose soul is unmoved by circumstance,
who accepts pleasure and pain with equanimity, only
he is fit for immortality. (Bhagavad Gita 2:15)*

Krishna reiterates that practising equanimity, by exhibiting calmness and self-control, makes the person progress towards immortality. This is a reference to the end of the death and rebirth cycle.

Equanimity, or Emotional Intelligence (EQ) has been identified as a key skill for successful people.

Mediterranean people have the reputation of being hot-blooded, impatient, and loud. I actually believed it was true, and that we were genetically pre-dispositioned, victims of our genes. I was never that impatient, but I have to admit, compared to others, patience was not my strength. About fifteen years ago I read Daniel Goleman's *'Emotional Intelligence'* (R16) and I realised then that Mediterraneans are not the victims of their genes, but the victims of their belief systems.

This discovery was pivotal to my spiritual development. To put it simply, Emotional Intelligence helps us to recognise, understand and manage our emotions. Emotions will be covered in detail in the coming chapters.

Selfishness – The Desire for Approval

The ultimate and most well-known act of selflessness was the crucifixion of Jesus. His prophesied sacrifice was intended to teach humanity the purest nature of Love, Divine Love. Jesus was ready to give his life for us and go through all the pain and suffering of this selfless, altruistic act.

A selfish person, on the other hand, is self-centred. In order to get what they want, selfish people are manipulative and do not take people's feelings or emotions into consideration, nor do they care about the consequences of their actions. Such people lack empathy. They don't like to share but they always expect others to be at their disposal.

This is the defence mechanism of people that have been hurt. Selfish people suffer in their **desire for approval.**

Buddhism, Hinduism, and Christianity have selflessness or altruism as a prominent element of their teachings.

In Buddhism, *Anatta* is an important principle, which is to do with *'non-self'*; Buddhists believe that we are all one. Understanding that we are all one, the Buddha encouraged people to behave as one, in a selfless way.

> *Not by mere eloquence nor by beauty of form does a man become accomplished, if he is jealous, selfish and deceitful. (The Dhammapada 19:262)*

The Buddha reiterates that selfishness, jealousy, and other negative energies limit the chances of the soul to become *'accomplished'*; to reach the highest level of spirituality.

> *He who is incapable of hatred towards any being, who is kind and compassionate, **free from selfishness**, without pride, equable in pleasure and in pain, and forgiving ... (Bhagavad Gita 12:13)*

In the above Bhagavad Gita passage, Krishna repeats that selfishness is a negative energy that has no place in progressing along our spiritual path.

> *And He sat down, called the twelve, and said to them, "Whoever wants to be first must be last of all and servant of all." (Mark 9:35)*

In the passage above, Jesus is teaching his disciples how to serve others in a non-self-serving way.

Depending on the level of soul contamination, a selfish person may not be able to see that his or her actions are causing pain to others. This kind of person needs help and guidance, not rejection and judgement. A person with more clarity of soul can develop empathy and learn how to feel other people's pain.

Greed – The Desire to Acquire

Greed is the **desire to acquire** material things and become wealthy. Greedy people associate material things with happiness or with a specific social status. This again is a product of their insecurities.

We often say, *"I love food"*, *"I love fashion"*, and so on, but we find it difficult to say to someone *"I love you"*. People in general tend to love physical, material things and commonly find it difficult to express their feelings when it comes to humans.

The worst part is that we actually associate ourselves with material things, with what we wear, with how we entertain ourselves. I am modern, therefore I only listen to this type of music. I am elegant, therefore I only wear this brand, and so on. I have heard people say, *"My dress sense reflects my personality"*. I find it very hard to draw a comparison between fashion and personality. Do they mean that those people that are not fashionable do not have a *'good personality'*?

In my country, in my parent's generation, it was common practice for parents to try and marry their children into *'good families'*. By *'good families'* they meant rich and educated families. Parents used to prevent their children from marrying into families that they did not consider as *'good'*, in other words poor and uneducated. I was born into a family of hardworking, uneducated parents; parents who had strong ethical values and taught us valuable life lessons. I am eternally grateful to my parents for the way they brought me up and the lessons they taught me. I consider my family to be a *'good family'*. Despite the shortage of money and the hardships they went through, they managed to raise nine children.

Greed is keeping us attached to our physical bodies and moves us further away from our spiritual side.

Most religions have generosity, the polar opposite of greediness, as a central part of their teachings.

> *Take heed that you do not do your charitable deeds*
> *before men, to be seen by them. Otherwise you have no*
> *reward from your Father in heaven. Therefore, when*
> *you do a charitable deed, do not sound a trumpet*
> *before you as the hypocrites do in the synagogues*

*and in the streets, that they may have glory from men.
Assuredly, I say to you, they have their reward. But
when you do a charitable deed, do not let your left
hand know what your right hand is doing, that your
charitable deed may be in secret; and your Father
who sees in secret will Himself reward you openly.
(Matthew 6:1-4)*

Jesus discusses generosity several times in the New Testament. He
also taught that generosity has to be performed in secret. You don't
need to *"sound the trumpet"*, otherwise it has no meaning, and adds
no value to your spiritual development. If giving to charity is done
as 'marketing' for the company, or to look good in front of others, it
actually causes damage and can create karma. When one is generous,
he or she must have no motive other than the genuine desire to help
others.

Dana (Devanagari: दान), which means generosity or charity, also
plays a major role in Hinduism. Believers are encouraged to practice
Dana and provide support to the needy and those in distress.

*Although these men, blinded by greed, see no guilt in
destroying their kin, or fighting against their friends.
(Bhagavad Gita 1:38)*

A strong message about greediness is recited by Krishnan in the
above passage. Greedy people are ready to destroy others, including
family and friends, in order to get material things. This is such a
common occurrence nowadays. Families are split over inheritance,
sibling against sibling. In business we see the best of friends become
estranged and the worst of enemies over financial disputes. Is any of
this worth the damage caused?

Know this, O good man: evil things are difficult to control. Let not greed and wickedness drag you to protracted misery. (The Dhammapada 18:248)

The main doctrine of Buddhism is detachment from desires which bring misery and suffering. In the above passage, the Buddha says just that. Greediness does not bring happiness; it brings suffering and misery.

Oppression – The Desire to Control

When we truly love, we allow people to be themselves. People are born with the gift of free will. We tend to drive our children's decisions based on our own agenda and how *'proper'* a child should behave or what decisions they should make. *"You have to become an engineer; your father is an engineer"*. Such demands completely disregard the choices and interests of our children. Our *'blueprint'* draws us towards certain professions. If your child says that he/she wants to be an artist or a musician for the right reasons, then what right do we have to stand in their way? My younger son, when he was about nine, said that he wanted to be a *"famous footballer"*. When I asked why, he said *"they make lots of money!"* He later discarded that idea, because he himself realised that he wanted this for the wrong reasons.

Our children have selected us to be their parents for their learning. All we need to do is give them love and teach them how to be compassionate, loving and honest human beings. We don't need to change them or make decisions on their behalf.

And the LORD God commanded the man, saying, "Of every tree of the garden you may freely eat; but of the tree of the knowledge of good and evil you shall not eat, for in the day that you eat of it you shall surely die". (Genesis 2:16-17)

In Christianity, one of the lessons of the metaphorical *'fall'* of Adam and Eve, was free will. God told them what was right and wrong and gave them the freedom of the Garden of Eden. They chose to eat from the forbidden tree, the karma, and their punishment was to forfeit everlasting life and to experience death. This story represents the cycle of death and rebirth, the principle of cause and effect.

> *But beware lest somehow this liberty of yours become a stumbling block to those who are weak. (1 Corinthians 8:9)*

Saint Paul in the above passage reiterates that we should not allow our freedom to become a burden to others. In this day and age, free will has been misinterpreted. We use our freedom of speech to insult those that are different from us. We feel that it is our right to express ourselves in any way we want, irrespective of the pain that we may cause.

Free will also plays an important role in Hinduism. Guidelines are provided for seekers to follow the correct path, but people may behave and act in any way they wish, and freely make their choices. Such choices and actions will determine the cycles of death and rebirth.

We are not alien to the experiences of *oppression*. Even though we are in the 21st century, there are many countries whose people live under oppressive governments, and oppression is also present at an individual level.

Domestic violence is a common and extreme case of oppression, when the individual becomes dangerous to himself and others. Oppression also exists in the workplace and oppressive managers create negative and demotivated work environments.

People who behave this way, have a sense of entitlement, and get satisfaction from their actions. Their **desire to control** blinds them to the truth.

In the Greek Orthodox marriage ceremony, the priest will recite the words *"Η δε γυνή να φοβήται τον άνδρα"*, meaning *"the woman shall fear her husband"*. Informal custom in Cyprus is for the woman to step on her husband's foot at the very moment the priest says those words, to signify her objection. I forgot to step on my husband's foot - something I still regret to this day!

Joking aside, Jesus never made such statements or implied any form of inequality. He taught that God made all persons equal, regardless of gender and race. On the spirit side, there is no male or female, black or white, Christians or Buddhists.

There are a few references in the New Testament that imply that women should be submissive to their husbands. There are also several references that the husband must love his wife. See the one from Ephesians below. The Church has not taken an explicit stance on the subject of a woman's position in relation to a man, but the fact that women to this day have not been allowed to join the clergy could lead to the conclusion that the Church may consider women to be *'beneath'* men.

> *Husbands, love your wives, just as Christ also loved the Church and gave Himself for her. (Ephesians 5:25)*

> *Do not lie to one another, since you have put off the old man with his deeds, and have put on the new man who is renewed in knowledge according to the image of Him who created him, where there is neither Greek nor Jew, circumcised nor uncircumcised, barbarian, Scythian, slave nor free, but Christ is all and in all. (Colossians 3:9-11)*

In the passage above, Saint Paul says that God created us in his image without exception. *"There is neither Greek nor Jew, slave nor free but Christ is all and in all."* We are all equal. In the passage above, Saint Paul teaches that men should love their wives. This is in response to the Old Testament's references allowing men to *'put their wives away for any reason'*.

The Old Testament is quite rigid and extreme on the treatment of women.

> *O daughter of Babylon, who are to be destroyed,*
> *Happy the one who repays you as you have served us!*
> *Happy the one who takes and dashes Your little ones*
> *against the rock! (Psalms 137:8-9)*

> *If a man is found lying with a woman married to a*
> *husband, then both of them shall die, the man that*
> *lay with the woman, and the woman; so you shall put*
> *away the evil from Israel. (Deuteronomy 22:22)*

The Church needs to look at itself and review its stance towards such inequalities. They are not in line with the teachings of Jesus. On several occasions he criticised the Old Testament and its rigid views.

Lust – Sexual Desire

This is a controversial subject and I have left it for last for a reason.

To be clear, there is no sin or karma in sex between two people that love each other. If it were not for the sexual act, none of us would exist.

From a spiritual perspective, sex carries karma under the following circumstances:

a) When an individual has sex purely for the purpose of satisfying their physical desires and without any emotional attachment to the other person. Even if the sex is consensual, the two individuals are taking advantage of each other's bodies, for their own *'selfish'* reasons. Here I am talking about one-night stands, with people that hardly know each other or who have no feelings towards each other.

b) Adultery carries karma. The person who commits adultery is breaking spiritual laws of oneness and entanglement. Entanglement is a deep subject, but in short, a married person that has intercourse with someone other than his partner allows energies from other family units to be entangled in his/her family unit.

c) The most serious type of sexual karma is that relating to rape.

Other than the above, sex is natural between two people that have feelings for each other.

I need to discuss the stance of the Christian Church towards divorce and adultery, because there is a misunderstanding in what Jesus taught on the subject:

> *The Pharisees also came to Him, testing Him, and saying to Him, "Is it lawful for a man to divorce his wife for just any reason?". And He answered and said to them, "Have you not read that He who made them at the beginning made them male and female?", and said, "For this reason a man shall leave his father and mother and be joined to his wife, and the two shall become one flesh? So then, they are no longer two but one flesh. Therefore, what God has joined together, let not man separate." They said to Him, "Why then did Moses command to give a certificate of divorce, and to put her away?" He said to them, "Moses, because of the hardness of your hearts, permitted you*

to divorce your wives, but from the beginning it was not so. And I say to you, whoever divorces his wife, except for sexual immorality, and marries another, commits adultery; and whoever marries her who is divorced commits adultery." (Mathew 19:3-10)

In the above text, Jesus was tested by the Pharisees (G13). They were already looking for ways to accuse him of blasphemy, as Jesus had on several occasions criticised the teachings of the Old Testament. In this passage Jesus was asked if a man can divorce his wife **for any reason**. The Old Testament allowed this because in those days, the position of the woman in society was beneath that of the man, and women were often rejected by their families when their husbands divorced them. When interpreting scriptures, one must understand the social structure of those days. We also need to understand that the world was a very different place. People lived simple lives, and materialism was limited to the very few who made the aristocratic upper class. However, lust is not a new thing. It has always existed and has driven men and women into abandoning their partners. For this reason, Jesus's response to the Pharisees was worded to allow a man to divorce his wife, if she has committed a serious wrong, for example adultery, and **not just for any reason**.

Therefore, the person that *'puts his wife away'* for no good reason will commit a sin or a karma.

The Pharisees went on to say that Jesus contradicted the teachings of Moses, who allowed divorce. Jesus's response was to emphasise that from the earliest times it was always considered to be adultery for a man to leave his wife for no good reason; nothing had changed. Moses saw the *'hardness'* in humans and this is why he allowed it.

Jesus was clearly saying that divorcing for no good reason is equivalent to adultery. People have the free will to make their own choices, but the consequences will be defined by the principles of karma. The Church does not have the right to intervene in personal decisions such as these.

I would like to share a personal story with you. I am the youngest of nine children from a poor family. When I was about three years old, on Easter Saturday, my mother went to church. After the church service she proceeded to take Holy Communion (G5). The priest, who had known her a long time, refused to give her communion, because he suspected that she has been taking contraceptives so as not to conceive. You can imagine how angry my mother became. After all, this priest only had six children! She told him that he was not the one feeding her family and it was not his decision how many children she would have. She stopped going to church, and it was only after the 1974 war in Cyprus, when we became refugees and moved to another area, that my mother started going to church again. It's been more than fifty years since this incident and things have changed, but occasionally I still hear similar stories of intolerance within the Church.

The sexual revolution that started in the 60s and was intended to liberate people from the bonds of rigid traditional code and religious superstition, at the same time has caused a lot of pain. Divorces have increased exponentially, leaving many more children disadvantaged and suffering as the ultimate victims.

Jesus and the other teachers taught Divine Love. There will be no need for divorce if the partners in a relationship live by the principles of Divine Love.

• CHAPTER 9 •

Soul Liberation through Divine Love

I was raised in a conservative family. We were very close and loved each other, but saying *"I love you"*, was not something we were brought up to do. It's only in recent years that we have learnt to express our emotions and say those beautiful words.

In 1974, Turkey invaded Cyprus and occupied forty percent of the Island. We were forced onto buses and moved to a neighbouring village, where we were kept until the United Nations intervened and we were evacuated to the southern part of the island. When we arrived in this other village, Turkish soldiers called everyone to the village square and started selecting men to board a truck. My father was selected and my siblings and I were shouting and holding on to him. We did not understand why they were taking him, but we instinctively knew that he should not go on that truck. We started crying and calling out to him, *"Papa, Papa".* He turned and gave us a sad *"it's OK"* look. A Turkish officer present understood that he was the father of several children and his compassion kicked in. He instructed the soldiers to remove my father from the truck.

All the men who got on that truck, including my uncle, my father's brother, were never seen alive again. It was only a few years ago that their graves were found and their bodies identified by DNA testing; they had all been shot in the back of the head. The other families could not save their loved ones, but we were fortunate; we were many and our combined voices were heard. Our love saved my father.

Love is all there is. Our soul is love energy waiting to be liberated. While writing this book, I have spent a lot of time researching Love. What do we understand when we talk about Love? Most books are concerned with romantic love. Romantic love is the soul blueprint's magnetic way of bringing souls together to progress their learning. Without romantic love, our learnings would not be possible.

About twenty years ago I was attending a training course, and the trainer showed us a video of Dr. Leo Buscaglia, a university professor, author, and motivational speaker. That video had a significant impact on me. It was a motivational presentation about an hour long about Love. He explained how he was raised in a very loving family. Love was very important to him and he understood the meaning of true love, but it was not until one of his students, a bright young lady, committed suicide that he realised how disconnected we are from each other. No one had been aware of or understood her suffering. He subsequently got permission to teach a class about Love at the university he was teaching at, and also wrote a book called *Love* (R13).

That training session made me think of how many people out there are suffering, and if we all exercise Divine Love, we will have fewer suicides, fewer divorces, fewer wars, less discrimination, less sickness, less suffering ….

Figure 12 illustrates the three types of love, physical, philosophical, and divine, and the relationship between them.

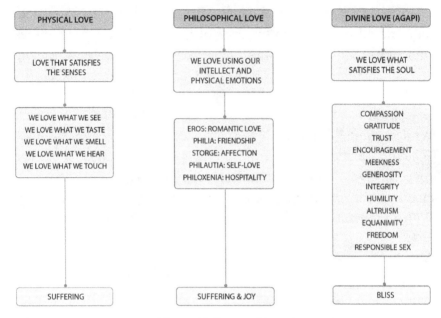

Figure 12: Types of Love

PHYSICAL LOVE

We tend to identify ourselves with material things, for example, food, entertainment, clothes, cars, houses (the list is endless), and with our external beauty.

We love food, we love perfumes, we love clothes, we love designer goods, we love music, we love to touch and to be touched, or we love things that feel good on our skin. But we find it very hard to say *"I love you"* to our loved ones.

People that are attached to their physical bodies, and love (or dislike) based on the signal given by their senses and are unable to show love and compassion to human beings, live in suffering because they are driven by their desires.

160

PHILOSOPHICAL LOVE

Romantic Love - Eros

Romantic Love has been talked about for thousands of years. The ancient Greek philosopher Plato was more concerned with *Eros*, Romantic Love, rather than the other types of love. For Plato, this was the key to the immortality of the human species, as it led to procreation. He also declared that Eros could be transformed into the best type of friendship, another type of love.

The ancient Greeks had Aphrodite, the Goddess of Love, who in mythology was born off the shores of my island, Cyprus. Love and romantic scandals were the norm on Mount Olympus, where the ancient Greek gods lived.

As already mentioned, romantic love is very important as it is the magnet that brings souls together to experience and learn. However, romantic love is not true love if it is missing elements of Divine Love.

To develop the romantic relationship further also requires compassion, kindness, and other associated feelings between the partners. Romantic love cannot develop without appreciating the other person and being grateful for having them in your life, without trusting them and having faith in them, without being humble and meek towards them, without generously sharing your knowledge and your possessions, without putting them first and giving them the freedom to be themselves, without being honest and patient with them. Romantic love can never be true love without these elements. The absence of these attributes is the main reason for the majority of divorces. Many couples marry for the wrong reasons, without feeling or exercising true love. Without true love there is a strong possibility that the couple will divorce and even if they don't, one or both partners will be unhappy. There is an old Cypriot saying, *"If you see a happy couple, you should know that one of the two is suffering quietly".* This is a little extreme but does convey a valuable message - people who are together are quietly suffering when true love is absent.

Friendship – Philia

Another ancient Greek philosopher, Aristotle, was more interested in *Philia,* commonly known as *friendship.* The type of love we have for our friends. We want to be with them and share happy and not-so-happy moments. People who have no siblings consider their friends as siblings and share most things with them.

When we are on the spirit side, deciding where to be born, the family, the race and so on, we also make contracts with souls that will come back as our friends. This type of friendship becomes the *'magnet'* to bring those souls together to share experiences and learnings.

Some friendships last a lifetime, some only for a short period. It's all part of our spiritual journey, for our learning. We often get hurt and break off our friendships, but if we were exercising Divine Love our friendships would be strong and long-lasting.

Affection - Storge

This is the type of love between family members. The love of parents towards their children and vice versa, and the love between siblings. This is the type of love that makes us want to sleep next to our children and watch over them when they have a fever, the type of love that gives us sleepless nights out of worry for them. We want to provide the best for them. We want them to be happy.

Once I asked my Higher Self at the end of a session, *"Do you have any last advice for me today?"* and it responded, *"Let go of the burden. It makes your energy very heavy."* It meant that I was always worrying about my children and that emotional energy made my energetic field *'heavy'*.

Affection is very important, but we also need to be careful. By providing our children with what they want without questioning, just to make them happy, we are contributing to their continuing attachment to the needs of their physical body; this hinders their spiritual development.

We must also understand that our children have their own spiritual learnings. It's the role of the parents to point them in the right direction by teaching them all aspects of Divine Love, and to avoid making them overly dependent on material things that will increase their suffering.

Showing affection towards our loved ones is not true love unless it contains all the aspects of Divine Love, as highlighted in Figure 12.

Self-love – Philautia

Aristotle argued that people that love themselves only for personal gain are not practising true self-love or *philautia*. True self-love is when one loves oneself in order to fulfil one's values and principles.

Self-love is very important for our spiritual development. Most religions refer to it in their scriptures. Jesus, for example, said:

> *"You shall love your neighbour as yourself" (Mathew 19:19).*

Jesus never concerned himself with romantic love, friendship, hospitality, and affection. Those are natural instincts, but to transcend these instincts, in order to reach a higher spiritual level, one must detach from the physical world. Detachment can happen only when we practise Divine Love, which dissolves our karmas and progresses the soul along the path to its original state of pure Love. All other types of love are beneficial as long as they are based on Divine Love.

Self-love is important, but not for our physical self, our appearance. Preoccupation with the physical self only brings suffering. Beauty will fade one day, and beauty professionals often exploit ageing to cash in on our insecurities. Self-love is concerned with loving our souls. By loving our soul, our true self, we aim to become better human beings.

On a number of occasions, I have heard people say, *"I hate myself"*. How would you expect people to love you when you hate yourself?

Hospitality – Philoxenia

The word *'philoxenia'* comes from the Greek word *'philos'* meaning friend, and *'xenos'* meaning *'stranger'*. It refers to being a friend and giving love to strangers.

In my country, when we have guests, we say *'eho xenous'* meaning *'I am entertaining strangers'*.

> *When you give a dinner or a supper, do not ask your friends, your brothers, your relatives, nor rich neighbours, lest they also invite you back, and you be repaid. But when you give a feast, invite the poor, the maimed, the lame, the blind. (Luke 14:12-13)*

In the above passage, Jesus taught the value of inviting without expecting a return invite. He also urged us to invite those *strangers* that require food, more than our *'rich neighbours'*, and not to forget those who truly need help.

So, while it's great to invite our friends and relatives for dinner and show we are excellent hosts, we should also offer support to the person that lives in your neighbourhood and struggles financially to feed his/her children. We think that this is the responsibility of the government, but it's also our responsibility to be generous to *'strangers'* that need our help.

These philosophical types of love will bring happiness and friendship to others. However, they also come with suffering. In the absence of Divine or True Love we tend towards trying to please others, and that brings suffering, especially if it's combined with physical love.

DIVINE LOVE – AGAPI

Agapi, or Divine Love, is the type of love taught by Jesus, the type of love that you give to everyone, not just your friends and family.

Love is Jesus's path to enlightenment or sainthood. It is the centrepiece of Christianity.

> *But I say to you, love your enemies, bless those who curse you, do good to those who hate you, and pray for those who spitefully use you and persecute you, that you may be sons of your Father in heaven; for He makes His sun rise on the evil and on the good, and sends rain on the just and on the unjust. (Matthew 5:44-45)*

There are many references to Divine Love in the New Testament; the following are two examples from the Epistles, the teachings of Saint Paul:

> *Therefore, as the elect of God, holy and beloved, put on tender **mercies, kindness, humility, meekness, longsuffering;** bearing with one another, and **forgiving** one another, if anyone has a complaint against another; even as Christ forgave you, so you*

also must do. But above all these things put on love,
which is the bond of perfection. And let the peace of
God rule in your hearts, to which also you were called
in one body: and be thankful. (Colossians 3:12-15)

Love suffers long and is kind; love does not envy;
love does not parade itself, is not puffed up; does not
behave rudely, does not seek its own, is not provoked,
thinks no evil; does not rejoice in iniquity, but rejoices
in the truth; bears all things, believes all things, hopes
all things, endures all things. Love never fails. But
whether there are prophecies, they will fail; whether
there are tongues, they will cease; whether there is
knowledge, it will vanish away. (1 Corinthians 13:4-8)

Saint Paul describes the qualities of love: forgiveness, kindness, humility, meekness, justice. He also says that love *"does not envy, love is not rude, love does not think in an evil way"*.

You see, Jesus is not talking about the love most of us understand, the love displayed by hugs, kisses and expensive gifts. Divine Love is the love that detaches us from our physical self and helps us transcend to higher levels of spirituality, to progress towards our *'graduation'* from this earthy school.

Jesus said that those who achieve the highest level of spirituality will experience Heaven and will be called Sons of God. This is because the essence of the soul, when liberated from the physical body, is essentially the same as the soul of the Father - pure Love, pure Bliss. This is also the meaning of the phrase below from Genesis. It's our souls that are made of God's image, not our physical bodies. Our physical body is just the *'uniform'* we wear for our experiences and learnings in our earthly school.

So God created man in His own image. (Genesis 1:27)

The Soul is a speck of God, pure Love, pure Bliss.

> *And we have known and believed the love that God has for us. **God is love**, and he who abides in love abides in God, and God in him. (1 John 4:16)*

In his letter to John, Saint Paul wrote that God is Love. He understood what the soul is. He understood that the path back to God was through Love.

Love is the oxygen of our soul. Without *love*, our soul *suffocates* in the negative energies of our *desires*. Studies have proved that children who are raised in orphanages from birth, are more likely to suffer from delays in achieving full cognitive function, motor development and basic language skills. Children raised in foster homes and given love and attention develop normal IQ, language abilities and emotional functioning. Our soul is Love energy. Our body requires food for energy; our soul requires Love.

Compassion

> *Then the King will say to those on His right hand, "Come, you blessed of My Father, inherit the kingdom prepared for you from the foundation of the world: for I was hungry and you gave Me food; I was thirsty and you gave Me drink; I was a stranger and you took Me in; I was naked and you clothed Me; I was sick and you visited Me; I was in prison and you came to Me." Then the righteous will answer Him, saying, "Lord, when did we see You hungry and feed You, or thirsty and give You drink? When did we see You a stranger and take You in, or naked and clothe You? Or when did we see You sick, or in prison, and come to You?" And the King will answer and say to them, "Assuredly, I say to you, in as much as you did it to*

one of the least of these My brethren, you did it to Me". (Matthew 25:34-40)

The ultimate explanation of compassion is found in Jesus's words in the above passage. *"I was hungry, and you fed me, I was thirsty, and you gave me a drink, I was naked, and you gave me clothes, I was in prison and you visited me, I was homeless, and you gave me shelter."* The meaning is clear.

Krishna emphasised that a good Hindu should show compassion and be free of hatred.

> *He who is incapable of hatred towards any being, who is kind and compassionate, free from selfishness, without pride, equable in pleasure and in pain, and forgiving ... (Bhagavad Gita 12:13)*

Krishna said that in order to attain enlightenment, one must develop two qualities - wisdom and compassion. Wisdom happens naturally. While the person is detaching from the physical body, he/she moves away from ignorance and towards wisdom. Compassion is the other important quality that a good Hindu should develop.

Compassion literally means to *'suffer together'*. Compassion is to feel the pain of others, to be empathetic and understand them totally without judgement. Kindness and compassion are not the same thing. You can be kind to a stranger, but you don't really want to share their pain. You are being nice to them without any attachments. With compassion, you share their pain and want to help them to ease their pain.

As part of their spiritual path, Buddhists have to practice *Karuna*, which means both compassion and self-compassion. Divine Love is not only for others, but also for ourselves. We live in suffering if we don't truly love ourselves.

Gratitude

> *Then He took the cup, and **gave thanks**, and said,*
> *"Take this and divide it among yourselves; for I say*
> *to you, I will not drink of the fruit of the vine until the*
> *kingdom of God comes." (Luke 22:17-18)*

Jesus taught his disciples to be grateful for what they had. At the last supper before his arrest, and ultimate suffering, he gave thanks to God for the supper, knowing it was his last meal.

> *Do not lay up for yourselves treasures on earth,*
> *where moth and rust destroy and where thieves break*
> *in and steal; but lay up for yourselves treasures in*
> *heaven, where neither moth nor rust destroys and*
> *where thieves do not break in and steal. (Matthew*
> *6:19-20)*

In the passage above, Jesus reiterates that material things decay; they don't last. But developing spiritually will bring one the *'treasures'* of Heaven. Jesus discouraged people from focusing on materialistic desires. Material things keep a person attached to his/her physical body and, as a result, the soul cannot be liberated.

A key concept of Buddhism is the suffering brought on by our desires. Gratitude is a key attribute of Buddhism.

Jealousy is the result of being ungrateful for what one has. The more we have, the more we want. For a poor person, having a plate of food is everything. For a rich person, having an expensive US$3,000 per head meal in a high-end restaurant is nothing special. For a poor person, a bicycle is a luxury; for a rich person an expensive sports car is the norm and to be expected. What does *'enough'* mean? This is an individual perception. The more we have, the more we want, and eventually, despite all we have, it is never *'enough'*. Ungratefulness leads to jealousy and suffering.

This reminds me of an excellent movie I recently saw, based on a true story. The movie was titled *'The Boy Who Harnessed the Wind'* and was the story of a young African boy who turned his father's bicycle into a wind turbine to pump water from the ground to save his father's crop and rescue his family from starvation. When you see a movie like this, you realise how lucky we are.

We are bombarded daily by commercials, cleverly designed to make us want more. These commercials play with our emotions and create insecurities. They define how we should look, what we should wear to *'fit in'*. The fashion industry is worth approximately 2.5 trillion dollars and the cosmetics industry is worth over half a trillion dollars per year. We have become slaves to these giant industries that have decided how we should look and what we should wear. The pharmaceutical industry is worth over $1.2 trillion. Our body is a sophisticated machine that can heal itself, but instead, we have turned to chemicals which are promoted by a sector whose primary purpose is to make large profits. Clearly, the medical profession is an essential element in society, but we do need to be careful about how much faith we put in non-essential medicines when we can heal our bodies through our thoughts and emotions.

So next time you say to yourself *"I wish I had more"*, think of a person that has much less than you and be grateful for what you have, because there is no such thing as enough. Gratitude is a quality of the soul and does not depend on how much one possesses. Gratitude and appreciation for what you already have will lead to a better quality of life. Bitterness and desire for what you don't have will generate suffering and create karmas that will hinder your spiritual development.

Every night before you sleep, give thanks for what you have; your gratitude will be repaid with divine support during times of need.

Trust and Faith

Trust is the building block of human and divine relationships. On a number of occasions during therapy sessions, I have experienced the Higher Self telling me that my client *"must trust herself and others"*.

Trust, belief, and faith are synonymous in the New Testament. Faith does not refer to religious faith; it refers to believing or trusting. These three words are mentioned many times in the New Testament and are key elements in the teachings of Jesus.

> *For assuredly, I say to you, whoever says to this mountain, 'Be removed and be cast into the sea,' and does not doubt in his heart, but believes that those things he says will be done, he will have whatever he says. Therefore I say to you, whatever things you ask when you pray, believe that you receive them, and you will have them. (Mark 11:23-24)*

In the above passage, Jesus talks about the power of faith. Today we call this *'the Law of Attraction'*; if one truly believes in something, it can happen.

Meditating daily for something you need does not mean you will get it. Meditation *'broadcasts'* a signal, with energy sent into the universe. However, if your emotions and beliefs are broadcasting a different signal, for example, *"I am not worth it"*, conflicting messages are broadcast and the intention of the meditation is not achieved. This is discussed further in Chapter 15.

> *But the boat was now in the middle of the sea, tossed by the waves, for the wind was contrary. And when*

the disciples saw Him walking on the sea, they were troubled, saying, "It is a ghost!" And they cried out for fear. But immediately Jesus spoke to them, saying, "Be of good cheer! It is I; do not be afraid." And Peter answered Him and said, "Lord, if it is You, command me to come to You on the water." So He said, "Come." And when Peter had come down out of the boat, he walked on the water to go to Jesus. But when he saw that the wind was boisterous, he was afraid; and beginning to sink he cried out, saying, "Lord, save me!" And immediately Jesus stretched out His hand and caught him, and said to him, "O you of little faith, why did you doubt?". (Matthew 14:24-31)

In this well-known passage, Jesus's walking on the water is intended to teach his disciples that anything is possible if one believes. Peter initially started walking on the water but sank when he became afraid and lost his faith.

Our life is nothing but a well-written movie script, and we are the actors. In movies we see superheroes do unbelievable things and we secretly wish that we also had such powers. We want to climb buildings like Spiderman and fly like Superman. We have discussed how highly developed souls have the powers to do such things.

We trust our politicians when they promise a robust economy, lower taxes, and reduced unemployment. We trust our doctors and our therapists because we believe that they know what's best for us.

Trust is a key element in any relationship; without it the relationship will deteriorate, and partners will resort to argumentative, judgmental and jealous behaviours.

We should always believe that people have good intentions, and we should give them the benefit of the doubt; to do otherwise would result in a life of suspicion and suffering. If a person turns out not to be as trustworthy as we believed, we should be grateful to that person for the valuable lesson he or she taught us.

But trust is not a one-way street; it works both ways. If we want people to trust us, then we need to do what we say we will do. We need to be reliable, honour our promises, and be open and transparent in our communications.

Trust is built by respecting other people's time, values, beliefs, religions, and cultures. You won't be trusted if you believe that your *'everything'* is better than the other person's.

For people to trust you, you have to become a good listener and first understand them before you offer a solution. Don't jump to a conclusion before listening and properly understanding.

A person that trusts and wants to be trusted, shares his/her feelings when the other person hurts them, and doesn't suffer quietly. The other person does not have a crystal ball or psychic abilities to read the other's feelings. You must communicate your feelings, otherwise you are equally responsible for the bad behaviours of the other person.

In Hinduism, '*Sraddha*' (Sanskrit: श्रद्धा) means faith. This term is also used in Buddhist teachings. Faith plays a major part in both religions, and also in Christianity.

> *Just as a storm cannot prevail against a rocky mountain, so Mara can never overpower the man who lives meditating on the impurities, who is controlled in his senses, moderate in eating, and filled with faith and earnest effort. (The Dhammapada 1:8)*

The Buddha in the above passage says that Mara (the temptation or Devil), cannot control our senses if we have faith. It is our physical senses that keep us attached to our physical nature, and thus causes us suffering.

Encouragement

In the corporate world, it is common for managers to flex their muscles when they interact with their subordinates, to satisfy their need for power. One day some years ago, I asked one of the managers I worked with at the time why he was so strict with his employees. He said, *"this is the only way they will respect me"*. Will people respect you when you are excessively hard on them, or will they fear you? Will they be efficient or demotivated and unproductive?

'Respect' is a word often misused. If we exercise true love, we don't expect people to respect us, because such a need for respect is not important to us. Why should they respect us anyway, are we better than them? Respect from another human being is not necessary if we operate purely from a level of Divine Love. However, we must respect other people's values, cultures, belief systems, opinions, and religions. It is clearly wrong to believe that our views and opinions, religion and belief systems are correct, and everyone else's are wrong. There is nothing right or wrong, it is all a matter of personal perspective.

People who exercise true love, give encouragement to their friends, families, and colleagues. They don't put them down. They don't expect or demand personal respect.

Jesus encouraged his disciples at every opportunity. There are several such references in the New Testament:

> *Peace I leave with you, My peace I give to you; not as the world gives do I give to you. Let not your heart be troubled, neither let it be afraid. (John 14:27)*

Therefore do not worry about tomorrow, for tomorrow will worry about its own things. Sufficient for the day is its own trouble. (Matthew 6:34)

In the first passage above, Jesus encouraged his disciples not to worry or be afraid. He was giving them the courage to carry on, knowing that they would face certain death. All his disciples other than Saint John suffered violent and painful deaths. Jesus warned them many times that they would suffer and die in his name, but through his Divine Love they were able to accept their fate without fear.

In the second passage above, he again encourages his disciples not to worry about tomorrow. This is the principle of 'being in the present moment' that is also a fundamental principle in Buddhism. Jesus, on a number of occasions, encouraged his disciples to live for the present and not worry about the future. *"Tomorrow will worry about its own things."* In other words, why worry about tomorrow when no one knows what tomorrow will bring?

When people are depressed or have troubles on their mind, they need love and encouragement. They don't need negativity; they have enough of their own. When we meet a person that is really suffering with such issues, we tend to share our own bad experiences, to show them that they are not the only ones suffering. We mean well; however, this doesn't help them. They become even more depressed and just being close to them and telling them everything will be OK is sufficient. There is no need to say much, just listen and show empathy.

In the workplace, even a pat on the shoulder and a *"well done, good job"* is sufficient to increase the confidence and positive feeling in the group. Open recognition can have a very big impact. People just need some simple encouragement and acknowledgement when they do something worthwhile.

Meekness

Meekness is a major teaching of the great masters.

> *You have heard that it was said, 'An eye for an eye and*
> *a tooth for a tooth.' But I tell you not to resist an evil*
> *person. But whoever slaps you on your right cheek,*
> *turn the other to him also. (Matthew 5:38-39)*

People think that being meek is a weakness and that it makes them appear submissive. In the above passage, Jesus rebukes the teachings of the Old Testament that require equal retribution - *'an eye for an eye'*. He taught that we should forgive those who wrong us, even if they repeat the wrong.

Is Jesus encouraging us to be submissive? Not at all. The power of meekness overpowers aggression. Imagine this scenario. Someone approaches you, shouting aggressively. You don't understand why. Instead of switching into defence mode, you say, *"You seem very upset. I don't know what has made you so angry, but tell me all about it and whatever it is we will find a solution."* How do you think this conversation will continue? In most cases, the person will calm down and even apologise for overreacting. Jesus's statement was metaphorical, but the meaning is clear; we should not become defensive or aggressive when we are faced with someone who is upset. We should instead maintain a calm attitude. This is the only way to solve a problem, through calmness and understanding.

A meek person demonstrates the qualities of humbleness and patience.

> *Blessed are the meek, for they shall inherit the earth.*
> *(Matthew 5:5)*

There are several passages in the New Testament about meekness. In the above passage, Jesus reiterates the importance of meekness in the development of the soul.

The Buddha himself exercised the ultimate meekness that earned him the name *Preacher of Meekness*. When a jealous king tortured him, he did not complain.

> *Just as jewels and gold are the ornaments of a woman, meekness and humility are the ornaments of a Vaisnava (a devotee of Lord Krishna). The symptoms of a devotee are that he is humble, tolerant, merciful, and friendly to all living entities. He has no enemies; he is peaceful, and he abides by the scriptures. (Srimad Bhagavatam 3.25.21)*

The above passage from the Hindu religious scriptures states that a person that is following a path of spiritual growth must show meekness and be humble, tolerant, and merciful. This is a common theme across all the major religions.

Generosity

We associate generosity with providing material things to others, things of monetary value. We tend to define generosity in materialistic terms even when it involves simple acts, such as providing food for the poor. The donation of funds to charitable causes is indeed noble when done for the right reasons and with the right thoughts and feelings. But generosity is not limited to the giving of material things. Visiting a lonely person, or someone in prison or in a rehabilitation centre, or giving your time to cheer someone up who is suffering from illness or depression - these are equally beneficial acts. Emotional support is as important as financial. Not everyone has extra money to give to charity, but we can all spare a little time to spread some love and kindness.

Generosity and kindness go beyond our fellow human beings. We also need to be generous and kind to the environment and the other inhabitants of our planet. We are not being generous to the birds we keep in cages as our pets. We are not being generous to our planet when we cut down the trees in our jungles. We are not being generous to our environment when we pollute and emit greenhouse gases. There are many, many such examples in our everyday lives.

Ellen Degeneres finishes each episode of her show with the words *"be kind to one another"*. She displays acts of generosity in each episode; she rewards special people that showed extraordinary character. Generosity and kindness have a domino effect, they spread like wildfire; people emulate good behaviours.

> *And whoever gives one of these little ones only a cup of cold water in the name of a disciple, assuredly, I say to you, he shall by no means lose his reward. (Matthew 10:42)*

> *Take heed that you do not do your charitable deeds before men, to be seen by them. Otherwise, you have no reward from your Father in heaven. Therefore, when you do a charitable deed, do not sound a trumpet before you as the hypocrites do in the synagogues and in the streets, that they may have glory from men. Assuredly, I say to you, they have their reward. (Matthew 6:1-2)*

In the first passage above, Jesus reiterates that small things, like a glass of water for a thirsty person, are important acts of generosity. In the second passage he teaches that charitable work should be done quietly. Do not *'sound the trumpet'*. You are not doing it for the eyes of others, you are doing it because you genuinely want to.

The Buddha taught seekers to practice generosity. The act of generosity plays a very important part in Buddhism.

If beings knew, as I know, the results of giving and sharing, they would not eat without having given, nor would the stain of selfishness overcome their minds. Even if it were their last bite, their last mouthful, they would not eat without having shared, if there were someone to receive their gift. (Itivuttaka 26)

In Hinduism, the word Dana (Devanagari: दान), means generosity and charity. The passage below is from the Rigveda which is an ancient Indian Mahabharata.

An assurance unto all creatures with love and affection and abstention from every kind of injury, acts of kindness and favour done to a person in distress, whatever gifts are made without the giver's ever thinking of them as gifts made by him, constitute, O chief of Bharata's race, the highest and best of gifts (dāna). (The Mahabharata 13:59)

The above passage beautifully explains generosity and its importance to our spiritual development.

Integrity

One of the ten commandments given to Moses says, *"Thou shalt not steal"*. Is this what integrity means? The answer is that it means a lot more. In several passages of the Gospels, Jesus reiterated that Moses has given the people the *'law'*, in other words what societies use even to this day as the foundation for maintaining a just, fair and safe society.

Jesus was looking beyond the law. His goal was to teach the path to enlightenment, the path to spiritual liberation.

Did not Moses give you the law, yet none of you keeps the law? Why do you seek to kill Me? (John 7:19)

For the law was given through Moses, but grace and truth came through Jesus Christ. (John 1:17)

In the first passage above, Jesus asks the Pharisees why they seek to kill an innocent man if they know and obey the laws given by Moses. Jesus came to show us the path. He said, *"I am the light"*, to take us out of the darkness, *"I am the good shepherd"*, to guide his sheep to safety, *"I am the word"*, to show us the truth and move us from ignorance to wisdom.

Integrity is not only about not stealing. It's much, much deeper than that. Promising to do something and not doing it is dishonest (the opposite of integrity). Spreading rumours about a person behind their back is dishonest. Being unfaithful to your spouse or partner is dishonest. Trying to cheat the tax authorities is dishonest. Blaming someone else for your own mistakes is dishonest. Sharing confidential information with a third party is dishonest. And the list goes on and on …

The Buddha discusses ethical behaviour in his Eightfold Path to liberation. It is clearly referenced in these three paths:

Right Speech – no lying, no rude speech, no transfer of harmful information.

Right Action – no killing, no stealing, no sexual misconduct.

Right Livelihood: Earn your money in an honest way, without engaging in illegal activities or activities that harm others.

Altruism

Altruism is not a word we hear in our typical daily conversations. People who exercise altruism are those who put the wellbeing of others above their own - those people who think and act for the benefit of others.

In Christianity, Jesus's sacrifice on the Cross was the ultimate example of altruism, the ultimate lesson of Love and Forgiveness, exemplified by the well-known plea from Jesus as he was about to die: *"Father, forgive them for they know not what they are doing"*. With his death on the Cross, he showed us the path to enlightenment through Divine Love.

"Love those that persecute you" is another of Jesus's sayings, which highlights his message of love and forgiveness.

The Buddha said:

> *There are these four types of people found in the world. He who is concerned with neither his own good nor the good of others, he who is concerned with the good of others but not his own, he who is concerned with own good but not the good of others and he who is concerned with his own good and the good of others is the chief, the best, the topmost, the highest, the supreme. (Anguttara Nikaya II:95)*

In the above passage, the Buddha teaches the principle of equal treatment of oneself and others, and not neglecting either.

In Hinduism, '*Atmatyag*', or '*selflessness*', is one of the four highest acts of humanity, alongside Love, Kindness and Forgiveness.

One finds it difficult to act in an altruistic manner in today's stressful, materialistic society. Every family has its own problems to deal with, and personal family issues will naturally take priority. It is understandable that we cannot always put the wellbeing of others above our own. We can, however, do the best we can and give importance to helping others where possible.

One should never ignore a plea for help and should do whatever is within one's ability to support. Financial help is not always possible, but a few kind words of encouragement or comfort in times of difficulty or distress go a long way. We all have the ability to exhibit altruistic behaviours in our own different ways.

Equanimity

'Equanimity' refers to the attributes of patience and calmness.

Equanimity (*upekkha*) is another key element of Buddhist teachings. Gil Fronsdal, a Buddhist teacher, summarises the essence of equanimity as follows:

> *Neither a thought nor an emotion, it is rather the steady conscious realisation of reality's transience. It is the ground for wisdom and freedom and the protector of compassion and love. While some may think of equanimity as dry neutrality or cool aloofness, mature equanimity produces a radiance and warmth of being. The Buddha described a mind filled with equanimity as "abundant, exalted, immeasurable, without hostility and without ill-will.*

In Hinduism, the word for *'equanimity'* is *'samatvam'* (समत्व). In the Bhagavad Gita, Chapter 2, Krishan says to Arjuna:

> *Perform your duty equipoised, O Arjuna, abandoning all attachment to success or failure. Such equanimity is called yoga. (Bhagavad Gita 2:48)*

Hindu monks achieve equanimity through yoga, the scientific way of attaining enlightenment. It does not mean that the average person cannot achieve equanimity by practising patience and calmness in their daily lives.

> *By your patience possess your souls. (Luke 21:19)*

> *But he who endures to the end shall be saved. (Matthew 24:13)*

Jesus was also an advocate of patience and endurance. In the first of the New Testament passages above, he teaches that patience is a virtue that allows our souls to be redeemed. In the second of the two passages, he refers to the virtue of endurance.

> *Love suffers long and is kind; love does not envy; love does not parade itself, is not puffed up (1st Corinthians 13:4)*

Saint Paul, in the Epistle to the Corinthians, writes that true love experiences and endures suffering. Patience and endurance are key attributes that we must have to progress spiritually.

In recent times the concept of emotional intelligence (EQ) has become an increasingly important quality in everyday life. Simply put, Emotional Intelligence is the ability to control one's emotions and demonstrate patience and calmness in any situation. This is considered a key attribute in the maintenance of strong relationships.

There is a scientific basis to Emotional Intelligence. This is referred to as *'amygdala hijacking'* (the location and relative size of the amygdala is illustrated in Figure 13). Daniel Goleman, in his book *Emotional Intelligence* (R16), describes the amygdala as that part of the brain that regulates the fight or flight response. The word *'amygdala'* comes from the Greek word *'amygdalo'*, which means *'almond'*. The amygdala is the shape and size of an almond and is the part of the brain that manages emotions. When we experience stress, the amygdala *'hijacks'* the neocortex of the brain, preventing it from making sound decisions. Because the amygdala operates faster than the neocortex, the person reacts negatively and adopts a defensive, aggressive, depressed, withdrawn, or other abnormal posture when under stress.

When we pause and listen to what the other person is saying, and understand his or her point of view, it gives the neocortex time to catch up with the amygdala and respond with a rational response. When we put ourselves into the other person's shoes and look at the situation from their point of view, we realise that most of the time we are overreacting and causing stress for ourselves and others.

Genes do not control your emotions. Patience is a choice, and it is our responsibility to choose patience over other negative reactions.

Equanimity does not only help our soul transcend, but also helps us build strong relationships with those around us. A patient disposition also results in improved health. Impatient people are in constant fight or flight mode, producing high levels of the steroid hormone cortisol. This hormone causes high levels of system toxicity which can eventually lead to illness and disease.

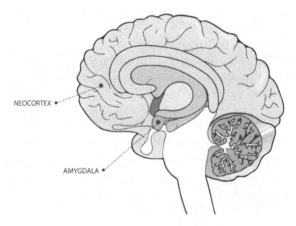

NEOCORTEX ●

AMYGDALA ●

Figure 13: Amygdala Hijack

Freedom

When we truly love someone, we allow that person the freedom to be themselves. We are all born with the gift of free will and need to be allowed to learn our lessons in life. Offering advice is positive support but imposing our opinions on others against their will has the opposite effect because this overrides their free will. We are all here in this earthly school for the same purpose, our spiritual development. Oppressing people and not allowing them to be free hinders their ability to develop, and creates karmas.

We can offer advice and show love to someone who is displaying symptoms of self-destruction. A person who is exhibiting these tendencies feels lonely, unloved, and rejected. The last thing that person needs is for someone to try and forcibly change them. More than anything they need true love. True love is accepting others the way they are. It does not try to change them, only to show them the way, as Jesus did. He was *'the light'*, showing us the path to redemption of our souls.

In the same way, we should lead by example and be the light helping others who are suffering to find their way.

We tend to try to *'mould'* our children to become the adults we want them to be. This is not freedom. *'Programming'* of our children's belief systems starts in the home and continues at school and in the wider community and society as a whole; however, the earliest and most enduring influences are from the parents. Our role as parents is not to mould but to ensure we don't create fears and insecurities in our children. The behaviours and actions of parents play a major role in the future wellbeing and success of their children.

For example, many parents are tempted to push their children towards a certain career path. We are all born with our specific *'blueprints'* that also include our career choices to allow us to progress our spiritual growth. This is the *'magnet'* that draws us towards specific professions. If our child makes a wrong choice of career, we can advise them but should not impose our will. They will eventually find their way, and the path they travel will be an important part of their learning.

We are all provided with gifts in the form of talents and abilities. Our gifts are not given to us for our personal enrichment; their prime purpose is for us to help others. For example, if one is drawn towards medicine, it is because this is an area in which one will be able help others as part of their learning, with the prime focus being on the support to others and not materialistic personal benefit. Unfortunately, medicine is a lucrative business, and there are many opportunities for doctors to personally benefit in ways which may not always be aligned with the best interests of their patients, for example in their dealings with pharmaceutical companies. Such temptations exist and whereas most medical professionals will do the right thing, there are exceptions, which occasionally surface in the media. Such instances once again illustrate the existence of free will, and in such cases, the choices made will adversely impact the individual's spiritual progression.

I was surprised when I was told that I am a 'green soul' and that my path is to help others physically and emotionally - not by acting like Jesus (I don't have such powers), but by being the facilitator and mediator between my clients and the divine spirits.

Oprah Winfrey used her gift of free will to spread kindness and generosity through her show. I was watching the Oscar Awards ceremony a few months ago and Joaquin Phoenix utilised his speech time to spread awareness about animal and environmental issues. He said that powerful and influential people should use their voices to support those creatures in our world that cannot physically express themselves. He couldn't have said it better. Becoming rich while utilising our natural gifts is a bonus; however, the priority is to help others who are less fortunate and need support.

When making career choices, we need to think carefully about our choice of employer, and whether they act in an ethical manner, refrain from exploiting their employees, refuse to promote violence, eschew the use of child labour, aim to protect the environment, promote healthy life styles, etc. Corporate Social Responsibility (CSR), Environmental, Social and Governance (ESR) and other such company standards are becoming more and more important as shareholders and society as a whole are holding companies to account for their corporate behaviours and impact on our communities and our planet. It is no longer enough to be materially successful; outcomes also need to be ethical and sustainable.

The Old Testament metaphorical story of Adam & Eve shows us that God has given human beings freedom of choice, but making the wrong decisions has consequences and negatively impacts our spiritual development.

There are references in the New Testament to our freedom of choice. I particularly like this one from Saint Paul in his Epistle to Galatians:

> *For you, brethren, have been called to liberty; only*
> *do not use liberty as an opportunity for the flesh, but*
> *through love serve one another. (Galatians 5:13)*

Saint Paul says that we have been born free, but we should not use this gift of freedom to satisfy our physical needs, but to satisfy our spiritual ones by helping and serving others.

In Hinduism, free will is clearly defined as the ability to make choices. The right choices lead to the liberation of the soul, the wrong choices lead to karma and the cycle of death and rebirth.

In Buddhism, freedom is the fourth element of true love, *'Upeksha'*. This is a key Buddhist concept.

Responsible Sex

In the previous chapter, we discussed the impact of lust on our spirituality, and how *'empty'* sex, forced sex and infidelity cause karmas.

'Empty sex', one-night stands for the sake of gratifying sexual desires, in spirituality is considered as taking advantage or exploiting someone else's body to satisfy one's own needs, even if the act is consensual. Infidelity causes karmas by bringing energies from other families into the adulterer's family. This in turn creates an entanglement of energies and may generate karmic behaviours.

Enlightened individuals living their last life on this plane generally abstain from sex. This comes naturally to them as the concentrated energy *(kundalini)* moves from the Root Chakra, through the spine and towards the Third Eye Chakra. Thus, they are able to control their sexual urges. This is not to say that married couples or those that are engaging in responsible sex cannot be living their last lives. However, there is a common theme between Hinduism, Buddhism and Christianity, that those living their last life in this place will completely detach from physical needs, including sex.

The Catholic Church demands the clergy practice celibacy. We have discussed this earlier; this is unnatural and causes pain and suffering if the clerics are not living their last lives.

• CHAPTER 10 •

Final Step to Enlightenment

When I was about seven or eight years old, I overheard the adults talking about someone's daughter who chose a monastic life when a marriage proposal was withdrawn. In my young mind, I associated nuns and monks with pain and disappointment. I believed that people who chose this path did so to be away from society and avoid being hurt. However, in time I realised that this isn't entirely true. There might be some instances of people retreating into a monastic life to avoid society, but the more common reason for people choosing this path is because they wish to detach from their physical needs to accelerate their spiritual path. People close to their last level of spirituality have no interest in a materialistic way of life and living the life expected of them by society at large.

We often visited monasteries when I was younger. Secretly, I was wondering if I would make a good nun! Where I come from, nuns and monks live very simple lives in a self-sufficient monastic economy. They produce what they eat, and they sell the excess to provide for the maintenance of the monastery. I always felt very calm and serene whenever I visited a monastery. Now I understand why; it's because of the high vibrational energy of the nuns or monks, coupled with the blessed environment.

In the last stage of our spiritual development, the soul naturally chooses a life that is detached from physical pleasures. It's a natural progression. The soul is already back to a near-original state and only requires detachment from physical pleasures to complete its journey.

Spirituality is about the *'spirit'*, the soul. It's the science of turning *'inside out'*, operating from the spirit. It is not the same as simply meditating and doing yoga, unless this is done on a full-time basis, with trained gurus in a monastery.

People seek to find abundance through meditation, the law of attraction. Abundance is not just wealth; there is also abundance of love, happiness and joy. There is nothing wrong in having wealth; we all want to live a comfortable life and enjoy our life journey. Your meditation on abundance can work, as long as your belief system and your *'intention'* are sending the same broadcasting message. If your belief system is saying *'I am not worth it'*, it does not matter how much meditation you do, it is not going to work. You are broadcasting conflicting messages to the universe. You have to adjust your belief system, the *'programme'* that drives everything you do. You can change your belief system through self-hypnosis, or meditation, before you go on and ask for abundance.

Abundance in material things, however, keeps us tied to the physical body and bound by our physical needs and wants. Therefore, when we meditate for abundance, we must ensure that our intentions are not only for material things, but also positive emotions such as love and happiness.

From a spiritual perspective, there is nothing wrong with material things as long as we don't *'love'* them and we don't identify with them.

> *"No servant can serve two masters; for either he will*
> *hate the one and love the other, or else he will be loyal*

to the one and despise the other. You cannot serve God and mammon." Now the Pharisees, who were lovers of money, also heard all these things, and they derided Him. And He said to them, "You are those who justify yourselves before men, but God knows your hearts. For what is highly esteemed among men is an abomination in the sight of God." (Luke 16:13-15)

In the above passage, Jesus tells the Pharisees that no one can serve two masters. This means, you cannot seek spirituality and be emotionally attached to material things.

When a rich man who lived an ethical life asked Jesus how he could enter in the Kingdom of Heaven, Jesus said to him:

"If you want to be perfect, go sell what you have and give to the poor, and you will have treasure in heaven; and come, follow Me." But when the young man heard that saying, he went away sorrowful, for he had great possessions. Then Jesus said to His disciples, "Assuredly, I say to you that it is hard for a rich man to enter the kingdom of heaven". (Matthew 19:21-23)

Jesus did not mean that the soul of this man can never become enlightened, just not in this life. People born into a wealthy family made this agreement on the spirit side before their incarnation. Being rich can teach us many lessons. Did we obtain our wealth in an ethical manner? Did we exploit others in our efforts to become rich? Did we share our wealth with others? A wealthy life comes with its own lessons.

He who is spiritual, who is pure, who has overcome his senses and his personal self, who has realised his highest Self as the Self of all, such a one, even though

he acts, is not bound by his acts. Though the saint
sees, hears, touches, smells, eats, moves, sleeps and
breathes, yet he knows the Truth, and he knows that
it is not he who acts. (Bhagavad Gita 5:7-8)

Krishna very clearly explains the last stage of spirituality. A saint, even though still in a physical body, is not bound by his physical senses. *"He knows the Truth."*

Physical detachment or non-attachment is a key principle of Buddhism. The word *'nekkhamma'* means *'renunciation',* that is, giving up on physical desires in order to achieve Nirvana.

All three religions agree that liberation of the soul, attaining enlightenment or sainthood or Nirvana, requires detachment from physical needs.

Individuals living their last life generally choose a monastic life. This is not a fixed rule, but typically they prefer to be detached from society. The soul cannot be liberated while still enjoying physical desires. People in this last stage of spirituality are able to easily control their physical desires as the energy is no longer concentrated in the Root Chakra (discussed in Chapter 12), which controls our physical needs. Many people on the last stage of their spiritual journey, observe celibacy, or complete abstinence from sex.

For there are eunuchs who were born thus from their
mother's womb, and there are eunuchs who were
made eunuchs by men, and there are eunuchs who
have made themselves eunuchs for the kingdom of
heaven's sake. He who is able to accept it, let him
accept it. (Matthew 19:12)

A eunuch is a man that has been castrated, but Jesus's meaning is that some people are born unable to perform sexually. Some others have become physically castrated by other people, but there are those that are able to control themselves sexually by detaching from their physical needs. He clearly refers to the last category as those that are behaving like eunuchs by choice in order to complete their spiritual journey.

Sexuality is very important. Without sexuality, none of us would be here. I am the youngest of nine. There must have been a lot of sexuality in order for me to even exist! Jesus does not imply that people should stop having sexual relationships, this is a natural urge.

The above passage from the Gospel of Matthew is one that the Catholic Church uses to demand celibacy from its clergy. A person that is not yet enlightened but is eager to join the clergy has to sacrifice the most natural physical urge. This is a huge sacrifice. How will a person whose soul is not in the last stage of its spiritual journey act if asked to suppress this natural urge? Such an enforced sacrifice suppresses the gift of free will given to us by God.

• CHAPTER 11 •

An Introduction to
the Energy Body

The purpose of this book is not to delve into the scientific theories of quantum physics, and I am certainly no expert in this area. It is, however, necessary to have some basic knowledge in order to understand the impact of emotions (which are essentially forms of energy), on our physical well-being. Countless books have been written on this subject and from book to book there will be some differences. It is necessary to look at the big picture when relating these theories to our inner selves.

The human being has three layers of energy:

a) The Physical Body
b) The Energy Body (or Subtle Body)
c) The Soul (the Spirit)

The soul resides in our heart, waiting to be liberated. Liberation only happens when the heart returns to its original state of crystal clear, pure love energy. Please refer to Figure 14 which illustrates the differences between the Physical Body and the Energy Body.

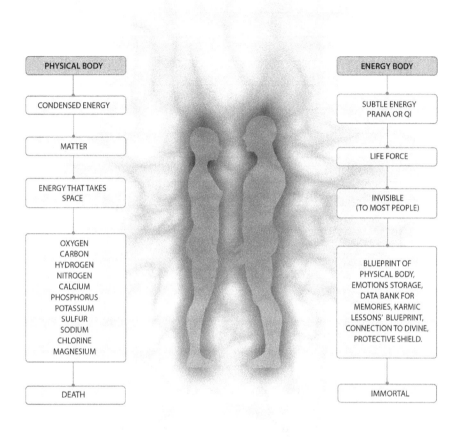

Figure 14: Physical vs Energy Bodies

Physical Body

It was not too long ago that scientists believed that our bodies were made of gross matter. *'Matter'* refers to anything that occupies space and has mass.

ELEMENT	SYMBOL	PERCENTAGE IN BODY
OXYGEN	O	65.0
CARBON	C	18.5
HYDROGEN	H	9.5
NITROGEN	N	3.2
CALCIUM	Ca	1.5
PHOSPHORUS	P	1.0
POTASSIUM	K	0.4
SULFUR	S	0.3
SODIUM	Na	0.2
CHLORINE	Cl	0.2
MAGNESIUM	Mg	0.1
TRACE ELEMENTS INCLUDE : BORON (B), CHROMIUM (Cr), COBALT (Co), COPPER (Cu), FLUORINE (F), IODINE (I), IRON (Fe), MANGANESE (Mn), MOLYBDENUM (Mo), SELENIUM (Se), SILICONE (Si), TIN (Sn), VANADIUM (V), ZINC (Zn)		LESS THAN 1.0

Figure 15: Physical Body Elements

Our body is actually made of several, non *'human'* elements as highlighted in Figure 15. These elements can be found in the environment and they are the same elements required for the survival of all species, whether animal or vegetable.

When Buddhists and Hindus refer to *'oneness'*, they are referring to this aspect of our physical existence. There is nothing in the physical body that can be called *'human'*; our bodies are made of elements that exist in the environment. People that have unexpected out-of-body experiences afterwards reveal that, even though they still identify themselves as individual physical beings, they see themselves as one with the rest of the universe. They don't see boundaries between them and the other life forms in the universe. Our physical body is just a *'uniform'* made of physical elements that functions to allow the soul to travel and experience.

The Christian Church suggests that the dead body will be resurrected, to come back to life in the days of the Final Judgement. This belief comes from the fact that the Church does not understand the meaning of the word *'resurrection'*. It means *'rebirth'*, with the soul returning in a new body. It does not mean that the dead body will come back to life. Origen, the Christian mystic, and theologian who lived in the early centuries of Christianity, said:

> *Just as the food which we eat is assimilated into our body and changes its characteristics, so also our bodies are transformed in carnivorous birds and beasts and become parts of their bodies; and again, when their bodies are eaten by men or by other animals, they are changed back again and become the bodies of men or of other animals.*

In other words, when someone dies the body returns to its original elements. It is not physically possible for the same elements to return together in the same form as before. As noted earlier in this book, Origen was excommunicated for his beliefs.

Basic chemistry tells us that all elements are made up of *atoms* which define their properties. Figure 16 illustrates the structure of the atom. This consists of a *nucleus*, which contains positively charged *protons,* and *neutrons* which are uncharged. The atom is orbited by negatively charged *electrons.* The attraction between the positively charged protons and negatively charged electrons creates a stable atomic structure.

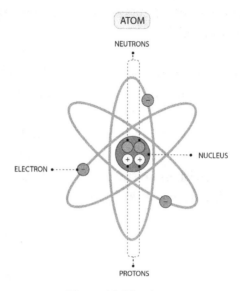

Figure 16: The Atom

Simply put, the atoms bind with each to form molecules, groups of molecules form cells, and groups of cells form an organism (Figure 17).

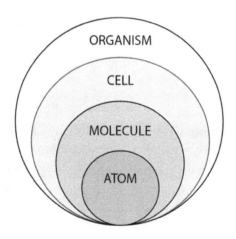

Figure 17: The Organism

Now we come to the relevance of all of this with the rest of this section. If you were able to view the entire human body through a powerful microscope, you would see 99.9999999% of it is empty space. Our body is essentially compressed energy, and all those elements are nothing but energy vibrating at different frequencies.

Albert Einstein believed that everything in the physical world, animate and inanimate, is made of and controlled by energy. Einstein was quite explicit when he said:

> *Everything is energy and that's all there is to it. Match the frequency of the reality you want, and you cannot help but get that reality. It can be no other way. This is not philosophy. This is physics.*

Energy Body

For most people it is hard to accept that there is something called the energy or subtle body which exists beyond our physical form. This is because our energy body is invisible to most people. Donna Eden, the co-author with Dr David Feinstein of *Energy Medicine* (R23), has the ability to see the body's subtle energies. She learned to use this gift to heal her clients and restore physical and emotional health, and over the years she has trained thousands of people across the world.

Religious icons or pictures of saints or enlightened people are commonly depicted with a golden or yellow halo around their heads. People that are able to see energy can see the light emanating from the bodies of living saints (i.e., those that are living their last life in the physical world). Enlightened souls can see the energies of other people, and some people that are truly gifted are able to see other people's energy bodies and their colours and layers.

The energy body is very complex and cannot be compared with the basic forms of energy we are familiar with in our day to day lives. The energy body is *'intelligent'* energy.

Eastern nations have known about the energy body for thousands of years. Acupuncture and Chinese medicine, as well as other types of healing such as sound healing, reiki healing, crystal healing, theta healing, energy healing and so on, are based on the understanding that our energy body is a carbon copy of our physical body, and it is the energy body and not the physical body that one must fix. Refer to Figure 14.

The Mind

The ancient Greeks had a saying, *"Νους υγιής εν σώματι υγιεί"*. Literally translated, this means *'healthy mind in a healthy body'*. Our physical health is linked to our mental health. This section will describe how our mind can influence our health, both positively and negatively.

The energy body controls the mind, which stores all our memories and belief systems (our body programme), in the mental layer of its aura. The mind is part of, and one with, the energy body.

Our physical body cannot function without the energy body. It holds our thoughts, emotions, and belief systems, as *'programmes'* and *'software'* that drive everything we do. There is no such thing as external reality; it is within us. Our own programmes create our reality.

When you want to type a letter, you will search for the applicable programme on your computer's software through your keyboard and monitor (the input). Then you will type your document. Similarly, when your brain receives a signal from your five senses, it releases the energy of thought. Then it looks into the subconscious mind (the programme) to find information, memories, or belief systems to associate it with. Figure 18 illustrates this analogy.

For example, if you have seen a dog, your brain will search in your subconscious mind to find information relating to dogs. If the memories are positive and generate pleasant emotions, then the

200

person will be receptive and open to the dog. If the memories are painful, for example having been bitten by a dog in the past, or having witnessed someone else bitten, then the sight of the dog will generate the emotion of fear or anxiety.

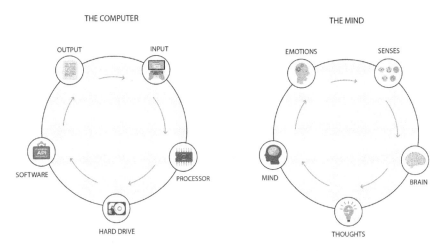

Figure 18: The Mind (The computer analogy)

This is how we learn, by association or repetition. From the day we are born, we associate signals we receive from our senses with emotions, and we create a belief system. These become the programmes that run our lives. This explains why reality is an individual perception. Reality is not something that is external; it is within us.

A woman who experienced an abusive father may associate men with abuse or unpleasantness, and may develop a belief that *"all men are bad"*. This in turn may lead to difficulties in developing stable relationships with male friends or partners. Our belief systems are energy that vibrates at a certain frequency and broadcasts a signal within the universe. This will attract those kinds of people into her life who will validate her belief that all men are bad. This woman is also likely to date men similar to her father.

"All men are bad" is this woman's perception, but this doesn't make it true. Something that is true for me, isn't necessarily true for others.

Our belief systems, from this life or other lives, are the blueprints that we bring with us as part of our karmic learnings. They are the *'programmes'*, the beliefs that run the show.

Hypnosis works by changing a negative recollection associated with a painful experience into a positive one. Programmes are not written in stone; they can be changed through meditation or self-hypnosis or other techniques.

Energy Systems

Our Energy body is governed by the chakras. The development of the chakra system concept originated in India several thousand years ago and is mentioned in the Vedas (G23). *'Chakra'* is a Sanskrit word meaning *'wheel'*. This is exactly what they are; they are wheels of energy that spin clockwise and anticlockwise.

When chakras spin clockwise, they generate electricity and distribute it via a complex network of Meridians (see Figure 20) (these operate similarly to the circulation of blood around our bodies), and Nadis. Chakras may malfunction, or become blocked, stop spinning or spin anticlockwise. When they spin anticlockwise, they also take negative energies from the environment and bring them into our bodies.

There is a total of 114 chakras, but we are mainly concerned with seven, which are the main *'power stations'* of our body.

Each chakra has a specific role to play and each is connected to one of the layers of our aura (see Figure 19).

Below is a brief explanation on each chakra, which also includes some of the transcripts from conversations with my Higher Self.

Root Chakra (*Muladhara*)

D: I learned in books and courses that blockage of the Root Chakra is caused by fears. Is this correct?

HS: Yes, that's exactly right. The Root Chakra is at the base of the spine and when you have fears, insecurities, worries and anxiety about your children, it malfunctions and creates a barrier between you and your fear.

D: This makes sense.

HS: Did you know that when someone's fight or flight response is activated, even their sweat smells different?

D: No, I did not know this.

The Root Chakra is at the base of our spine and is the chakra of survival. It takes care of our physical needs. It's connected to the Etheric Layer of our aura, which is the exact blueprint of our physical body.

When the Root Chakra malfunctions, it can cause physical conditions such as obesity, anorexia and constipation. It can also cause issues with the large intestine, feet, bones, and legs. One common condition is sciatica, which causes pain that radiates from the lower spine along the path of the sciatic nerve.

The Root Chakra is also linked to the adrenal glands, which are small glands located on top of each kidney. They produce adrenaline and cortisol to help us deal with stressful situations. They also produce sex hormones. A blocked Root Chakra deprives the adrenal gland of vital energy. Adrenal gland disturbance can cause the production of too much or too little of these hormones, which in turn results in high blood pressure and muscle and bone weakness.

Sacral Chakra (*Svadhishthana*)

D: I read that the Sacral Chakra can be blocked by guilt. Is this correct?

HS: If you take a step back, you realise that in your Heart Chakra you have a small brain. The same cells you have in your brain also exist in your heart. When you feel fear, you first feel it with your heart. Guilt is an emotion you feel in your heart and you have to send it somewhere. Any emotion, such as fear, guilt and anxiety, has to be sent somewhere in your body. Different emotions are stored in different places.

D: If I understand correctly, you are saying that all our emotions, including guilt, are processed in the heart and then sent to the appropriate chakras to deal with them?

HS: Correct.

D: So, guilt is processed at the Sacral Chakra?

HS: Yes, but guilt is not the only emotion that causes the Sacral Chakra to block. Rejection, unrequited love, and humiliation can cause this chakra to block.

D: Earlier you said that the emotions are stored in different parts of the body. I thought that the emotions are supposed to reside outside the body, in the aura.

HS: Correct, but how would they leave the body when the person is not healed?

The Sacral Chakra is located below the lower abdomen and governs our sensuality. It becomes blocked by chronic guilt, feelings of romantic rejection, unrequited love, and humiliation. It is associated with the emotional layer of our aura, where our emotional energy is stored.

When this chakra malfunctions, it may cause hormonal disturbance and consequent sexual issues, cancer and urinary conditions. The Sacral Chakra is linked to our ovaries/testes.

Solar Plexus Chakra (*Manipura*)

HS: The Solar Plexus Chakra is generally blocked by issues relating to money. This chakra for a successful individual is different from that of people who have financial and job problems.

D: Are you saying that the Solar Plexus Chakra of a successful person is stronger?

HS: Yes, but it is also a different shape.

D: I understand. But what emotions actually block it or cause it to malfunction?

HS: It gets disturbed when the person cannot provide for his family ... cannot provide for them in the way he wants to. It also malfunctions when a person has low self-esteem, depression, and disappointment. There are many other reasons that can cause it to block, but these are the main ones.

The Solar Plexus Chakra is located in the area of the stomach. It drives our will power and becomes blocked by low self-esteem, disappointment, and depression, and as the Higher Self indicated in the dialogue above, money related issues. I found in my work that impatience, anger, and stress also block this chakra.

This chakra is linked with the mental layer of our aura, where all our memories, experiences and beliefs are stored. Our mind.

When the Solar Plexus Chakra malfunctions, it causes issues with the digestive system, liver, and gall bladder. It also affects the pancreas and may cause diabetes.

The Heart Chakra (*Anahata*)

HS: When you have a lot of emotions you can cause damage and disease to the body. Someone who has experienced a broken heart a number of times can actually have a heart attack.

D: I know a couple of ladies that have had breast cancer after a divorce. Both of their husbands left them for other women. I am guessing the cancer had been caused by the heartache.

HS: Correct, but also hatred towards the man and his new partner. They feel betrayed and rejected. The women you are referring to will also create karmas for themselves by not forgiving and letting go.

D: Is there anything else that will affect this chakra?

HS: Feeling unloved and lonely can also cause the Heart Chakra to block.

The Heart Chakra is located near the area of the chest. This chakra is our love centre, giving and receiving love. It becomes blocked when someone is feeling unloved and lonely. Grieving, loss, heartache and betrayal by a spouse/partner can also cause this to malfunction. When I say '*loss*', I don't mean death only; it could also be due to loss of a job, home etc.

The Heart Chakra is linked to our astral body, which is the gateway to the astral plane.

When the Heart Chakra malfunctions, it can cause serious conditions, such as breast cancer, lung diseases, heart conditions, circulation problems and issues with our arms. It also disturbs the thymus gland, which is a small gland in the top part of the chest under the breastbone, which is part of the lymphatic and endocrine systems and can cause diseases in these areas.

The Throat Chakra (*Vishuddha*)

D: I read that the Throat Chakra is our communication centre. It gets blocked when people bottle up their feelings and don't express themselves, or when they display the other extreme and express themselves in damaging ways that hurt those around them. Is this correct?

HS: Yes … and when people don't cry ... they don't express their feelings and keep things inside them. They 'swallow' things instead of releasing them.

The Throat Chakra is located in the area of the throat where our thyroid gland is.

It is connected with our communication. This chakra is often blocked in people who are withdrawn and not very expressive, as described above, and also in those individuals who are over-communicative and suppress others, and don't have good listening abilities.

This chakra is connected to the etheric layer of the aura and is the blueprint of our physical body on the spiritual plane.

When the Throat Chakra is blocked, it can cause sore throat, neck, and shoulder pains. It is connected to our thyroid gland and blockage of this chakra can lead to thyroid issues.

The Third Eye Chakra (*Ajna*)

D: What emotions causes the Third Eye Chakra to block?

HS: This chakra is not related to emotions. The Third Eye Chakra is linked to the pituitary gland. The main cause of blockage is the quality of drinking water. Nowadays, the water you drink has a lot of fluoride, which 'litters' the pituitary gland and disturbs the function of the Third Eye. It is also disturbed when a person refuses to see what is right in front of him. When he knows what the truth is and he is not willing to accept it, he is living a lie, and this will also create blockages of this chakra.

D: I did not know about the relationship between the water and pituitary gland. Interesting!

The Third Eye Chakra is located between the eyebrows. An active Third Eye Chakra helps us with our *'sixth sense'*, our intuition. It becomes blocked when we are unable to see the truth. We are *'lying'* to ourselves about something, which deep down we know to be wrong. According to the information provided by my Higher Self above, it seems that it is also disturbed by the water we drink, because of the high levels of fluoride.

The Third Eye is our antenna to the Divine. Successful meditation and prayers depend on this chakra functioning properly. If this chakra becomes blocked, our *'broadcasting'* to the Divine or the universe will be impaired. This chakra is linked to the Celestial Layer of our aura.

A malfunctioning Third Eye Chakra can cause problems with the eyes, vision issues and headaches. The Third Eye is connected to the pituitary gland, a pea-sized gland found at the base of the brain. The pituitary gland is called the master gland because it controls several other hormone-releasing glands, such as the thyroid gland, the ovaries, testes, and adrenal glands. When the pituitary gland malfunctions, it disturbs the endocrine system of the body. It also disturbs the production of hormones, such as the growth hormone, follicle stimulating hormone and prolactin.

The Crown Chakra (*Sahasrata*)

The Crown Chakra is not located in our body; it is above our head. This becomes blocked when we are not following the path of our blueprint. When we are not on the right road towards spiritual growth.

This is linked to our spiritual aura layer and holds the blueprint for our spiritual path.

A blocked Crown Chakra can cause depression, confusion, insomnia, and nightmares.

Our Crown Chakra is linked to the pineal gland. When the Crown Chakra is blocked, we tend to experience broken sleep and nightmares, because the gland's production of melatonin is out of balance.

The Role of the Chakras

The chakras are the power stations of our body. As an analogy, imagine the power station in your area distributing electricity to your home, and from the circuit board in your home, electricity is sent to all the sockets and light bulbs. This energy from the chakras is called the *'life force'* or *'prana'* (G14). Paramhansa Yogananda calls the energy *'lifetrons'*.

The chakras send energy to the meridians, which are energy pathways in the body. These pathways have energy (*prana*) flowing through them to all our organs. Chinese medicine identifies 12 major meridians, which correspond to lungs, spleen, heart, kidneys, pericardium, liver, large intestine, stomach, small intestine, bladder, gallbladder and San Jiao (triple warmer), which controls our fight or flight response, an organ for which western medicine has no equivalent. Chakras also provide energy to the Nadis system, which provides the vital life force to the cells in our bodies. We have approximately 72,000 nadis in our body.

In addition, the chakras provide energy directly to our endocrine system. Figure 19 illustrates how our main chakras align with our endocrine system. If a chakra becomes blocked, it deprives the associated gland of the life force energy, and with time this becomes *'diseased'*. The most commonly related conditions are thyroid and insulin disturbances and high cholesterol.

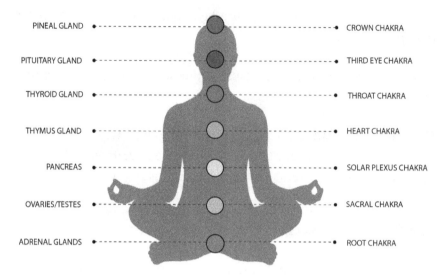

Figure 19: Chakras vs Endocrine System

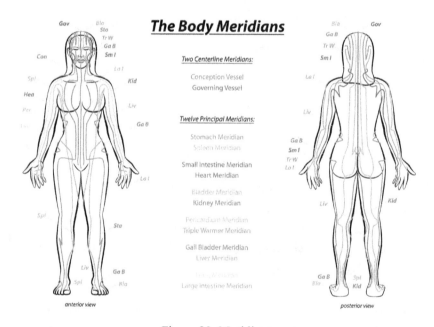

Figure 20: Meridians

Our body replenishes the '*life force*' (*prana*) and the life force creates a protective shield around our body, the aura, which protects us from negative energies in our environment. When this shield weakens, our bodies are contaminated by negative energies in our environment. Similarly, our own energies leak from our bodies and we become lethargic and tired. Paramhansa Yogananda explains this in the *Second Coming of Christ:*

> *Man's body is like an automobile battery, which is able to generate some electricity from its components and the distilled water supplied it from outside. But the power available from these chemical reactions is only temporary; they have to be continually recharged with electric current from the car's generator, or else the battery "dies." Similarly, the life in man's body is not maintained solely by means of indirect sustenance (food, liquids, oxygen, and sunshine) but by the direct source of vibrating life current, the "word" of God.*

> *Electricity from the generator recharges the automobile battery and restores its power to generate more electricity from its chemicals and distilled water; likewise, Cosmic Energy coming into the body through the medulla enables the body to convert food and gross elements into life-giving energy. This same Cosmic Energy, in its universal creative role, made solids, liquids, and gases what they are; when we ingest them, the intelligent life energy in the body must convert those solid, liquid, and gaseous forms of nourishment into energy that can be utilised by the body. The body's intelligent life energy is prana, lifetrons, deriving from the life-giving functions of the astral body. The difference between materially active forms of energy (electricity, light, heat, magnetism) and life energy (prana) is that the former are merely mechanical forces while the latter, being lifetronic, possesses an inherent divine intelligence.*

Our protective shield exists in many layers (see Figure 21)

Each of these layers corresponds to one of the chakras. These layers are our *'database',* a storage location, analogous to the computer Cloud.

Chakras are like any engine that can be damaged by wear and tear and misuse. Therefore, we should always keep our chakras in good condition. We are directly responsible for the functioning of our chakras.

The constant spinning of our chakras keep the life force in our body flowing. A healthy chakra spins clockwise. A blocked chakra spins anticlockwise or doesn't spin at all. When any of the chakras malfunction, a few things can happen:

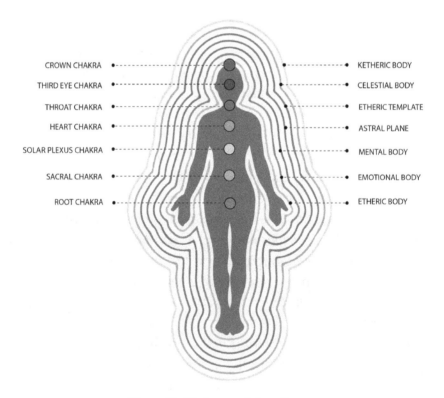

Figure 21: Chakras and Aura Layers

(a) The endocrine gland directly relating to a particular chakra (refer to Figure 19), will not receive the required energy and this will cause health issues. As an example, I will relate a personal experience. I was brought up to always hold my tongue and not answer back. Bottling up my emotions created negative outcomes; whenever I checked my chakras my Throat Chakra was blocked, and this eventually created a problem with my thyroid.

(b) Blocked chakras will not provide vital energy to the meridians and nadis, and other organs and parts of our bodies such as our muscles will also be impacted.

(c) Our emotions are stored in one of the layers of our energy body. One of the functions of the chakras is to remove the energy from our emotions from our bodies and store it in the second layer of the aura. If one or more chakras are blocked, this cannot happen and the energy remains trapped in the body. It finds refuge in organs, muscle, or other tissue and this creates health issues.

d) Chakras work in coordination with each other. For example, if the Sacral and Heart Chakras are not aligned, this may cause one or both partners in a relationship to be unfaithful, even though they may love each other dearly. The Sacral Chakra is linked with sexuality and the Heart Chakra with love. The disconnect happens when the two are 'not talking' to each other.

The functions of each of the chakras are described in Figure 22.

	1st CHAKRA ROOT MULADHARA	2nd CHAKRA SACRAL SVADHISHTHANA	3rd CHAKRA SOLAR PLEXUS MANIPURA	4th CHAKRA HEART ANAHATA	5th CHAKRA THROAT VISHUDDHA	6th CHAKRA THIRD EYE AJNA	7th CHAKRA CROWN SAHASRARA
LOCATION	BASE OF THE SPINE	LOWER ABDOMEN	STOMACH	HEART	THROAT	BETWEEN EYEBROWS	TOP OF THE HEAD
CHAKRA FUNCTION	SURVIVAL	SENSUALITY	WILL POWER	LOVE	COMMUNICATION & CREATIVITY	INTUITION	UNDERSTANDING
CHAKRA BLOCKED BY	FEARS, ANXIETIES, INSECURITIES, WORRIES	GUILT, ROMANTIC REJECTION, HUMILIATION	IMPATIENCE, ANGER, STRESS, LOW SELF-ESTEEM, DEPRESSION, DISAPPOINTMENT	FEELING UNLOVED, GRIEF, LOSS, HEARTACHE, BETRAYAL, LONELINESS	BOTTLE-IN, NOT EXPRESSING, NOT CRYING	WATER HIGH IN FLUORIDE, NOT ABLE TO SEE THE TRUTH	NOT ALIGNED WITH SPIRITUAL PATH
CHAKRA RIGHTS	TO HAVE	TO FEEL	TO ACT	TO LOVE	TO EXPRESS	TO SEE	TO KNOW
BODY PARTS AFFECTED	LEGS, FEET, BONES, LARGE INTESTINE	WOMB, GENITALS, KIDNEY, BLADDER, LOWER BACK	DIGESTIVE SYSTEM, LIVER, GALLBLADDER	LUNGS, HEART, CIRCULATION, LYMPHATIC & IMMUNE SYSTEMS	THROAT, EARS, MOUTH, NECK SHOULDERS	EYES, BASE OF SKULL	CEREBRAL CORTEX
CHAKRA MALFUNCTION CAUSES	OBESITY, ANOREXIA, SCIATICA, CONSTIPATION, HYPERTENSION	SEXUAL PROBLEMS, URINARY TROUBLE	DIGESTIVE TROUBLES, DIABETES, CHOLESTEROL	ASTHMA, CORONARY DISEASE, LUNG DISEASE, BREAST CANCER	SORE THROAT, NECK AND SHOULDER PAIN, THYROID TROUBLES	VISION PROBLEMS, HEADACHES	DEPRESSION, CONFUSION, INSOMNIA, NIGHTMARES
ENDOCRINE SYSTEM	ADRENAL GLANDS	OVARIES / TESTES	PANCREAS	THYMUS GLAND	THYROID GLAND	PITUITARY GLAND (MASTER GLAND)	PINEAL GLAND
ENDOCRINE IMBALANCE	DISTURBS THE PRODUCTION OF ADRENALINE, CORTISOL, ALDOSTERONE, DHEA AND ANDROGENIC STEROIDS	DISTURBS THE PRODUCTION OF ESTROGEN AND PROGESTERONE / TESTOSTERONE	DISTURBS THE PRODUCTION OF INSULIN	DISTURBS THE PRODUCTION OF THYMOSIN, AND THYMOPOIETIN	DISTURBS THE PRODUCTION OF THYROXINE	DISTURBS THE PRODUCTION OF ALL HORMONES	DISTURBS THE PRODUCTION OF MELATONIN
AURIC LAYER	ETHERIC BODY	EMOTIONAL BODY	MENTAL BODY	ASTRAL BODY	ETHERIC TEMPLATE	CELESTIAL LAYER	KETHERIC LAYER
AURIC LAYER FUNCTION	PHYSICAL BODY'S BLUEPRINT	STORES ALL EMOTIONS	STORES MEMORIES, BELIEFS & EXPERIENCES	THE GATEWAY TO ASTRAL PLANE	BLUEPRINT OF PHYSICAL WORLD ON THE SPIRITUAL PLANE	CONNECTION WITH THE DIVINE, YOUR BROADCASTING ANTENNA	BLUEPRINT OF OUR SPIRITUAL PATH

Figure 22: Chakras and their function

Kundalini (कुण्डलिनी)

Kundalini is shown as a *'coiled snake'* at the bottom of our spine, where the Root Chakra is (illustrated in Figure 23). This is concentrated energy, which naturally moves upwards through the body with the spiritual development of the seeker. Once the energy reaches the Crown Chakra through the spinal cord, it penetrates the pineal gland. A chemical reaction in the hormones *'switches off'* the physical body's senses and activates the energy body's senses. A person that reaches this level of spirituality will often and without warning undergo a wonderful *'out of body'* event and becomes part of the *'one'*.

Figure 23: Kundalini Energy

I was trying to comprehend this concept and was struggling to understand what happens during kundalini. I had assumed that the soul was in the body's pineal gland during kundalini, and the chemical reaction pushes it out.

However, a subsequent conversation with my Higher Self clarified this:

D: Does the soul reside in the pineal gland?

HS: No.

D: Ah … I thought that the soul resides in the pineal gland.

HS: It's in the centre of the heart.

D: This is confusing. When people have an out of body experience, I thought that the soul exits the body. Somewhere I also read that the soul gets bored at night and leaves the body!

HS: The soul never leaves the body. How would you have vivid dreams otherwise? The soul only leaves at death.

D: So, what leaves the body when people have out of body experiences? I understood that the energy that travels from the spine pushes the soul from the pineal gland out of the body.

HS: This is not correct. The pineal gland only has hormones. What you are describing is astral travel.

D: So, you are saying that the energy body does not have to leave the body to experience an out of body experience.

HS: Correct.

D: So, where does the soul go after death? And what happens to the energy body?

HS: They are one. They cannot exist without each other. The soul experiences through the energy body when outside the physical body. It moves back to the community after death.

D: This is what we call the spirit side?

HS: Correct. It prepares for the next incarnation. Souls make contracts with other souls before they return.

D: How about when the soul 'graduates'? Where does it go?

HS: It evolves into a different type of being. It becomes an angel.

D: And it moves to what we call 'Heaven', a different plane of existence?

HS: Correct.

It took a while for me to understand this concept. My Higher Self was explaining that our energy body expands several feet outside our body. In our conscious state, we experience though the physical body's senses. When we are asleep, we are in a *'semi-dead'* state, and the energy body that never sleeps takes over. We don't recall any of this when we wake up in the morning. When we have a kundalini experience, our brain is super active because of the activity of Gamma brain waves (refer to Figure 24). The kundalini energy creates a chemical reaction in our pineal gland, which forces the physical senses to *'switch off'*. This means that even though we are still conscious, we are not experiencing through our physical body's senses, but through our energy body. The chemical reaction that happens when the kundalini energy interacts with the hormones in the pineal gland expands our consciousness, and we operate from our energy body instead of our physical body. The soul never leaves the body during such experiences.

Figure 24 illustrates the different waves used by the brain. When our brain is in Delta mode, we are asleep, and all our senses and certain body functions are switched off - *'semi-dead'* as my Higher Self said. Theta state is the one that is activated in hypnosis, when the individual is conscious but in a deep state of relaxation. In Alpha state, we are in a meditative state, or a light state of hypnosis. Beta is the awake state when our brain is active. As described earlier, Gamma state is when our brain waves are super-fast and operating at a very high frequency. People that are having a kundalini experience are operating in this state.

Having a natural kundalini awakening is not the same as having an *'induced'* one. Many people have induced kundalini experiences through kundalini yoga or by taking certain herbal supplements called psychedelics. Spiritual Gurus advise against these. Kundalini multiplies your emotional state at the time that you experience it. If you feel blissful it multiplies that feeling, and you will have a wonderful experience that will assist physical and emotional healing. However, a person that is depressed or carries emotional baggage will not have the same experience; such people's lives often change for the worse after experiencing an induced kundalini.

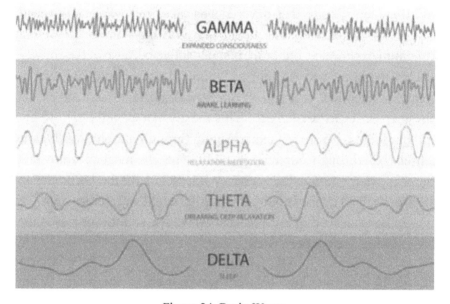

Figure 24: Brain Waves

Dr. Rick Strassman spent five years researching the effects of DMT (N,N-Dimethyltryptamine), a powerful plant-derived psychedelic chemical, that scientists assume is also manufactured by the brain. He was eager to understand the link between the mystical experiences that people have when they take psychedelics and near-death experiences (NDE). He recorded his research in his book *DMT: The Spirit Molecule (R24)*.

> *I believed the source of this DMT was the mysterious pineal gland, a tiny organ situated in the center of our brain...I therefore wondered if excessive pineal*

> *DMT production was involved in natural occurring 'psychedelic' states.*

I believe that during a naturally-occurring mystical experience or near-death experience, the chemical reaction between the kundalini energy and the hormones in the pineal gland generate DMT. Individual experiences after having taken psychedelic drugs vary from person to person. Many people report that their lives changed for the worse after having taken psychedelic drugs. This section is not intended to discourage people from having mystical experiences. I am no expert in this area; my intent is only to relay information I have read or found during my research.

Emotional Energy

Dr. Bruce Lipton's *Biology of Belief* has allowed us to understand how our thoughts and beliefs control our biology and ultimately, our health. We now understand that we are not the victims of our genes. Our beliefs, the programmes we create in our mind, are able to create neural pathways in our brain and thus control the behaviour of our DNA.

Emotions play an important part in our wellbeing. Emotions are the outcome of the interaction between thought and the mind (figure 18).

As discussed in previous chapters, I am not considering feelings such as hatred and jealousy as emotions. This book is focused on the spiritual rather than the psychological side of things. Emotions have a purpose, either positive or negative. The feelings (desires) shown in the first column in Figure 26 have no other purpose other than contaminating our soul and our bodies and derailing our spiritual path.

Emotions have a real purpose to play (See Figure 25). Anger, for example, is important for us to draw boundaries to stop people crossing them. Similarly, fears exist for our safety, and grief for our healing.

EMOTION	PURPOSE
ANGER	PROTECTION AND DRAWING BOUNDARIES
FEAR	FOR OUR SAFETY
GRIEF	HEALING
SADNESS	CONNECTING WITH THOSE WE LOVE
DESPAIR	PRIORITISE
SHAME	SOCIAL ACCEPTANCE
GUILT	SELF-RESPECT
ANXIETY/WORRY	PROBLEM-SOLVING
DISGUST	REJECT UNHEALTHY SITUATIONS
SURPRISE/SHOCK	FOCUS AND ANTICIPATE

Figure 25: Emotions and their purpose

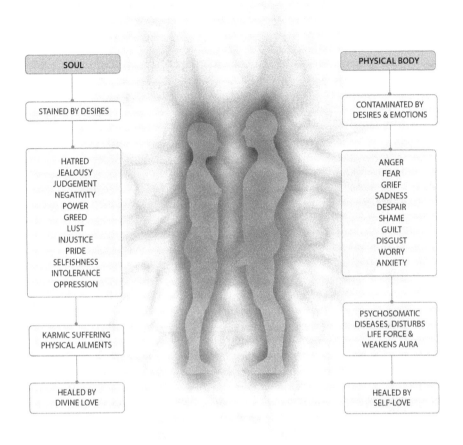

Figure 26: Desires vs Emotions

Emotions in small doses are fine. However, we tend to burden ourselves with the ills of society. We live with chronic emotions, such as fears, grief, and shame, which cause our chakras to malfunction.

Earlier we discussed our physical body, and the general principles of the atom. Figure 27 illustrates the electrons harmoniously orbiting around the atom. In the presence of emotional (trapped) energy, the energy system malfunctions, and the electrons become unbalanced. Their orbits are no longer harmonious, and this creates an energetic imbalance. Our body vibrates at a certain frequency, and this imbalance results in two key problems: (a) The energy of our emotions is at a lower vibration than that of our bodies, and the trapped emotions are therefore lowering the vibrations of our body - the aura of our bodies thus weakens; (b) The imbalance caused by disharmonious orbit of the electrons causes the cells to become inflamed and leads to illness and disease.

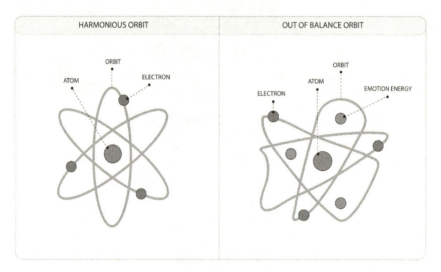

Figure 27: Harmonious & Out of Balance Electron Orbit

In one of my conversations with my Higher Self, while trying to understand this phenomenon, I asked:

D: I am still trying to understand how emotions are impacting our health. Is my explanation of the effects of harmonious and unbalanced electrons orbit correct?

HS: Yes, it is correct, but the trigger of emotions is thought.

D: OK, I know that thoughts are the cause, but I only wanted to understand if this model is correct and I am not misleading people with false information.

HS: It's correct but remember to talk about thoughts!

As my Higher Self said above, thought is the culprit. Our emotions are the bioproduct of our thoughts. When our senses send a signal to our brain, it creates thoughts, which in turn trigger emotions.

Ultimately, the culprit of our physical imbalance is thought, not emotion. Our thoughts are also responsible for the creation of our belief systems. This is the essence of Dr. Bruce Lipton's *Biology of Belief.* Dr. Lipton explains how our thoughts and belief systems are responsible for changing our biology at a cellular level and creating the majority of the diseases we suffer from. Only about 1% of all diseases are genetic. Approximately 20% are the outcome of our lifestyle and what we eat, smoke, take in as chemicals, pollution, and so on. The remaining 79% of diseases are psychosomatic; we create these with our thoughts.

Mindfulness, or focusing on the present moment, is an important principle in Buddhist teachings, and a wonderful tool to manage our thoughts. These concepts will be discussed in Chapter 15.

To summarise, our physical wellbeing is threatened by our thoughts in the following ways:

a) Our thoughts trigger our emotions. Trapped emotions disrupt the flow of energy through the complex energy system of the chakras, meridians and nadis.

b) Our thoughts also influence our belief system, which also leads to illness and disease.

I would like to share with you an interesting case. A client of mine recently contacted me to inform me that she was diagnosed with endometrial cancer. This is a young woman, in her thirties, positive by nature, a vegetarian, and generally fit and healthy.

Due to the covid-19 restrictions, I could not meet her. I do not carry out hypnosis sessions virtually and there was nothing much I could do for her other than reiki and coaching. Two days after this discussion I was connecting with my Higher Self to discuss a few other issues. I decided to ask about this particular client and added this to the *'agenda'*.

I started my discussion with other items on the list:

HS: Have you not got anything more pressing to discuss?

D: Pressing?

HS: Yes, a sickness.

D: Oh ... yes! I wanted to get the small issues out of the way first! Shall we do it this way?

HS: Yes.

It was obvious that my Higher Self was expecting this subject to be raised. I took a little time to discuss the other items on the list and then I continued with my client's case:

D: One of my clients has been diagnosed with endometrial cancer, she is very young and ... (my HS interrupted).

HS: I know everything. What do you want to ask?

D: In order for me to be able to help her, I would like to understand if this is a karmic issue, a psychosomatic issue, or whether the disease has been caused by an external factor. Are you able to provide this information?

HS: She had her love rejected. This has caused her Sacral Chakra to destabilise. Her emotions have manifested as negativity, which has taken over her body. The low vibrations in the area allowed viruses to thrive.

D: But she was told she has cancer.

HS: Yes, she does have cancer. Her cancer is a viral infection.

D: Can this cancer be healed?

HS: Yes, it's reversible, but she tends to be negative. She must make changes in her attitude. You know how to coach her.

D: Will it help if she activates her chakras? Can I do remote reiki on her?

HS: Yes, but it is not sufficient. When you are able to meet her, you must do hypnosis and cut the cord. You must also do sound healing and use crystals. (Cord cutting is a technique we use in hypnosis)

D: OK, I will do so, but in the meanwhile can she get someone else to do it.

HS: No one understands her as much as you. She must change her diet and take supplements. Write down what I am going to say and pass it on to her.

D: I am already writing and recording.

HS: She must stop drinking milk.

D: Dairy products in general?

HS: Anything which has milk.

D: Can she drink other types of milk, such as coconut milk and almond milk?

HS: She can only drink coconut milk. She can eat almonds and walnuts in nut form.

D: Great. Anything else?

HS: No sugar and meat. (I did not hear the second word well and I thought it said 'milk')

D: OK, no sugar and milk.

HS: MEAT. She must follow a vegetarian diet. She must eat foods high in sulphur, like broccoli, cauliflower and horseradish.

D: Ah…OK, no meat. She is vegetarian. She eats fish occasionally. Can she eat fish, such as salmon?

HS: No salmon. Fish high in omega oils such as mackerel and sardines.

D: I will inform her. How about omega oil supplements?

HS: No. Only fresh fish. Do you know the main reason that she must not eat any meat?

D: Not really!

HS: Vegetables, fruits and spices remain in the intestines for less than 12 hours, which means all the toxins leave the body. When people eat meat, it stays in their body for 24 hours.

D: It makes sense. Anything else?

HS: Twice a week and for six weeks, she should eat no food. Only water with some lemon juice, cayenne pepper and clove oil. Her cells will regenerate during this period.

D: I will pass the information on. Anything else?

HS: In the morning she can have a smoothie with avocado, wheat germ, alfalfa and spirulina.

D: OK…

HS: She must take antiviral and immunity supplements. She must eat fruits that contain vitamin C, such as Camu berries and Elderberries. The best way is to take vitamin C intravenously. Twice a week and for 6 weeks, she must take 7.5-10mg.

D: Yes, I got it. Anything else?

HS: She must take oregano oil, goldenseal root, olive leaf extract, maitake mushrooms and echinacea. She must take calendula. It's a very strong antiviral.

D: That's great. I guess she can follow the instructions for the dosage.

HS: Yes, the oils she can put on her salad. What will help her a lot is papaya and pineapple enzyme first thing in the morning. She can also have chia seeds. They are very beneficial.

D: She needs to have the chia seeds in the morning?

HS: Any time of the day.

The Higher Self then switched from answering questions to teaching:

HS: Do you know why emotions hurt people?

D: Well, I know how they block the chakras and that they cause hormonal discrepancies.

HS: When someone has been hurt because of love, the first thing the body does is to release its own hormones. When a woman is single for a period of time, a lot of testosterone is released in the body … and what happens to her fight or flight mechanism … she becomes more like a fighter and because of the high testosterone, the oestrogen is suppressed. Hormonal imbalance pushes someone to another place.

D: So, the problem is both the chakras and the hormones.

HS: Correct. When there is a fight or flight response, the adrenal glands release toxins. Over a period of time; those toxins are supported by hormones.

D: When the body is in fight or flight mode, it also releases cortisol. High levels of cortisol are equally damaging, right?

HS: Yes, for anyone under stress for a long period of time cortisol can be very damaging for the body.

D: Yes, I read this.

HS: When a man and a woman are together, their DNAs are present in each other, and are retained for several months after they have broken up. When one of them leaves the relationship, he or she has left his or her DNA inside the other, who is trying to reject it in the same way his or her love was rejected.

As you can see, there is a combination of reasons that led to the development of cancer.

The client is now being treated with conventional therapy prescribed by her doctor, simultaneously with the treatment provided by my Higher Self.

I am sharing these details to demonstrate how unbalanced chakras created by our thoughts and emotions can cause physical ailments. I am not suggesting nor do I advocate that the *'prescription'* provided by my Higher Self for this particular case is the solution to all types of cancer. Hopefully, I will be in position to share more information in the future.

Fight or Flight Response

Our physical body is born with a primitive mechanism called *fight or flight*. When our early ancestors were faced with danger, their body responses would adjust to deal with it. If, for example, they were hunting and were faced with a wild animal, they had to quickly decide if they would fight or run (flight). In response to fear or stress, the body starts releasing hormones to deal with the situation. The *sympathetic nervous system* will send a signal to the adrenal gland to release adrenaline. Adrenaline pumps energy into the heart, lungs and muscles to give strength to the person to either fight or run. In order to do this, energy has to be redirected from somewhere else. Therefore, the body turns off any unrequired functions - other systems, such as the reproductive, digestive, and urinary facilities. This explains why scared children cannot sometimes control their urine when they get scared; their bladder functions switch off to direct the energy to the systems requiring energy. This is also why people with high levels of stress have digestive issues. The digestive system cannot cope if it is constantly switching on and off, which is what happens with people who are prone to repeated attacks of stress.

The body also switches off unnecessary endocrine functions (see Figure 28), such as the metabolic system (the thyroid function) and pancreas (insulin production). These then create additional stress for the body. This is the reason that some people who are prone to stress cannot lose weight. Like any machine, the body will eventually malfunction when it is continuously switched on and off.

Once the threat has passed, the body turns on the *parasympathetic system*. This triggers the release of another hormone, cortisol, which helps to relax the body and bring the heart rate, body temperature and breathing back to normal. In small doses, cortisol is beneficial, but in high doses, it is toxic just like any other medicine. High levels of cortisol in the body can have severe consequences and has been linked to Cushing's Syndrome and other conditions, such as osteoporosis, high blood pressure, weakness and depression, reduction of sex drive, and so on.

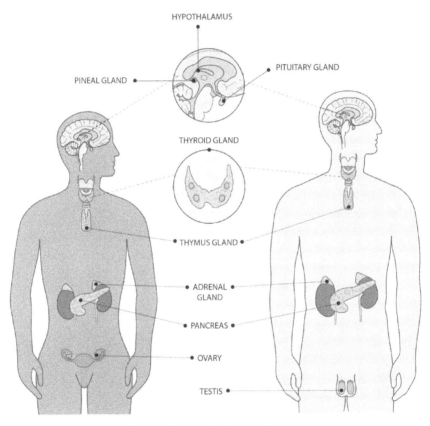

Figure 28: The Endocrine System

When one is in a state of constant stress, he/she will experience fears and other strong emotions that trigger a *fight or flight* response. Our early ancestors had to worry about food; their fight or flight response would be activated only while hunting. In modern society, with all the stresses and strains, fears and other negative emotions, people experience regular fight or flight response mechanisms. Imagine the impact on our health. Solutions to this and other conditions will be discussed In Chapter 15.

CHAPTER 12

An Introduction to Emotions

Scientists have been trying to understand emotions for hundreds of years.

Different dictionaries have different definitions for the word *'emotion'*. For example:

> *A strong feeling deriving from one's circumstances, mood, or relationships with others.*

Or:

> *A conscious mental reaction (such as anger or fear) subjectively experienced as strong feeling usually directed towards a specific object and typically accompanied by physiological and behavioural changes in the body.*

What causes emotions? What is the purpose of emotions? Over the past hundred and fifty or so years, psychologists and scientists have developed several theories.

Theories of Emotions

Charles Darwin's Evolutionary Theory

According to Charles Darwin, the 19th century English biologist, geologist and naturalist, emotions have evolved over time and they exist because they play an adaptive role. Emotions motivate people to respond quickly to environmental stimuli, to help them improve their chances of survival. Furthermore, he suggested that facial expressions and body language are the *'languages'* of our fear, anger and other primal emotions.

James-Lange's Theory of Emotion

Psychologists William James and Carl Lange put forward the theory that emotions are a result of a physiological reaction to events. Their theory suggests that an external stimulus will lead to a physiological reaction. In simple terms, the theory suggests that people have physiological responses to stimuli which result in emotional experiences.

Flowchart 1: James-Lange's Theory of Emotion

Cannon-Bard's Thalamic Theory

Walter Cannon and Philip Bard came up with the Thalamic Theory of Emotions. They suggested that when our brain receives a stimulus, it results in a physiological reaction, such as sweating, trembling, or a racing heart. The resultant emotional experiences occur simultaneously with physiological reactions.

Flowchart 2: Cannon-Bard's Thalamic Theory of Emotions

Schachter-Singer Theory

This theory suggests that the physiological changes occur first and the individual then identifies the reason for these changes.

Flowchart 3: Schachter-Singer Theory of Emotions

Cognitive Appraisal Theory

A modern approach to emotions was proposed by psychologist Richard Lazarus in 1991. According to this theory of emotion, thinking must occur first before we experience the emotion. A stimulus leads to a thought, which leads to the physiological response and then the emotion.

Flowchart 4: Cognitive Appraisal Theory of Emotions

This is a complex subject, and the intent is not to go into this in any great detail. This brief summary of the theories has been included to highlight that there is no consensus on this subject, but how important are the differences? Does it really matter if we sweat before or after we have an emotion? What does it matter if emotions have evolved over time or not? Isn't the purpose of psychology to help relieve people from the thoughts that cause emotional and physical suffering? In more recent studies, scientist have used technology to find out how emotions are created, and which part of the brain is responsible for their creation.

Scientist are approaching the study of emotions purely from a *'matter'* perspective. They are assuming that the brain is responsible for creating the emotions. However, what is missing is the idea that emotions are energy and that they do not reside in the brain. Emotions reside in the aura; the energy of emotions is created in the heart, in response to thoughts interacting with the mind.

HS: If you take a step back you realise that in your Heart Chakra you have a small brain. The same cells you have in your brain also exist in your heart. When you feel fear, you first feel it with your heart. Guilt is an emotion you feel in your heart and you have to send it somewhere. Any emotion, such as fear, guilt or anxiety, has to be sent somewhere in your body. Different emotions are stored in different places.

D: If I understand correctly, you are saying that all our emotions, including guilt, are processed in the heart and then sent to the appropriate chakras to deal with them?

HS: Correct.

See Flowchart 5 below for visual representation of this theory.

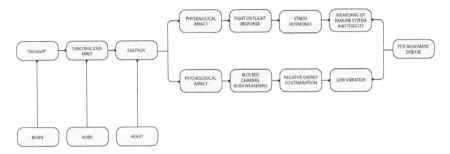

Flowchart 5: From Darkness to Light Theory of Emotions

Emotional energy, once it serves its purpose, moves out of the body through the chakras. If one or more chakras are blocked, then emotional energy becomes trapped in the body and causes disturbance, both physical and emotional. The physician Dr. Bradley Nelson, in his book *The Emotion Code* (R14), recorded his experiences of using his technique to treat people by helping them to release trapped emotions.

Therefore, emotions are simply energy which changes in form and vibration. When water is boiled, it changes from a fluid to a gas and evaporates. During condensation, the gas is converted back to a liquid and can be further converted to solid ice by freezing. Similarly, in response to the stimuli received by our senses, a message is received and encoded by the brain into a thought, then the thought interprets this message by looking into the past memories recorded in the subconscious mind, and emotional energy is created to deal with the situation. The emotions will trigger the appropriate endocrine response to deal with fear (fight or flight response) or other hormones appropriate to the situation.

Therefore, thought is the culprit. So, what do we do? Stop thinking? This is clearly not possible, as without thought we cannot function. Our thoughts help us to interpret the messages received by the environment, to allow us to plan our lives and solve our problems.

Depending on which source is used as the reference, an average person will have approximately 40,000 thoughts a day. Only 5% of our thoughts are related to stimuli received from the environment. We operate from our subconscious mind for the other 95%, either daydreaming or in a state of self-hypnosis, glued to past memories. Therefore, even without a stimulus received by our senses, we are still developing emotions that trigger physiological responses.

Buddhism's philosophy of mindfulness, and the focus on remaining in the present moment, is important because thought creates suffering by keeping us in the past, with its associated painful memories, and thus in a state of constant physical and emotional suffering.

Being in the present moment sounds fantastic, but this is easier said than done. How do we stop those painful memories from occurring? How do we erase them?

Our emotions have a purpose; they are our defence mechanism. As with everything, moderation is required, otherwise the outcome will be contamination of our energy body and illness and disease of our physical body (see Figure 26). Chronic emotions such as grief and fear cause our chakras to malfunction and thus obstruct the flow of the vital energy force into the organs, endocrine system, muscles and so on.

Our mind does not recognise the difference between a real event and watching a movie. For example, if you are watching a sad or scary movie, you are operating from your subconscious mind and are in a state of hypnosis. The emotions of sadness or fear that you experience while watching a movie will have the same impact on your energy flow as a real event. This highlights the importance of being selective about what you watch.

The list of negative emotions is endless. For the purpose of this book, I will refer to the most important ones and those that cause our chakras to block.

Emotions by themselves don't create karmas, but they are at times connected to desires. As an example, feeling guilt and shame is linked to lack of self-love. Divine Love is not only for others; it starts with the individual. If you don't show Divine Love to yourself and accept yourself totally and unconditionally, you are causing injustice to yourself and this creates karma.

Anger is often connected with oppression, intolerance, and power. Therefore, anger by itself may not cause the karma, but represents the way our karmas are manifested.

Our emotions are a choice we make; they are not a natural mechanism. We can control them. It is not our genes that are responsible for our emotions.

Anger

Even though anger is the emotion that enables us to draw boundaries, it is important to first exercise patience, and only apply anger when the other person is not willing or prepared to take a reasonable position.

Anger is sometimes caused by desires. Anger is often used as a tool by those who wish to exert power or display superiority to overpower others. Others may display anger when things are not going their way. People that have a natural tendency to oppress others will use anger to generate fear in order to keep people *under control*. Intolerant people also express anger. Therefore, even though anger itself does not carry karma, the reason why a person gets angry does.

'Chronic' anger blocks the 3rd chakra, near the Solar Plexus.

Fear

Having rational fears is normal. Fears keep us safe and keep us from doing things that may cause us to harm ourselves. However, irrational fears lead to a permanent state of anxiety and adversely affect our quality of life.

There is a difference between phobia and fear. Fear develops when we have a negative experience, one that we remember; the reason for the fear is known. On the other hand, a phobia has no known reason. In hypnotherapy, we find the root cause of phobias in past life experiences or experiences from an early age, and the individual does not remember them.

It's difficult to ask someone not to have a phobia, because it is encoded in their subconscious mind. Such cases of those suffering from dilapidating, extreme cases of phobia, require professional help from a Clinical Hypnotherapist, EFT (Emotional Freedom Technique) Specialists, NLP Practitioners, or other healing modalities.

Many fears derive from the fear of death. Prior to my contact with my Higher Self, I had lots of fears - fear of death, fear of darkness, fear of dogs, fear of public speaking, along with many insecurities. The communication with my Higher Self liberated me, and my fear of death disappeared. Now I have no other fears and my phobias have been resolved under hypnosis. I am a free person.

Chronic fears block the 1st chakra, the Root.

Grief

We generally associate grief with the loss of a loved one. Women also grieve when they miscarry. We also grieve for many other losses, such as leaving a home when relocating, or losing a job.

Our loved ones sometimes have to leave this earthly school earlier than we expect them to. There are many reasons for an early departure. Sometimes the soul is on a short *'contract'* in this life to help a family member with his/her learnings. Typically, we lived previous lives with most of our family members. Souls help each other to develop. If you have suddenly and unexpectedly lost someone close to you, it is important to evaluate the life of your loved one and your own life and ask yourself, *"If I were to learn something from the death of my loved one, what would it be?"* The answer is there. Your loved one is listening to you and is always there for you; you can ask him or her.

Sometimes souls choose to exit their physical body earlier as the circumstances at the time are not allowing them to learn. They prefer to move back to the spirit side and reincarnate again to continue their learnings. Sometimes they reincarnate relatively quickly, in the same family, as children or grandchildren.

Our loved ones are always there, and they watch over us. They are trying to guide us and if you ask for help, they will find a way to help you.

Grief is our natural healing mechanism. People that are finding it hard to let go, and carry *'chronic grief'*, will cause their 4th chakra, the Heart, to malfunction.

People frequently mourn lost jobs, lost homes or over a lost love. These are understandably very stressful situations. We have all been there at one time or another. I have learnt not to worry about things that are beyond my control. We cannot turn the clock back. If we could, we would have dealt with situations differently, but what kind of a lesson would that have been? The goal is to learn from every difficult situation. Ask yourself, *"what have I learnt from this situation?"* There is always a hidden lesson, and when you find it, you will progress along the path of liberation.

I wrote earlier about my father - how the cries of his children saved his life; yet he was to die only 12 years later, heartbroken. My father was a farmer. He worked very hard to raise nine children. When we became refugees, we lost everything. Our home, our land ... everything. We moved to another area with only the clothes we were wearing.

My father had looked forward to the day we would return to our home and our land and farm. He was connected to the land. He loved it. In the summer of 1985, Turkey declared independence for the occupied northern part of our island. That broke him, and he lost hope. I will never forget the look on his face when he heard the news on the radio. His hopes vanished, and I had never seen him so lost. He died a few months later from heart failure. He was a healthy man, very active and had never suffered from heart issues until the day of his heart attack. His love for his home, his farm and his land killed him.

Sadness

It's normal to feel down when you hear of sad events. Sadness shows our sensitive side. A compassionate person will naturally experience sadness; he/she is sharing the pain of others. Sadness is a way of expressing our solidarity with those who suffer, by suffering with them.

Sadness is natural in small doses but harmful when the feeling is intense and over a long period. Whether we turn on the television or read the newspaper, we are regularly exposed to negative news. We live in a state of sadness and anxiety most of the time. It's one thing knowing what is going on around the world and keeping in touch with current affairs, and it's another to be in a state of fear, sadness, negativity, and anger. These feelings contaminate our physical body and soul.

In these times of digital and mass media, it is common for politicians to win office by misinforming the public and manipulating the facts. Campaigns are designed to ignite our worst fears and generate sadness, anger, and other negative emotions. Elections increasingly polarise the population and aim to divide rather than unite. Campaign managers and politicians cause significant damage to the collective consciousness, for the sole purpose of winning elections. Society as a whole needs some serious soul searching; there must be far better ways of choosing our leaders than this.

We need to stop reacting to whatever we read or watch on television. It's not within our power to change or influence such events. Why be angry or sad if we cannot do anything about these? What will be achieved other than causing emotional and physical distress?

We often take on our shoulders all the ills of society, but we are not superheroes. We cannot save the world, or make society work as it should. Our purpose is to grow spiritually in this earthly school, to move to the next 'grade'. Desires and emotions are keeping us in the same 'class', life after life, repeating the same mistakes and trapping us in the karmic cycle of death and rebirth.

Despair

Sometimes our life throws things at us for a purpose; to give us a jolt and wake us up. When we despair and feel trapped without a way out, it is important to remember that despair is nothing but an emotion that stimulates us to discover our priorities and take action. The journey is one of self-discovery.

The very first time I spoke to my Higher Self, I had the opportunity to talk about the actions that I have regretted, and which caused karmas. I was surprised to be told that it is possible for me to progress spiritually in this life. My Higher Self said, *"Those are forgiven. We have sent those people in your life for your learning."* There are no coincidences; situations are deliberately intended for our learning, but how we deal with them is purely our choice. I have gone through a lot of self-discovery, remorse, and forgiveness. This is the reason I was forgiven. It did not happen just like that. I am no different from anyone else.

I participated in a hypnosis class, during which one of the participants volunteered to be hypnotised by the instructor. A couple of years earlier, this individual had suffered from depression and despair. He hated his job but could not see a way out. One day he had an accident and nearly died. His Higher Self told him that his accident was pre-planned for the purpose of persuading him to leave the job he hated. It worked! After recovering from the accident (the plan was not for him to die), he resigned from his job, and is now happily employed as a therapist.

When you are in despair, evaluate your life and ask yourself *"What is the universe trying to teach me?"*. Every challenge in our lives is provided for us to wake up and seek the right path. If one door closes, a more significant one opens.

Shame

While checking the chakras of one of my clients, I found that her 3rd chakra, (near the Solar Plexus) was blocked. I asked her if she was carrying any emotions of shame. She said, *"yes, I am embarrassed to ask my clients to pay me, and I am working without getting paid."*

Embarrassment is when we feel ashamed to do something because we are shy and don't want to be judged. This causes us to keep everything inside us and quietly suffer.

Shame is more than just embarrassment; it is also a deep feeling of humiliation, and it could manifest for two reasons: a) we feel ashamed for something we did b) someone else did something to us that made us feel ashamed of ourselves. Body shaming is a common example.

Shame is a very strong emotion that causes physical and emotional distress. The person carrying shame is miserable and is stuck in the past, buried in negative thoughts and emotions.

It is important to remember that everything that happens in our lives happens for a reason. Life is a well-orchestrated play, and we are the actors. Whatever happens in the past, stays in the past and we move on.

Guilt

Guilt is a common emotion and one that causes our 2nd chakra to block. Parents often feel guilty about the way they have raised their children: *"I wish I had spent more time with my kids", "I wish I could have done things differently".* We can't turn the clock back but it's never too late to rebuild relationships with children and others close to us, no matter how old we or they are. What stops us from taking action is the fear of rejection. What if they are still holding grudges? Always remember that our children have chosen us for their learnings, and they also have their own journeys. Our responsibility is to teach them how to be humble, compassionate and forgiving. We can choose to continue to suffer from feelings of guilt to the end of our lives, or we can put these behind us and rebuild our relationships with them.

Children don't come with a user's manual. We all make mistakes; it's how we acknowledge our mistakes and correct them that matters. It's never too late to show our true, loving, compassionate and humble selves.

We also often feel guilty for things we have said or done to our parents. Fear and ego stop us from saying *"I am sorry".* We keep postponing that painful conversation for another time. When they are gone, in addition to guilt we feel angry with ourselves for not having had that conversation. Pick up the phone now. Make that visit you have been putting off for another day.

We feel guilty for things we have done or should have done in our relationships. We feel guilty for the way we treated a colleague. We feel guilty for what we said to a friend. Just pick the phone and call them. You are an apology away from liberation. Go and visit them and release yourself from those emotions of guilt.

Apology is a powerful tool. If we don't use it, we will continue to punish ourselves and suffer from physical and emotional torment. It's never too late to apologise.

Anxiety and Worry

I have included these two emotions together, as they are connected. Worry is the emotion that manifests itself in our thoughts, whereas we feel anxiety physiologically, and the symptoms are recognisable - panic attacks, racing heart, trembling hands, etc.

We can potentially worry about many things. Worry is generally linked to our physical and financial security. Worry and anxiety lead to stress, which in turn generates a *fight or flight* response. As we explained earlier, *fight or flight* is the mechanism that helps us to physically deal with stress.

Imagine a typical situation in today's stress-laden world - constantly worried about the security of your job, the security of your family, the future of your kids, the state of your family's health etc. Providing for our families is a basic human need and worrying about this is understandable ... but within reason. And it doesn't stop there. You wake up in the morning and you are already stressed about your financial situation. Your child spilled milk on their uniform and you get angry. You are late for work and you are angry with other drivers for cutting you off. You go to work, and you bump into your boss in the elevator and he gives you a dirty look about something that happened yesterday, adding to the stress you already have about job security. You have a bad day at work; nothing goes right. You go home in the evening and your spouse starts talking about his/her day. You lose your temper and, filled with guilt and remorse, you withdraw to another room and spend the night brooding.

Sound familiar? This is a common day in the lives of many and illustrates what worry does to people. And, as if this is not enough, for the whole day, your body has been *'manufacturing'* cortisol and adrenaline. Your body is full of toxins, and your *fight or flight* response has been working overtime throughout the day.

Worry is normal in small doses; it is a support mechanism for helping us to find solutions to problems. When you feel stressed, withdraw for a few minutes to a quiet place where you can do some breathing exercises to clear your mind and turn the *fight or flight* response off.

Disgust

We all feel disgust at times. What we eat and drink is one source of disgust that comes to mind, but there are other causes which relate to signals we get from our other senses; what we see, smell, hear, or touch. Such feelings are normal.

Disgust is also linked to desires which can cause karmas. All our reactions are based on the programmes created in our subconscious minds. These are nothing more than a matter of individual personal perceptions. Something that is disgusting for you may be normal for another person because it aligns with his/her own belief systems.

Someone likes sushi, another person dislikes it. Someone yearns to build a classic home, another only likes modern ones. One person loves rock music and another can't stand it and only wants to hear classical. Some people enjoy beach holidays, others can only handle quiet, out of the way mountain retreats and others may prefer cultural excursions. The list is infinite and it is all a matter of perception and personal preference. However, preference becomes an issue when an alternative becomes a dislike and then a source of disgust because it conflicts with an individual's belief system. A person who is easily disgusted will show their disbelief and disapproval physically and will irritate or anger others. It is not our place to change people's likes and dislikes; if we dislike something, then we should try to avoid it, but we should not pressurise others to change their *'likes'* to suit ours. It is not our place to interfere with the likes and preferences of others.

Years ago, when we lived in Bahrain, a friend was flying to Sydney via Bahrain. I suggested that she stopped over for a couple of days in Bahrain to stay with us. This immediately generated a look of disgust on her face, and she expressed strong opinions about that wonderful country that she had never visited, which were ignorant, prejudiced and false. Of course, I told her in no uncertain terms how wrong she was, with the intimation that the invitation was withdrawn. Her disgust was coming from a belief system that she had subconsciously developed over the years from I don't know where. In a few words and one facial expression, she expressed her intolerance for something she had no knowledge of and had made no attempt to understand. It is shocking to a rational mind that someone can be so judgmental towards a whole people and a place she has never visited; unfortunately, this all too common and is the source of many of the problems we face in today's world.

Surprise/Shock

There are numerous examples of people suffering from serious, non-curable diseases that were caused by a shock to the system.

246

Common examples include diabetes, heart disease, psoriasis or other autoimmune diseases, and many types of cancers. The list goes on.

Shocks emanating from sudden unpleasant surprises are often beyond our control and can have catastrophic impacts on our health.

In our lives, we experience situations which are created as part of our learning and we need to deal with them. When we experience such situations, it is important to take time out to reflect on our lives, our behaviours, emotions, and actions. Any shock should be treated as a learning exercise for our spiritual development.

It is common for *'awakened'* people to have experienced severe depression or shock that has led to their awakening. Our Higher Selves will provide us with answers if we have faith and ask for help.

CHAPTER 13

Understanding the Impact of Thought

Wisdom is not connected to age; wisdom is an innate spiritual intelligence that lies within the soul of every human being on earth, hidden only by our contaminated thoughts. This is why one must look within for true knowledge (Andy, The Enlightened Gardener, by Sydney Banks)

I recently read a book by author and philosopher Sydney Banks, *The Enlightened Gardener* (R22). Mr. Banks utilises the voice of Andy, a simple gardener but a highly developed soul, to present the three principles of Mind, Consciousness and Thought. A group of four psychologists meet Andy, who changes their lives by presenting principles of wisdom unknown to them, which contradicted the teachings of basic principles they learned at university and have been applying ever since. One of the three principles presented by Mr. Banks was Thought. He demonstrates how our suffering is caused by unhelpful, negative thought patterns.

In this book we have discussed how emotions impact our physical and energy bodies and lead to physical and mental disease. We have also discussed how Desires lead to soul contamination and derail our spiritual development. As my Higher Self said, *"the cause of emotions is thought"*. You might question how it is possible to live without thoughts, and you would be right - it is not possible. Thoughts are a gift to help us plan our lives. Our mind is recording all our memories, and we would be life forms without identity if we were not able to think and recall those memories and remind ourselves of who we are. To remind ourselves of the good memories that bring us joy, and to recall the not-so-pleasant memories, allows us to learn from our experiences, to become better human beings and to accelerate our spiritual development. In Figure 29, you can see how our negative thoughts lead to desires and negative emotions. This contaminates the physical body by creating excessive levels of adrenaline and cortisol which negatively impacts the immune system. In addition to this, our chakras malfunction, which deprives our bodies of *'lifetrons'*, the vital energy required to maintain healthy body and mind. This leads to disease and suffering and slows down our spiritual development.

Conversely, we clearly see the impact of positive thoughts. These lead us to positive emotions and help us to exercise Divine Love, the path to spiritual development. On a physical level, when we exercise Divine Love and have positive emotions our bodies produce 'happy hormones', such as serotonin and dopamine, which boost the immune system. Our chakras function properly, and this leads to overall physical and mental wellbeing.

But how do we *'switch off'* from thinking negative thoughts? Memories are there and cannot be erased. The key is not to stop thinking or remembering, but not to experience emotions when those memories are recalled. Negative emotions are the result of unpleasant thoughts relating to something that happened in the past.

The Dalai Lama once said:

> *If there is not a solution to the problem, then don't waste time worrying about it. If there is a solution to the problem, then don't waste time worrying about it.*

This means that when you experience suffering because of a past event, you have two choices: (a) fix it or (b) move on. The coming pages will provide several tools to help you move away from unhelpful, painful thoughts.

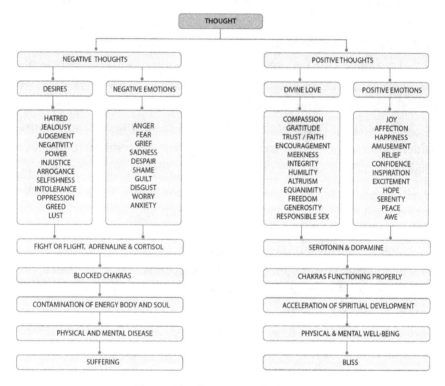

Figure 29: The Impact of Thought

CHAPTER 14

Practical Solutions for Liberating the Soul

From Darkness to Light

The great masters offer different paths for moving from the darkness to the light and clearing our souls of impurities caused by karmas. All these paths, whether progressing through Divine Love, or eliminating desires, or the scientific path of yoga, lead to the liberation of the soul.

Through the cycle of death and rebirth, we return again and again to continue our learnings. Our learnings are experiential; we have to experience in order to learn, and the required learnings are dictated by our karmas. There are many analogies from our physical world; for example, one cannot learn to be an architect from reading books alone, without practical knowledge and experience. The architect must design buildings in order to gain the experience to be able to call himself an architect.

Similarly, karmas must be experienced. If, in another life, you caused pain, physical or emotional, in this life you will experience the same pain you caused - the principle of cause and effect.

There are, however, simple solutions that provide practical means of accelerating our spiritual development.

Forgiveness and Repentance

Forgiveness is one of the foundations of the path to enlightenment taught by Jesus. It dissolves karma or sins, the way the scientific path of yoga does.

Jesus used the parable of the Prodigal Son in his teachings. In this parable, God is the father, and the Prodigal Son represents humanity, the sinful children.

> *A certain man had two sons. And the younger of them said to his father, "Father, give me the portion of goods that falls to me." So he divided to them his livelihood. And not many days after, the younger son gathered all together, journeyed to a far country, and there wasted his possessions with prodigal living. But when he had spent all, there arose a severe famine in that land, and he began to be in want. Then he went and joined himself to a citizen of that country, and he sent him into his fields to feed swine. And he would gladly have filled his stomach with the pods that the swine ate, and no one gave him anything. But when he came to himself, he said, "How many of my father's hired servants have bread enough and to spare, and I perish with hunger! I will arise and go to my father, and will say to him, Father, I have sinned against heaven and before you, and I am no longer worthy to be called your son. Make me like one of your hired servants." And he arose and came to his father. But when he was still a great way off, his father saw him and had compassion, and ran and fell on his neck and kissed him. And the son said to him, "Father, I have sinned against heaven and in your sight, and am no longer worthy to be called your son." But the father said to his servants, "Bring out the best robe and put*

*it on him and put a ring on his hand and sandals on his feet. And bring the fatted calf here and kill it, and let us eat and be merry; for this **my son was dead** and is alive again; he was lost and is found." And they began to be merry. Now his older son was in the field. And as he came and drew near to the house, he heard music and dancing. So he called one of the servants and asked what these things meant. And he said to him, "Your brother has come, and because he has received him safe and sound, your father has killed the fatted calf." But he was angry and would not go in. Therefore his father came out and pleaded with him. So he answered and said to his father, "Lo, these many years I have been serving you; I never transgressed your commandment at any time; and yet you never gave me a young goat, that I might make merry with my friends." And he said to him, "Son, you are always with me, and all that I have is yours. It was right that we should make merry and be glad, for your brother was dead and is alive again, and was lost and is found." (Luke 15:11-32)*

With this parable, Jesus summarises God's love towards us. It does not matter how much we sin or how many karmas we carry, He wants us back home. There is no such thing as eternal punishment. All that is required is genuine remorse and our karmas will be erased. Life is all about learning our lessons. Remorse for wrongdoing proves that the person has learnt his or her lesson. When you sit for an exam and pass, there is no need to repeat that particular subject and you progress to other lessons. The clearing of karma is the same concept. The father said, *"my son was dead, and he is alive again".* When Jesus said that someone was dead, he meant that he was in the cycle of death and rebirth, buried in sin. Being alive means achieving the highest goal of spirituality.

It does not matter how many times you sin, if you ask for forgiveness, you will receive it. God is pure love, pure bliss. He is not the cruel and vengeful God portrayed in the Old Testament.

> *Then Peter came to Him and said, "Lord, how often shall my brother sin against me, and I forgive him? Up to seven times?" Jesus said to him, "I do not say to you, up to seven times, but up to seventy times seven".*
> *(Mathew 18:21-22)*

Jesus taught that there is no limit to how many times we should forgive someone. If we don't forgive, then not only do we carry a karma, but we will also not be forgiven for our sins.

In Christianity, one of the seven Sacred Mysteries performed by the Church is Confession. The Church encourages people to confess their sins in the presence of a priest. The priest then becomes the channel to God, for the forgiveness of the sins confessed. However, we do not require a priest to be able to confess our sins. God is everywhere, and when we are genuinely remorseful and ask for forgiveness, it will be granted, regardless of where we are, as long as we in turn forgive those you have harmed us. There is nothing wrong with making confessions in the presence of a priest if that's what you want, but the key element is to be genuinely remorseful.

Other great masters also taught forgiveness as an important part of spirituality.

> *Humility, sincerity, harmlessness, forgiveness, rectitude, service of the Master, purity, steadfastness, self-control (Bhagavad Gita 13:8)*

In the above passage, Krishna explains the importance of forgiveness as one of the important behaviours for the seekers.

The Buddha said this to a man that asked for his forgiveness: *"I cannot forgive you because I have no grudge against you"*.

These words should not be taken to mean that the Buddha was against forgiveness. He was making the point that if one's heart is full of Love and one doesn't bear grudges against others, there is no need for forgiveness. The Buddha was already enlightened, with a crystal-clear soul. For those of us who are not yet enlightened, it is important to be forgiving. There will be a day, in this life or another, that we will be saying the same thing the Buddha said, *"there is nothing to forgive"*.

Living Forgiveness

It is important to remember that you will not be forgiven unless you genuinely forgive others. This reminds me of a conversation I had with a client's Higher Self. The Higher Self said that she had to resolve the karmic issues she had with her father that she had been carrying over several lives. This was surprising as my client maintains that she has forgiven him, and she is in regular contact with him. The Higher Self said, *"No. What she is doing is superficial. Only for her to feel good. He is not feeling it."* Thus, a genuine forgiveness or repentance is required. Do it and believe it.

Exercise No. 1:

Make three lists:

- Make a list of those people who have hurt you, mentally and/or physically. They do not need to know; the important thing is for you to remember.
- Make a list of those you have hurt physically or mentally. It does not matter how small or big the issues were, or if the

persons listed are aware of the hurt. All that matters is that you and God know.

- Make a list of the physical ailments, emotional traumas and other misfortunes that may have been caused by karmas.
- Starting with the first list, every day, through prayer or meditation, forgive one person that hurt you. It is important to remember that the *'hurt'* is your perception. The person that you are referring to may not be aware that he/she has injured you. Going directly to that person and saying *"I forgive you"* may cause friction if the person does not think he/she has done anything wrong. The act of forgiveness is between you and God. At the same time, ask God to forgive you for your share of responsibility in the creation of the issue. Such situations are not always the fault of only one party.
- When you have completed the first list, move to the second list. Each day, during prayer or meditation, ask for forgiveness for those people you have hurt.
- Lastly, continue this exercise by asking the Divine for forgiveness for anything that you might have done in this life or another, that may be the cause of any physical ailments, traumas, or misfortunes you are experiencing.

Your repentance and forgiveness need to be genuine. God knows if you are genuine or not. So, how will you know if your forgiveness is genuine? When you think about the person whom you have hurt, or who has hurt you, if the forgiveness is not complete or real, you will still have feelings of guilt or pain. If you have these feelings, then repeat the above exercise until you do not experience those emotions when you think of that person. If these feelings continue, your forgiveness and repentance are superficial, and you need to persevere until you eliminate these feelings.

Hope

Hope is another form of positivity. In earlier chapters, we have discussed faith, and the need to believe in something for it to happen. Hope is a little different. Hope is being positive about the outcomes when you face setbacks. When things are not going well, when you or your loved ones experience health or financial issues or when nothing seems to be going right, it's easy to lose your way and become negative about everything.

Hope keeps you positive. Any setback is a lesson to be learnt, every challenge is an opportunity. Hope keeps you focused on your journey and stops you descending into self-pity and *'victim mode'*.

Hope is a strong wish for things to return to normal, and for all our misfortunes to be resolved.

> *For our sakes, no doubt, this is written, that he who plows should plow in hope, and he who threshes in hope should be partaker of his hope. (1 Corinthians 9:10)*

Saint Paul, in the above passage, explains that only when we act in hope, do we get what we wish for.

Positivity can also go in the opposite direction. Being overly positive without a logical basis, can create suffering. Positivity should always be exercised within sensible and logical limits.

Exercise No. 2:

Try the following as an exercise in hope. Every time that you have a strong wish, either for yourself or a loved one, create a short phrase and use it as a mantra (G9) during prayer or meditation. For example:

I hope to pass my exam

I hope to find a job

I hope to get better soon....

Become the Light

Jesus was the Light of the World. He was the light to show us the way out of darkness. Everyone's purpose in the physical world is to reach enlightenment, regardless of what religion we follow. This is a process that may take several lives to complete. By practising Divine Love, you are already on the good path. When you help others to find their way out of darkness, it helps you grow spiritually. You are *'scoring'* additional points.

With patience, we can help others out of darkness, towards the light. The world needs Light Workers. There are millions of Light Workers out there, helping the world to raise its consciousness level. The level of consciousness on our planet has fallen significantly in recent years. Events such as the environmental disasters and shocking loss of animal life in Australia, the massive fires in the jungles of South America and South East Asia, the many wars, the over-exploitation of the planet's resources and consequent damage to the environment; these and many other events have lowered the vibration of our planet. The Light Workers, through the wonderful tool of love, are playing an important role in reversing the negative impacts to the planet's vibration.

Become a Light Worker; you will be helping yourself and others. Allocate a little time each week or month towards helping someone. You don't necessarily need to be volunteering in a charity organisation if you don't want to. You can be a Light Worker while at work, at school, in the supermarket or walking down the street. Spreading love and compassion can be done just about anywhere.

Self-Love

I mentioned earlier that Divine Love is not only for others, but also for ourselves. Divine Love is not about our physical bodies; it is about our spiritual bodies - our souls.

The physical body is just a vehicle to get us from A to Z. One person may drive a Ferrari sports car and another a Fiat 500. The Ferrari might be much faster but may be derailed and not reach its destination if the driver loses control at high speed. The Fiat may travel much slower but stay the course and ultimately reach its destination first.

In the same way, when we are part of an average looking family (which we chose to be reincarnated into), it is very possible that we will also look average. We need to accept how we look and make the most of the gifts provided to us, so that we can reach the end of our journey.

Good looking people are born that way as part of their learning. How do they handle physical beauty? Does it make them arrogant? Do they only look for good looking partners and look down on those that do not match their physical attributes? Do they get stressed and anxious when age takes away their physical beauty?

Social media has decided how we should look and how we should dress. A person that loves himself/herself inside is not concerned about any of that. They don't need anyone's approval. They don't need to belong. They are happy the way they are, and they make the most of their life's journey.

When we buy a car, we look after it. We take it for regular service checks, we wash and polish it, but we fail to do the same for our bodies. Our body is the vehicle of the soul; if we don't look after it, it won't last long enough for the soul to learn the lesson it came into this life for. If you have self-love, you will not abuse or endanger your body. Moderation is the key in everything we do, whether it be the amount and quality of our food, the amount of alcohol we drink, smoking, physical exercise, stress and so on.

You may be kind and compassionate to everyone else, but you will remain attached to your physical body if you do not feel good about yourself, and this will not allow you to transcend.

It is important to love yourself unconditionally, and not allow others to put you down and make you feel bad about yourself. Look at yourself in the mirror every morning and say, *"Good morning, this is me and I am proud and happy to be who I am'!"*. Your soul is a wonderful energy of Love, a speck of God waiting to be liberated. Your true You is an immortal, wise and loving energy that strives to be reunited with its Source.

Exercise No. 3:

Complete the following exercise to see how much you love yourself. Read the questionnaire and rate yourself.

BEHAVIOUR	SCORE
I ACCEPT MY PHYSICAL FLAWS AND IMPERFECTIONS. I FOCUS INSTEAD ON MY OTHER QUALITIES.	
I KNOW THAT I NEED TO STRIKE A BALANCE BETWEEN MY PHYSICAL AND MENTAL NEEDS.	
WHEN PEOPLE GIVE ME COMPLIMENTS OR GIFTS, I RECEIVE THEM WITH GRATITUDE.	
I EAT HEALTHILY AND EXERCISE REGULARLY TO KEEP MY BODY IN GOOD HEALTH.	
I SET CLEAR BOUNDARIES AND, IN A CIVILISED MANNER, LET PEOPLE KNOW WHEN THEY HAVE CROSSED THEM.	
I MAINTAIN SHARPNESS OF MIND BY READING AND LEARNING ABOUT NEW SUBJECTS AND CONCEPTS THAT STIMULATE ME.	
I ALWAYS FORGIVE MYSELF FOR THINGS THAT I HAVE SAID OR DONE AND ENSURE I DON'T REPEAT THE SAME MISTAKES.	
I DON'T TAKE FEEDBACK FROM OTHERS AS CRITICISM. I SEE IT AS A WAY OF IMPROVING MYSELF.	
I ENJOY MY OWN COMPANY. I AM EQUALLY SATISFIED WHEN I AM ALONE AS I AM IN THE COMPANY OF OTHERS.	
I ALWAYS OFFER MY OPINION, BUT I ENSURE THAT I DON'T HURT OTHERS' FEELINGS.	
I LOVE HELPING OTHERS, BUT I ALSO KNOW WHEN TO SAY "NO" IN SITUATIONS WHERE I DON'T HAVE THE TIME TO HELP.	
I OFTEN LAUGH AT MY OWN MISTAKES.	
WHEN I FEEL DOWN, I FIND WAYS TO LIFT MYSELF.	
I ASK FOR OTHERS' OPINIONS BUT DON'T RELY ON THEM TO MAKE DECISIONS ON MY BEHALF.	
I INVEST TIME AND MONEY IN MY WELL-BEING, PHYSICAL OR MENTAL.	
WHEN I AM STRESSED, I FIND POSITIVE WAYS, SUCH AS EXERCISE, TO DISTRACT MYSELF INSTEAD OF ALCOHOL, SMOKING OR DRUGS.	
TOTAL SCORE	

5 : ALWAYS

4 : OFTEN

3 : OCCASIONALLY

2 : RARELY

1 : NEVER

Questionnaire 1: Self-Love

How did you do?

65-80: You love yourself totally and unconditionally.

49-64: You love yourself even though sometimes you are carried away by emotions.

33-48: You love yourself, but you are not always consistent in how you express it.

17-32: You show very little love towards yourself.

1-16: You have no love towards yourself.

PRAYER

Prayer as we know it is not the same as meditation. Prayer is more like a communication with the Divine. A prayer's purpose is to give thanks to God or to ask for help.

> *The Pharisee stood and prayed thus with himself, "God, I thank You that I am not like other men, extortioners, unjust, adulterers, or even as this tax collector. I fast twice a week; I give tithes of all that I possess". And the tax collector, standing afar off, would not so much as raise his eyes to heaven, but beat his breast, saying, "God, be merciful to me a sinner." "I tell you; this man went down to his house justified rather than the other; for everyone who exalts himself will be humbled, and he who humbles himself will be exalted." (Luke 18:11-14)*

Jesus taught the parable of the Pharisee and tax collector praying in the temple. Prayer is not about publicly displaying one's inflated devoutness to a God who knows the truth about all of us. It is about being humble and remorseful. That is how forgiveness is achieved.

But you, when you pray, go into your room, and when
you have shut your door, pray to your Father who is
in the secret place; and your Father who sees in secret
will reward you openly. (Matthew 6:6)

In the above passage, Jesus reinforced the private nature of prayer. One can pray in a quiet space where one can focus, detached from one's thoughts and have the discussion with the Divine.

And whatever things you ask in prayer, believing, you
will receive. (Matthew 21:22)

Jesus said that whatever you ask you will receive; however, there are conditions (the small print so to speak!). God is not our servant and is not interested in providing us with material wealth. Providing wealth means keeping you attached to your physical body, which is the opposite of what we need to achieve. God wants us to achieve liberation of the soul. Having said that, God wants us to enjoy the journey and have a comfortable and joyful life. Something that causes you to regress in your spiritual development will not be given. God will only provide things that accelerate your path, giving you comfort and security at the same time. The following are examples of good prayers:

The main purpose of prayer is to give thanks to God for what we already have. God knows our struggles and we will only receive what we are seeking if we are grateful for what we already have.

During the Last Supper, Jesus started with a prayer giving thanks to God. The Christian Church's practice of Holy Communion comes from the following New Testament passage:

And as they were eating, Jesus took bread, blessed,
and broke it, and gave it to the disciples and said,
"Take, eat; this is My body." Then He took the cup,

and gave thanks, and gave it to them, saying, "Drink from it, all of you. For this is My blood of the new covenant, which is shed for many for the remission of sins. But I say to you, I will not drink of this fruit of the vine from now on until that day when I drink it new with you in My Father's kingdom." (Matthew 26:26-29)

This practice is misunderstood. Simply going to Church and taking Holy Communion does not erase our sins. Holy Communion is highly symbolic. It becomes blessed when it's done with intention and feeling. Jesus was the first to give thanks at the Last Supper. Thus, gratitude for what we have is important for Holy Communion to be effective. It is the appropriate time to show sincere remorse and ask for forgiveness to those we have hurt. Only then can sins and karmas be erased. Without this sincerity of intention, Holy Communion is just a symbolic practice without any benefit or meaning.

Those who lose their jobs can pray to God for appropriate employment that will provide security for their families. God will lead those who pray with genuine intention to a path that will bring them closer to their goal.

If a member of your family is sick, you can pray for their quick recovery. Have in mind that sickness is also part of our learning, by feeling the pain we have caused to others in past lives. Therefore, if someone close to you is ill and this is connected to a karmic event, you can ask God to forgive your loved one for whatever they have done to deserve their suffering. Allow God to do His job; He grants such wishes.

Group prayers are very powerful. Prayer is energy directed to the Divine. Can you imagine if this energy is multiplied by a hundred? There are books written about real-life examples of the power of prayer. In the television series *It's a Miracle*, so many healings happened through individual and group prayers. One thing all the instances have in common is that the person praying is not asking to be healed. He/she is asking for forgiveness and thus allowing God to do His job. Similarly, in group prayers, all the participants ask God to forgive the person's sins. It is important to ask and not to beg.

The following is a prayer joke that I particularly like, partly because of the humour itself and also for the hidden message.

Once there was a great flood somewhere in the world. A man was fervently praying to be saved. The waters started rising and after a few hours, he had to move to the upper level of his house. The waters kept rising and he moved to the roof. During the whole time, he was praying for God to save him. After a few minutes, a police patrol on a boat approached him and told him to jump on. He said, "No thanks, God's help is on its way." The police patrol eventually gave up and left. The water had by now reached his waist. The same patrol boat comes back and the policeman tried to persuade him to jump on. "This is your last chance, jump on." The man said, "No thanks, God's help is on its way." A couple of hours later he drowned and went to the spirit side. He very angrily said to God, "God, all my life I obeyed and believed in you and lived a righteous life. Once in my life I asked for your help and you denied me. Why?" And God said, "I sent a boat twice, why didn't you jump on it!"

There is a meaning to this story; when you ask for help, the solution you have in mind may not be what God has in mind for you. Allow God to help you as He sees fit.

To conclude, prayer is powerful. Do it with a purpose of gratitude, remorsefulness and forgiveness and allow God to do the rest.

Exercise No. 4:

- You can pray sitting or lying down. Pray privately in a quiet space and light a candle.
- Take a few deep breaths. Breathe in from the nose, breathe out from the mouth. Repeat no less than 10 times.
- Rub your hands together until they generate heat.
- Utilising your stronger hand, activate your Crown and Third Eye Chakras to enable *'broadcasting'*.
- Firstly, open your Third Eye Chakra. Bring one of your hands 2 inches away from your forehead. Start a circular clockwise movement and repeat 20 times.
- Repeat the same on top of your head to clear the Crown Chakra.
- Now that your Third Eye and Crown Chakras, your broadcasting antennas, are functioning, you can offer your prayer. Firstly, thank God, or whoever you are addressing your prayer to, for the daily blessings you receive (we should be thankful for even the simple things we take for granted, such as food, drink, good health, etc). Then share what you need help with. Deliver your needs with emotion, believing that they will be granted. Don't offer solutions. The appropriate solution will be provided to you.
- Once you offer your prayer, stay in this relaxed, meditative mode for as long as you can and come out of it when you are ready.

Meditation

The word *'meditate'* appears three times in the English translation of the New Testament. It comes from the Latin word *'meditari'* which means to *'reflect on* or *study something'*. Similarly, in the Greek version of the New Testament, three words are used which relate to meditation - *προμελετᾶν, λογίζεσθε, μελέτα,* which mean, *'think about it, study it, plan it'.*

The Eastern religions apply the equivalent word for meditation in different ways. In Hinduism, *'dhyana'* means *'contemplation or reflection'*, which is the equivalent of the English application of the word *'meditation'.* Meditation is part of the science of yoga. Yoga is the *'union'* with the Divine, and meditation is one of the tools utilised in yoga to help the seeker to achieve *'Samadh*i' (*to direct together*) - an elevated state of consciousness, a state of oneness. During deep meditation, yogis achieve union with the cosmic consciousness.

> *Meditating on the Divine, having faith in the Divine, concentrating on the Divine and losing themselves in the Divine, their sins dissolved in wisdom, they go whence there is no return. (Bhagavad Gita 5:17)*

In the above passage, Krishna reiterates how a seeker can eliminate karmas through the scientific path of yoga, which includes meditation.

In Buddhism *'dhyana'* is the word used, which literally means *'training the mind'.* The purpose of meditation is to detach the mind from the physical senses and arrive at a state of perfect equanimity. Buddhist monks practice meditation for long periods of time each day, as part of their spiritual path on their journey to Nirvana.

Christian Saints also experience this state through deep prayer, and experience union with the universal cosmic consciousness.

Spiritually, monks apply meditation in a much deeper and more scientific way. For the average person, meditation is an excellent tool for reducing stress and anxiety. It brings peace and improves wellbeing.

Meditation is an effective tool to attract one's needs in life, by sending a frequency of intention to the universe. The universe in return sends the people and life events to the person to allow him/her to work towards achieving their intent.

As discussed earlier, your intention and belief systems need to be aligned in order to achieve your goal. Your belief systems, including your fears and phobias, are the programmes that keep you from changing your predicament. You can change your belief systems with meditation.

Meditation is easier for some people than others. It requires one to switch off all thoughts. Meditation does not necessarily need to be done in a lotus position, as is commonly perceived, and can also be achieved with appropriate background music. Have an intention of what you want to achieve in mind before you start. Meditation can help you erase damaging (limiting) belief systems.

There are several ways to meditate. The most common ones are described below:

Unguided Meditation

Unguided meditation is self-facilitated. The individual meditates in silence or by listening to some relaxing background music. In a quiet space, and a comfortable posture, the meditator focuses their attention on their breathing or their Third Eye for a period of time.

Guided Meditation

A trained practitioner directs the participants through guided imagery or visualisation. You can find guided meditation on *YouTube*, subscribe to an online meditation channel, or visit a holistic wellness centre in your area. Guided meditation is particularly beneficial for inexperienced meditators, or for those who find it difficult to focus their minds.

Focussed Meditation

The participants focus their attention on something, an object, a sound, or a sensation. An excellent way of practicing focused meditation is by concentrating one's attention on a burning candle.

Mantra Meditation

While you are focusing your attention on your breath or Third Eye (Exercise 9), silently repeat calming words or new belief systems.

Mindfulness Meditation

This meditation is a way of being mindful or living in the present moment. This type of meditation will be discussed in the coming pages.

Movement Meditation

Qi Gong and Tai Chi, both originating from Chinese tradition, are considered forms of meditation. They involve meditation, relaxation, and physical movements, which help the participants restore and maintain balance.

Meditation has been found beneficial in reducing stress, depression, and anxiety, and promoting emotional health. It helps improve attention span, focus and concentration. It also provides benefits in memory functioning, especially with respect to age-related memory loss. Meditation helps fight addictions, improves sleep patterns, and has been found to positively contribute to lowering of blood pressure and reduction of physical pain.

Exercise No. 5

Meditation can be an excellent way of achieving your goals, for example a new job, a new home, a new relationship, happiness, etc. Often, our inability to attract abundance into our lives relates to limiting beliefs. Prior to this exercise, for best results, do Exercise No. 13.

- Play background meditation/relaxing music (optional).
- Sit in a *'lotus'* position (crossed legged) on the floor or sit on a straight-backed chair.
- Take deep breaths … breath in from your mouth …. exhale from your nose.
- Set your intention for today's meditation. Visualize the ideal scenario of what you want to achieve in some detail. For example, visualize yourself in your ideal job role.
- Clear all those scenes from your mind and start your meditation.
- Focus on your breathing, notice your stomach rising and falling. Notice the air flowing in and out of your nostrils.
- Instead of focusing on your breathing, you can choose to focus your attention on your Third Eye.
- You can meditate for a minimum of 10 minutes per day. For best results, try to meditate for longer, say 20-30 minutes each day.

Practicing Mindfulness

'Mindfulness', or *'sati'*, is at the heart of Buddhism. Our suffering is caused by thoughts, of the past and future. Since you can't wind the clock back, and you cannot predict the future, what is the point of suffering?

In Buddhism, enlightenment happens when we are liberated from suffering, which is the opposite of the Divine Love taught by Jesus.

'Anapanasati' means *'mindfulness of breathing'*. Concentration and awareness of the action of breathing is a core practice in Buddhism

Mind precedes all mental states. Mind is their chief;
they are all mind-wrought. If with an impure mind a
person speaks or acts suffering follows him like the
wheel that follows the foot of the ox. (Dhammapada 1:1)

Buddhists meditate regularly, using the technique of being 'mindful' of their breathing, and completely emptying their heads of thoughts, with complete focus on the present moment.

Similarly, Hinduism refers to *'vartamana',* which signifies the living and present moment.

Therefore do not worry about tomorrow, for tomorrow
will worry about its own things. Sufficient for the day
is its own trouble. (Matthew 6:34)

Jesus in the above passage taught that we should not worry about tomorrow. Tomorrow will take care of itself. No one knows what tomorrow will bring. Why worry about it?

Scientific research shows that practicing mindfulness improves our overall well-being. It is an excellent tool for releasing stress, as well as other benefits such as a healthier heart, lower blood pressure, improved sleep, and reduction of chronic pain and digestive issues.

We have earlier discussed the damage and disruption that thought causes to our physical and spiritual bodies. Thought is the reason for our suffering and the distraction from our spiritual path. Control your thought and you are halfway there.

Many people say that they have tried mindfulness, but that they cannot clear their minds of thought. There is good reason for this. Most thoughts are based on events that happened in the past. Most of the time we are operating with our subconscious mind. We are attached to the people who hurt us, or vice versa. An invisible cord transfers negative energy between us and the people around us. We are all connected, and while this energy flows between people, being in the present moment is incredibly difficult. The only way to cut this invisible cord is to practice forgiveness and repentance. There is no other way. This was the route to my own liberation, and even though my mind is still thinking, it's not stuck in the past anymore. We need to think so we can plan, analyse, and learn, but not to worry or be angry or sad; all such thoughts need to be cleared from our minds.

Being in the present moment liberates one from painful thoughts and therefore assists in eliminating desires that cause suffering. To practice mindfulness, one doesn't need to be in a meditative state, but one must be focused and mindful of everything one is doing. A complete focus on that one thing you are presently doing will allow you to eliminate negative thoughts.

For example:

If you are walking, focus on your walk, count your steps, or observe the movement of your legs. Be mindful of your walking.

If you are eating, focus your attention on the flavour and scent of your food. Enjoy every bite. Be mindful of your eating.

In this way, being focused on the present allows you to develop a new habit of being mindful of everything you are doing right now, which eliminates suffering from thought.

For those of you who wish to learn to be present and practice mindfulness in a structured way, try this following exercise:

Exercise No. 6

- Sit in the *'lotus'* position (crossed legged) on the floor or sit on a straight-backed chair.

- Take deep breaths ... breath in from your mouth ... exhale from your nose.
- Focus on your breathing, notice your belly rising and falling. Notice the air flowing in and out of your nostrils.
- Now, become aware of any sounds, sensations, smells ...
- If your mind starts wandering, bring your attention back to your breathing again.

Do this exercise for 10 or more minutes each day. It will help you to stay focused on the present. Like most other aspects of our lives, something that is practiced daily eventually becomes a habit.

Yoga

The word 'yoga' (योग) literally means 'union, union with God. It's the scientific way of enlightenment originating in India. It was never the intention for yoga to be used as a fitness regime. When Paramhansa Yogananda moved to the US in the early 20th century, it was not his intention to export a fitness technique to the West, but rather to introduce an alternative path to enlightenment and accelerate the journey by combining the path of Jesus with the scientific path of yoga.

Having said that, yoga has many benefits for those seeking to accelerate their spiritual journey. The mechanism of stretching the muscles removes the blockages from the meridians and nadis and allows the energy to flow freely. It helps the seeker to align his/her chakras and have a better 'connection' with the divine, and yes, it's also a great fitness routine. Yoga is beneficial, both physically and spiritually.

Scientists have been studying the health benefits of yoga for some time, and now have evidence that it improves our overall wellbeing. It is now accepted that yoga provides health benefits in a whole host of areas, including improved blood flow, relief from depression, improved heart rate, lowering of blood pressure and sugar levels, increased regulation of the adrenal glands, enhanced immune system and improved functioning of the nervous system.

Physically, yoga improves flexibility, strengthens muscle and bone structure, and improves posture. It protects the spine and improves resistance to cartilage and joint damage.

CHAPTER 15

Practical Solutions to Heal Your Body and Mind

This book would be incomplete without practical ways to heal oneself. The techniques described in this chapter are based on person experiences and information provided to me by my Higher Self, and the Higher Selves of others.

In the following sections, I will provide practical exercises that will aid in the process of spiritual development and emotional healing. Healing our emotions is connected with the healing of our physical bodies and our relationships, which in turn will lead to longer and happier lives.

Challenge Vs Opportunity

When something bad happens to us, we take it to heart. *"It's my bad luck"* or *"Bad things always happen to me"*. In this way we are creating more belief systems, *'programmes'* that continue to send signals to the universe, and we will continuously attract people and events to validate our new belief system.

There is nothing called *bad luck*. We create our own reality with our thoughts. Our thoughts create the belief system, and this becomes our reality; we are locked into a vicious cycle.

To avoid this, think of the *'bad'* things that happen to you and ask the question, *"what is the learning from this experience? What is the universe trying to tell me?"* The answer will give you the solutions to your problems.

For example, if a person is repeatedly losing his/her job he/she might come up with answers like this:

- My values and the values of the organisation did not match. I am better off without that job.
- My attitude did not match the culture of the organisation; perhaps I should adjust my attitude the next time around.
- I should have trusted my gut feeling from the beginning and not have accepted that job.
- I should have been less defensive when the boss was giving me feedback.
- I could have been more helpful with my colleagues.

This is just an example; however, if you ask these questions every time you are faced with a challenge, this will help you find the solutions to your problems without creating additional negative belief systems.

Exercise No. 7

Think of an unpleasant experience that you had in the past. List down at least five positive lessons from this experience. What are the hidden lessons? Will this experience make me a better person, better parent, sibling, friend, or colleague? Do you have a share of the responsibility for the outcomes and do you need to learn to accept that outcomes are not always black or white, but sometimes grey?

Shedding of the 'Victim' Attitude

We tend to see ourselves as the victims of society, but the truth is we are not victims. We create our own reality with our thoughts which lead to our emotional outbursts. Is someone else responsible for your emotions? We tend to blame others, but they are our emotions, and we are the only ones who can manage them. No one can fix our emotions. They are ours, and we must take responsibility for them.

We tend to blame others for our emotions. *"Yes, but ..."* There is no *"but"*. It's our issue to resolve. If you believe that your friend or boss has not treated you properly, go and tell them. They may not even be aware; sulking does not help you or them.

I always used to deal with such situations by bottling up my emotions. This created health issues. My lack of communication caused my Throat Chakra to be blocked for a very long time (about half a century!) and I ended up with a thyroid problem.

A few years ago, after my awakening, I took action. I realised that if I had been communicative and told people who injured me that I didn't accept the way I was being treated, chances are they would have stopped. I decided not to go back and open old wounds, and I also took the decision to forgive all those people, who might not even had realised they had done something to hurt me and draw the line. From that moment onwards, I would calmly but immediately respond to anyone who said anything to insult or hurt me, and nip the situation in the bud. Something special happened once I forgave all those who had injured me and started talking back. All these people started being nice to me! People who I have not seen for many years started making contact with me.

There is a simple explanation for this. We are all connected by an invisible thread or cord. While I was still holding onto emotions, the negative energy continued to flow between me and those people.

Forgiveness cut the energy flow. I was not the only one that was liberated; they were liberated as well.

I also realised that the past situations were partly my fault. If I had done this years ago, I would have been living a happy life. My thoughts were keeping me in the past and attaching me to people who, in my mind, had caused me pain. This was my perception, but it did not mean it was true.

Once the flow of negative energy stopped, I also stopped thinking of these people. It was so liberating.

Exercise No. 8

The following exercise is based on, and extends, Exercise 1 in Chapter 14.

- Make a list of all those who have hurt you over the years, including everyone you can think of, no matter how long ago it was.
- Each day take one person from your list and forgive them through prayer or meditation. This can also be achieved through Ho'oponopono, an ancient Hawaiian technique for forgiveness. There are many books and online courses available, for example Joe Vitale & Dr. Ihaleakala Hew Len's book *Zero Limits* (R15).
- In addition to forgiving others, forgive yourself for holding on to these feelings and also accept your share of responsibility for the situation.
- Draw a line to define your limits; don't allow anyone to cross this line in the future, otherwise you will repeat the cycle of generating feelings of hurt and anger previously experienced. When people cross your *'red line'*, you will be gentle but firm in informing them that you do not appreciate

their behaviours. In most cases, they will either apologise or change their behaviours.

Changing Behaviours

Figure 30 illustrates the four types of behaviours exhibited by people in their interactions with each other.

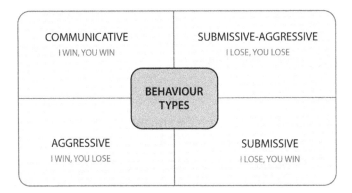

Figure 30: Types of Behaviour

Aggressive People

Aggressive people try to impose themselves on others by overwhelming them through shouting, threats, physical gestures, etc. They want to be in control, and their way of achieving this is by spreading fear. This is what we call an *'I win/You lose'* approach. This is a selfish way of dealing with things, and the person in question ends up with serious karmas, at the same time contaminating their own body with cortisol, blocking their chakras and creating the potential for falling ill and suffering chronic health issues.

Submissive People

At the other end of the behaviour scale, we have the submissive type. These people are the ones putting others first and ignoring their own needs. They display an approach of '*I lose/You win*'. These people feel frustrations and anger, but they don't express it. Submissive people also carry karmas; in their desire to please others, they don't express self-love. All the bottled-up emotions contaminate the body. Submissive people are regularly in *fight or flight* mode.

Submissive-Aggressive People

These people don't bottle up as such. They adopt an '*I lose/You lose*' attitude. Instead of dealing with the situation they sulk and bad mouth the other person(s) and try to find ways to punish them. They are carrying a lot of anger and resentment. As for the other categories already described, they are creating karmas for themselves, and damaging their own health, by overloading their bodies with cortisol and generating high levels of negative emotions.

Communicative People

And lastly, we have the communicative type. When something happens, they calmly and rationally put things on the table and deal with the situation immediately. These types do not get angry, nor do they bottle up feelings or bad mouth the other person. They tend to have long-lasting relationships and operate on a principle of '*I win/You win*'. Communicative people are the ones that positively progress their careers as a result of their collaborative approach. Their behaviour supports their spiritual growth and helps them maintain high levels of energy and physical health.

From this brief description, it is clear which behaviour type we should aspire to adopt.

Exercise No. 9

This is one of my favourite techniques:

- Recreate Table 1 on paper or an excel sheet (below).
- Over a period of one week, record all your emotions, using the descriptions from this book as your reference.
- Review each column and identify patterns of behaviour. Which emotions are more prominent? Who is the cause of your emotions? What was your response? Did you have any physiological changes? What thoughts did you have after an incident? The answers to these questions will identify the belief system that you have created.
- Now that you have identified the causes and outcomes, make an action plan and stick to it.
- The belief systems you created need to be eliminated. You can do this through meditation; the relevant techniques are described later in this chapter.
- Write down three positive lessons that each person or situation has taught you. For example, you are now more independent, more assertive, stronger, a better friend etc. Just remember that everything that happens to us, no matter how harsh it may be, is an opportunity for learning. During prayer or meditation, thank those people involved for the valuable lessons and forgive them.

WHO / WHAT WAS THE TRIGGER	EMOTION	BEHAVIOUR / RESPONSE	IMPACT	BELIEF	ACTION PLAN
TRAFFIC	FRUSTRATION	AGGRESSIVE	TREMBLING	IT'S MY BAD LUCK	MANAGE TIME BETTER
BOSS	ANGER	SUBMISSIVE	BOILING INSIDE	I AM NOT GOOD ENOUGH	SWITCH TO COMMUNICATIVE STYLE
SPOUSE	FEAR	SUBMISSIVE-AGGRESSIVE	BOTTLED UP	I AM WEAK	SWITCH TO COMMUNICATIVE STYLE, BE MORE UNDERSTANDING AS A FIRST STEP. IF NOTHING WORKS RE-EVALUATE YOUR OPTIONS
CHILDREN	ANXIETY	AGGRESSIVE	OUTBURST	I AM A BAD PERSON	SWITCH TO COMMUNICATIVE STYLE AND EXERCISE PATIENCE

Table 1: Changing Behaviours

Listening

In Chapter 9, we discussed how the amygdala hijacks the rational part of the brain, leading to outbursts and anger. Allowing the other person to complete their thoughts without jumping to conclusions will greatly increase the probability that the amygdala will not hijack your neocortex.

Hearing and listening are not the same thing. A person may be hearing but not really paying attention to what the other person is saying. They are preoccupied with their own thoughts and problems. How many times did you catch someone hearing you but not listening to what you are saying?

People that really listen are putting aside their own thoughts and problems for a period of time to listen to others. They are patient. They show compassion and empathise with the other person. People who share something important do so because they trust us. They lose trust if they sense that we are not listening. It would be better to inform the person that even though you really want to help him/her, at this time your mind cannot concentrate, and that you will be able to focus on the issue as soon as you clear your mind. In this way, you don't put yourself in the embarrassing situation of being caught not listening, and at the same time you maintain trust and rapport with the other person.

Listen and try to understand what the person is trying to say. Put yourself in their position and think the situation through from their perspective. You might find that they have a valid point to make. Becoming aggressive or defensive serves no purpose and will only cause physical and spiritual damage to you.

When you practice active listening and seeing things from the other person's point of view, and you still disagree with them, there is always the communicative way of responding. This way no damage will be done, and things will be sorted quickly and amicably.

People with good listening skills develop and maintain good relationships, in both their personal and professional lives. They become better problem solvers and gain the trust of others when making sensible and effective decisions with a *'cool'* head.

Exercise No. 10

Complete the following to understand how well you are listening:

Rate yourself from 1-5 and write your answer in the second column.

BEHAVIOUR	SCORE
I PAY ATTENTION TO THE OTHER PERSON, EVEN WHEN I AM NOT INTERESTED IN THE SUBJECT BEING DISCUSSED.	
I LISTEN TO THE OTHER PERSON, EVEN IF I DON'T AGREE WITH WHAT THE OTHER PERSON IS SAYING.	
I TRULY LISTEN TO THE WORDS THE OTHER PERSON IS SAYING, NOT FOCUSING ON THEIR PERSONAL APPEARANCE AND MANNERISMS.	
WHEN OTHERS SPEAK, I DON'T JUDGE THEM AND LABEL THEM FOR THEIR OPINIONS AND VIEWS.	
I MAINTAIN EYE CONTACT WHEN THE OTHER PERSON IS TALKING.	
I ALWAYS ALLOW OTHER PEOPLE TO FINISH BEFORE I STATE MY OPINION.	
I MAKE SURE THAT I ALWAYS RESPOND IN A PATIENT, CALM AND COMPOSED MANNER.	
I TRY TO UNDERSTAND THE OTHER PERSON'S FEELINGS AS WELL AS THEIR WORDS.	
I MAKE SURE I UNDERSTAND THE OTHER PERSON'S POINT OF VIEW BEFORE I RESPOND. I AM CALM, RELAXED, AND PATIENT WHEN I'M LISTENING.	
I GIVE PEOPLE MY FULL ATTENTION. I DON'T GET DISTRACTED BY THE ACTIONS OF OTHERS, OR BY INCOMING CALLS, MESSAGES, ETC.	
I NEVER INTERRUPT THE OTHER PERSON. I ALLOW THEM TO COMPLETE THEIR THOUGHTS.	
I DON'T RUSH TO CONCLUSIONS. I FIRST REFLECT ON WHAT THE OTHER PERSON SAID, BEFORE RESPONDING.	
WHEN PEOPLE TALK TO ME, I MAINTAIN EYE CONTACT AND SHOW GENUINE INTEREST IN WHAT THEY'RE SAYING.	
WHEN PEOPLE SHARE THEIR PROBLEMS WITH ME, I EMPATHISE AND SHOW COMPASSION.	
I KNOW WHEN A PERSON ONLY WANTS TO VENT HIS/HER FRUSTRATIONS AND OFFER MY SUPPORT IF THEY NEED IT.	
I ONLY SHARE SOLUTIONS WITH OTHER PEOPLE, IF I SENSE THIS IS WHAT THEY WANT.	
TOTAL SCORE	

5 : ALWAYS

4 : OFTEN

3 : OCCASIONALLY

2 : RARELY

1 : NEVER

284

Questionnaire 2: Listening Skills

How did you do?

65-80: You are an excellent listener. Congratulations!

49-64: You listen to others, even though sometimes, you get side-tracked.

33-48: You know how to listen but don't always do it. With some effort, you can become a good listener.

17-32: Your listening skills are below average and require improvement.

1-16: Your listening skills are very poor and require drastic improvement

Free Will

We are all born with free will. When we behave badly there is always a *'but'* or some justification because of the actions of others. *"Yes, I did, but it's because he said that to me"*, or *"What did you expect, when she went and did that?"*. These are common responses which illustrate reluctance to accept responsibility for our actions. It is easier to pass the responsibility to someone else and come across as the victim.

Since we all have free will, each of us has options available to us to handle such situations in more appropriate ways, but we commonly respond by going into *'victim mode'*. There are better ways to deal with such situations. We can adopt a communicative approach to resolve the issue, or initially behave in a submissive manner to reduce the other person's levels of aggression. We should always stop and put ourselves in the other person's shoes and see their point of view. We should always focus on what the other person is saying and allow him/her to finish speaking before reacting. There is nothing wrong with apologising for our share of responsibility. We have free will, and there are so many options available to us that would lead to a better outcome for both parties; instead we frequently adopt the most adversarial approach. We cannot change the way other people behave, but we have full control over our own emotions and behaviours. Instead of trying to change others, we can change ourselves; the benefits will be immediate and visible.

In my work, I have found that in a conflict situation between two people, when one of the parties changes his/her approach, the other automatically reciprocates. The negative energy that flows between the two stops. A negative approach will cause the other person to react in a negative and aggressive manner. Using free will to choose the right way will not only heal you, but it will also heal the other person; you will become a healer without even knowing.

There are times that a person may be suffering because of an abusive spouse. Many people experiencing such a relationship silently suffer with it because of their fear of the consequences of breaking away. This is understandable; fear drives most of our decisions. However, it is important to remember that everyone has options, even in such situations. A calm and understanding approach to the other person improves the interaction. This person could have been abused or bullied as a child. It is probably a desire to be accepted and loved that drives the anger and aggression. Try to see things from their perspective and show patience. If nothing works, then you still have the option (using your free will) to turn away from the person. By continuing to live with an abusive partner, after having tried everything in your power to solve the problem, you are not exhibiting self-love. This could lead to health issues and the creation of karmas.

The same principles apply to abusive bosses, friends, or even siblings and/or parents. Reason with them as much as is possible and if there is no way out, leave your job or distance yourself from the abusive relationship.

I was recently working with a client on resolving issues relating to her father. Prior to hypnotising her, I asked her to close her eyes and see things from the eyes of her father, to feel his emotions and understand why he was behaving the way he was. After a few seconds she said, *"He does not know how to be a father"*. I then asked her if she knew why. She continued, *"Yes, his father died when he was six and he never had a male role model"*.

Immediately, she felt differently about her father. Half of my work was done with this simple exercise.

This case shows us that it is not always black and white. We should try to see things from others' perspectives. We can utilise our free will to evaluate things properly.

Our Peripheral Control

From the time we wake up to the time we go to sleep, there will be instances when we will feel irritated, angry, disappointed, fearful, stressed, or any other number of emotions. There is always something.

We get stressed for all sorts of reasons, some of which are quite petty - when we are late for work, when other drivers delay us on the road, when the bank takes a long time to answer the phone, when one of our work reports misses a deadline, and many, many others. The upshot of this is we are hyped up when we go home, and we often take it out on our families.

We cannot and should not try to change another's personality; this is not possible and is also spiritually wrong. We often hear people saying something along the lines of *"I have been trying to get my spouse to change for so long, but he/she is not changing"*. We have no right to change anyone. Try to see things from the other's perspective; how would you react if someone tried to change you by telling you he/she knows best how you should behave?

The problem is not the personality. It's the behaviour. When it comes to people very close to you, you might be able to positively influence their behaviour. You may be able to partly influence the behaviour of those close to you - your children, spouse, siblings, parents and friends. However, you have full control over your own behaviour. Changing yours will automatically change others' behaviours too.

Sometimes we stress over trivial matters. For example, some people are obsessed with the cleanliness of their house. In their mind they are correct, but at the same time, they are stressing the people around them, and spreading negative energy within their household. Next time you get irritated, ask yourself, *"Is this important enough to get upset about and to spoil the relationship with my loved ones?"*

Exercise No. 11

In this exercise, use Table 2 below (similar to Table 1 but with the addition of two more columns), to define whether or not it was within your control to change or influence a given situation. Your response may change the action plan in the last column.

WHO / WHAT WAS THE TRIGGER	EMOTION	BEHAVIOUR / RESPONSE	IMPACT	BELIEF	IS IT WITHIN YOUR CONTROL?	REASON FOR YES / NO ANSWER	ACTION PLAN
TRAFFIC	FRUSTRATION	AGGRESSIVE	TREMBLING	IT'S MY BAD LUCK	NO	I CANNOT DO ANYTHING ABOUT THE TRAFFIC	MANAGE TIME BETTER
BOSS	ANGER	SUBMISSIVE	BOILING INSIDE	I AM NOT GOOD ENOUGH	NO	I CANNOT CHANGE MY BOSS BUT I CAN CHANGE MY APPROACH	SWITCH TO COMMUNICATIVE STYLE
SPOUSE	FEAR	SUBMISSIVE-AGGRESSIVE	BOTTLE IN	I AM WEAK	NO	I CANNOT INFLUENCE HOW MY SPOUSE BEHAVES, BUT I CAN INFLUENCE HER / HIM TO CHANGE BEHAVIOUR	SWITCH TO COMMUNICATIVE STYLE, BE MORE UNDERSTANDING AS A FIRST STEP. IF NOTHING WORKS RE-EVALUATE YOUR OPTIONS
CHILDREN	ANXIETY	AGGRESSIVE	OUTBURST	I AM A BAD PERSON	YES	I CAN CHANGE THE WAY I HANDLE MY CHILDREN	SWITCH TO COMMUNICATIVE STYLE AND EXERCISE PATIENCE

Table 2: Peripheral Control: Understanding what is within our control

Developing Self-control

Self-control is our ability to regulate our impulses, emotions and behaviours in order to improve our relationships with those around us, and also, of equal importance, our physical and mental health.

To master self-control, there are four simple skills that need to be learnt:

1. Knowing Yourself

To have self-control, it is important to have self-awareness. Understand what drives your impulses, emotions, and behaviours.

Do you tend to impulsively react to issues? Are you able to stay composed and positive in stressful situations? Are you able to exercise patience in frustrating situations? Do you tend to micromanage people around you? Do you accept responsibility or tend to blame others? Do you accept feedback without getting irritated, angry, or defensive? Do you often say things you don't mean?

Only when you are aware of yourself will you be able to successfully practice self-control. From today, start noticing your emotions and reactions. It will help you enormously in your journey to achieving self-control.

2. Understanding Others' Perspectives

When we only see things from our own viewpoint we often misunderstand the intentions of others. To develop self-control, one must start seeing the situation from the perspectives of the others involved.

Do you listen carefully and give the other person the opportunity to finish before you respond? Pause for a while to ensure you fully understand the point of view the other person is trying to put across. Before you respond to someone, do you ask yourself, *"How would I like it if someone responded to me in this way?"* Do you follow up with relevant and considerate questions to ensure you have understood the other person? Do you spend time to understand why the other person believes he/she is right? Do you often listen to someone having already decided to discredit or disprove what they are saying before they have finished? Do you often consider that people have different opinions, and that they are entitled to them?

Seeing things from another person's point of view is very important. We often jump to conclusions. This not only harms our relationships with others; it also creates mental and physical suffering. From today start to focus on effective listening without interrupting the other person. Allow him/her to finish their thoughts. Ask follow-up questions to understand the other person's point of view. Put yourself in the other person's position to truly understand the point he/she is trying to get across.

3. Developing Willpower

Willpower is the motivation to exercise one's will - the ability to control yourself. A person with strong willpower is able to override unwanted thoughts, emotions, and impulses. Self-control requires strong determination and discipline. People with low willpower often procrastinate and delay doing what they have agreed or promised to do; this invariably leads to relationship issues.

Do you often tend to procrastinate and put off doing something for later? Are you often unable to resist the temptation to respond without taking the time to think? Do you often get side-tracked and lose focus on your goals? Do you exhibit paralysis when under pressure or during periods of high stress? Do you give up easily when you face challenges? Is making decisions difficult for you?

In order to achieve self-control, one must first develop willpower. Analyse instances and situations that you showed a lack of willpower. Plan and stick to the plan and follow the timelines. Follow up on promises you made. Do what you say you will do.

4. Practising Compassion

In Chapter 9, we discussed the meaning of compassion in the context of Divine Love. Compassion is synonymous with empathy. It is not just being kind to someone. It's also about feeling their emotions and sensing their pain. Compassion is also equally relevant towards ourselves; one must forgive and accept one's shortcomings. Self-compassion is as important as compassion towards other people.

Do you enjoy helping other people? Do you wait for someone to tell you that they need help, or do you instinctively know? Do you listen to other people's problems and try to help them? Do you easily forgive those who have been unkind to you? Do you always listen in a non-judgmental way?

We tend to be judgmental and indifferent to our own and other people's emotions and pain if we do not exercise compassion for ourselves and others. Self-control cannot be achieved unless we feel the pain of the other person, and take a non-judgmental approach.

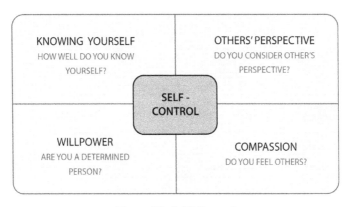

Figure 31: Self-Control

Exercise No. 12

Based on your answers in Tables 1 and 2, Table 4 lists all the situations for which you experienced strong emotions. Based on the discussion above, evaluate yourself on a scale from 1-10. This will help you identify your level of self-control in different situations. How well do you know yourself? Do you always consider the perspective of others or are you selective in what you accept? Do you have the willpower to exercise self-control? Do you have compassion with some people but not with others?

When you complete the list, review the outcomes, with particular attention to the low scoring areas that highlight the need for improvement. Analyse Table 4. Look for some patterns in order to understand how your behaviour changes in different situations and with certain people.

Look at the average of each column in Table 4 and refer to Table 3. If your average is between 1-3, then you have low self-control in this particular area. If your average is between 4-6, then you have moderate self-control. If your average is between 7-10, you have high self-control. This exercise will help you understand which areas require attention and improvement.

	LOW	MEDIUM	HIGH
AVERAGE RATING	1-3	4-6	7-10
KNOWING YOURSELF	LOW AWARENESS	SOME AWARENESS	HIGH AWARENESS
ACCEPTING OTHERS' PERSPECTIVE	LOW UNDERSTANDING	SOME UNDERSTANDING	HIGH UNDERSTANDING
WILLPOWER	LOW WILLPOWER	SOME WILLPOWER	HIGH WILLPOWER
COMPASSION	LOW COMPASSION	SOME COMPASSION	HIGH COMPASSION

Table 3: Self-Control Rating Table

CAUSE	EMOTION	IMPACT	KNOW YOURSELF	ACCEPTING OTHERS' PERSPECTIVE	WILLPOWER	COMPASSION
TRAFFIC	FRUSTRATION	TREMBLING	7	7	2	3
BOSS	ANGER	BOILING INSIDE	8	9	1	2
SPOUSE	FEAR	BOTTLED UP	7	1	1	7
CHILDREN	ANGER	OUTBURST	9	1	5	8
AVERAGE			7.75	4.5	2.25	5

Table 4: Understanding the Level of our Self-control

Countering Limiting Beliefs

Limiting beliefs/programming causes damage in our lives. Hypnosis can be used to replace such negative beliefs with positive ones.

With reference to our earlier example, if you have a fear of dogs, this is either because you had a bad experience earlier in your current life (even if you don't remember it), or a past life memory. Fears and phobias are beliefs, mind programming. Your mind associates dogs with danger or pain. After treatment by hypnosis or an equivalent process, your new programming could be *'Dogs are a man's best friend'*. We need to retain some measure of fear; fear is useful and keeps us from causing harm to ourselves.

Other examples of negative (old) and positive (new) belief systems:

Old: *I cannot lose weight*

New: *Weight comes off me easily when I wish it to.*

Old: *I am not good enough*

New: *I deserve love and happiness*

Your new statement should be short and precise.

Exercise No. 13

- You can do this lying down or sitting straight in a chair, whatever suits you best. Ensure that your back is straight to allow the flow of energy from the Root Chakra to the Crown.
- Rub your hands together until they generate heat.
- Utilising your stronger hand, activate your Crown and Third Eye Chakras to enable *'broadcasting'*.
- Firstly, open your Third Eye Chakra. Bring one of your hands two inches away from your forehead. Start a circular clockwise movement for approximately 20 circles.
- Take a few deep breaths and relax your muscles.
- *'Empty'* your head of any thoughts and observe your breath; focus on the movement of your stomach or place all your attention on your Third Eye (between your eyebrows). If you become distracted by any thoughts, sounds, smells or other sensations, quickly deflect them away and return to your breathing or attention on your Third Eye.

- While continuing to focus your attention on your breath or Third Eye, start chanting your new belief statement. You can do this in your mind. Do this for approximately 10 minutes.
- Repeat this for 21 days to embed the new belief.

If you are meditating for a different purpose, for example a new relationship or work promotion, first open your Third Eye and Crown Chakras and then visualize your ideal intended situation. Finally, clear these images from your mind and continue your meditation for a minimum of 10 minutes. Repeat this for 21 days.

Meditations don't need to be long. Ten minutes a day will be sufficient, although a longer period of meditation would be even more beneficial if this can be achieved.

Dietary Control and Vibrations

Anatomically, humans are herbivorous; our teeth, jaws and nails belong to those categories of animals that are vegetable eaters. Carnivorous animals have sharper teeth and nails, and they have jaws that only move vertically up and down to allow them to eat large pieces of meat without the need to chew. In addition, the stomach of a carnivorous animal is very acidic and able to better digest meat, and the smaller intestine allows the meat to be removed faster.

From a Christian spiritual perspective, eating meat is not a karma or sin. We are part of the food chain.

Jesus said:

> *Not what goes into the mouth defiles a man; but what comes out of the mouth, this defiles a man. (Matthew 15:11)*

Do you not yet understand that whatever enters the mouth goes into the stomach and is eliminated? But those things which proceed out of the mouth come from the heart, and they defile a man. For out of the heart proceed evil thoughts, murders, adulteries, fornications, thefts, false witness, blasphemies. (Matthew 15:17-19)

It is not what goes into your mouth, but what comes out that counts, Jesus said. The food gets digested and eliminated, but words cause pain and karmas. Jesus was not a vegetarian; at least, we know he ate fish. But the Bible tells us he fasted. The reason Jesus fasted is to do with the science of food digestion. The digestion process drives energy towards the internal organs and weakens the life force in the physical body, thus making *'connection'* to the Divine difficult. Jesus went for forty days without food and water. Divine souls can live with universal energy alone. In earlier chapters, we discussed examples of saints that switched from a *'calorie-burning engine'* to a *'universal energy-burning engine'* and lived for several years without food. An enlightened person can do this.

There is no evidence to show that the Buddha was a vegetarian; however, he encouraged vegetarianism because a central principle of Buddhism is the avoidance of causing suffering to any forms of life. Furthermore, Buddhism practices detachment from physical pleasures, including food, over and above that which the body requires for nutrition.

Hindus believe that eating meat generates karmas. True compassion cannot be practised when, at the same time, a person eats the body of another animal.

Hindus also believe that animals have emotions and fears. In the process of being transported for slaughter, they experience the full range of emotions, including fear, pain, anxiety and so on. When we eat meat, we ingest that negative energy. From a personal perspective, this has also influenced me to minimise my meat intake.

If you like to eat meat, plan to limit the frequency to once or twice a week. This will limit the amount of negative energy entering your physical body. Humans are not natural meat eaters; our bodies function more efficiently with less meat.

Fasting is beneficial in many ways. It builds up our resistance to temptation; if we can resist food, we can also resist other temptations.

> *Do not deprive one another except with consent for a time, that you may give yourselves to fasting and prayer; and come together again so that Satan does not tempt you because of your lack of self-control. (1 Corinthians 7:5)*

In the above passage, Saint Paul links fasting with resistance to temptations in general.

In the Greek Orthodox faith, when a person fasts, he/she becomes vegan for the particular period of fast, for example, during the lent period approaching Easter. However, in recent years, some people have created elaborate vegan recipes, such as vegan lasagne, vegan this, vegan that. This does not align with the purpose of fasting.

It is an interesting fact that while there isn't a consensus among religions regarding the acceptability of eating meat, there is agreement that fasting is a key consideration for those who are praying or meditating.

This reminds me of a recent case I worked on which involved a young lady in her early 20s, who had been suffering with bulimia for more than 10 years. I decided to contact the Higher Self for some information prior to deciding on the appropriate healing method to be used.

HS: She has disrespected food for a very long time. She has been throwing food away, while others around her were dying from hunger.

D: Surely not in this life. I can't imagine this happening in this life.

HS: No, it was in past lives, but she has not learnt. She still does not value food for what it is. She wastes food and does not respect it.

Food must be appreciated for what it is - for its nutritional value. We eat to live. We don't live to eat. When we buy a car, we ensure that it is regularly serviced. We change the oil and keep it clean. Our body is the *'vehicle'* that has been gifted to us to allow entry to this earthly school. It also needs care and maintenance so that it will last for the time required to allow us the opportunity to learn the lessons we have come to learn. Indulging occasionally is human nature, but continuous indulgence on a daily basis without any sense of responsibility towards the physical body causes karmas. We risk cutting our *'education'* short and having to repeat the *'class'*.

Not valuing food and wasting it while people around the world are hungry or starving also causes karmas. The earlier example of my client demonstrates this point.

Depending on the age of the person, the body contains between 55% and 75% water. Taking care of what we drink is important. I used to experience discomfort and heat in my wrists, and I eventually asked my Higher Self what was causing these symptoms. *"You must start drinking alkaline water. Your body has become acidic."* Although I had heard of alkaline water, I was not very familiar with this concept and actually thought that it was one of those marketing tricks! I switched to alkaline water and my wrists are feeling much better.

A Japanese scientist, Dr. Masaru Emoto, in his research and book *The Hidden Messages of Water* (R20), demonstrates how water changes its vibrational frequencies when exposed to various environments, such as music, words, emotions and prayers. Using a microscope, he examined the vibrational changes water undergoes when frozen water is exposed to loving, compassionate words, soothing music and prayer. He observed that the water crystalised into beautiful patterns. When the water was exposed to hateful and negative words and heavy metal music, the water crystals were of irregular shape. He also demonstrated how the water affects the person drinking it at a cellular level.

This demonstrates how our vibrational frequencies can change when we expose ourselves to unkind words and low vibrational music; there is a clear link because our bodies are largely made up of water.

In another conversation the Higher Self asked:

HS: Do you know why it is so important to drink plenty of good quality water?

D: I am guessing that the body is largely made of water and needs to be replenished.

HS: Water is a healer. When something is dirty, you wash it with water and it becomes clean. In the same way, your body needs cleaning of all the toxins.

For our physical and mental health, it is important to consume food of high vibrational frequency. Raw plant-based foods, such as fresh fruits and vegetables, nuts and seeds, green tea, legumes, olive oils and other essential oils are of very high vibrational frequency.

Meat, dairy products, sugar, rice, wheat, alcohol, coffee, sugary drinks, and processed food are all low vibrational food. Intake of these foods and drinks should be limited.

Exercise No. 14

By making some small changes in your diet, you will lead a longer and healthier life:

- Reduce the amount of low vibrational food you are consuming.
- Drink at least one and half litre of alkaline water (i.e. water with pH level greater than 7) and herbal teas.
- Go on a vegan diet twice a week, if possible. This will allow your body time to recover from the toxins ingested during the other days.
- Buy organic foods whenever possible. If this is not practical, read the food labels and ensure that the product contains no hormones or other damaging substances.
- Wash your vegetables and fruits with water, to remove any traces of pesticides.

Maintain your Physical Vibrations

A human voice is able to shatter a glass. If a person is singing at a matching pitch or resonant frequency with the glass, the sound of the voice vibrates the air molecules around the glass and this causes the glass to start vibrating. If the singing is loud enough, it can cause it to break.

In 1831, while a corps of British soldiers was marching across Broughton Suspension Bridge, the bridge collapsed and the soldiers fell into the river. Even though the bridge was a solid structure, the soldiers were marching at the same frequency of vibration as that of the bridge, which caused it to fail.

We discussed earlier that everything is composed of energy vibrating at different frequencies. The examples above demonstrate the powerful outcomes of matching those frequencies.

For our body and mind to be protected, our vibrational frequencies should be maintained at high levels. Our thoughts and negative emotions, the food we consume, the music we listen to, are all contributing to the weakening of our aura, blocking our chakras, and ultimately causing our vibrations to fall and cause physical ailments.

During one of our conversations my Higher Self asked:

HS: Do you know why it is rare for singers to have cancer?

D: Does it have to do with vibrations?

HS: Correct. Good music causes high vibrations. Bad music causes low vibrations. The lyrics of the song are also important. If the lyrics are spreading messages of hatred or negativity, the music is of low vibration. Low vibrations cause disease.

D: Perhaps it is rare for singers to have cancer, but there have been some famous singers who died of cancer.

HS: Yes, sometimes cancer is also karmic, but it can also be caused by low vibrational music. The body's vibrations get disturbed when the person sings at low vibration levels or listens to low vibrational music.

Exercise No. 15

To keep your body and mind healthy, your vibrations must be of high frequency. Here I provide some tips on how to improve your vibrations:

- Listen to high vibrational music. You can find such music on YouTube. 963 Hz, 528 Hz and 432 Hz are all high vibrational, healing frequencies. You can listen to such music during meditation or keep it playing in the background while you are working or studying.
- Sing and dance! Singing high vibrational songs improve your vibrations. Dancing is not just good exercise. Your body

releases *'happy'* hormones such dopamine and serotonin which help to boost your immune system.

- Keep your chakras active by managing your emotions, as discussed in previous chapters.
- Keep your chakras active, using the technique taught in Exercise No. 17.
- Seek professional help, such as sound healing, crystal healing, chakras healing, etc, to help you activate your chakras.
- Meditate regularly.
- Lie down and place crystals on your chakras. Crystals for chakra activation are sold in sets of seven pieces - one for each chakra. You can meditate in this position for 30 minutes, by visualizing white light penetrating each crystal, thus activating your chakras. Crystals are an excellent way of activating chakras if you are a visual person. Play high vibrational music at the same time.
- Join a yoga class or exercise regularly.
- Once a week, fill your bath tab with water and a handful of Epsom or sea salts. Lie in the bath for about 30 mins. This clears the negative energies from your aura.
- You can clean negative energies from your space by burning sage, also known as smudging. In Cyprus, people clean energies in their homes by burning dry olive leaves. Burning sandalwood is equally effective in cleaning energies.
- Regularly open your windows and allow fresh air to remove negative energies.
- Keep Epsom or sea salts in various parts of your space and replace at least once a month.
- Use essential oils in candles or diffusers to purify your space. Lavender is my favourite, but one can also use citrus oils, eucalyptus, chamomile, or peppermint.
- Declutter your home. Our subconscious mind associates cluttering and untidiness with a *'cluttered'* state of mind. This causes negative emotions and therefore weakening of the aura.

Turning off the Fight/Flight Response

In Hinduism and Buddhism, breathing is an art. It's the fuel of the heart. Engaging in breathing exercises brings inner peace.

I have explained in this and earlier chapters the damage that the *fight or flight* mechanism can cause to our health because of the constant and high levels of stress, fear, and anxiety.

Changing attitude is the ultimate goal; however, there is a quick solution whenever you feel that your *fight or flight* response has been activated. You will notice this in your physiological changes: rapid heart rate, body temperature changes, sweating, etc.

Exercise No. 16:

Take a few minutes break from whatever you are doing. Go to a quiet place where you will be alone. Sit straight or lie down, and do the following:

- Take a deep breath while you count fast from 1-10.
- Hold this breath and count from 1-10.
- Slowly release the breath and empty your chest while counting from 1-10.
- Hold your empty chest while counting from 1-10.
- Repeat this activity 20 times.

By the time you finish, your *fight or flight* mechanism will have been shut down and your body activity will be back to normal.

Balancing Your Chakras

Chapter 12 highlighted the importance of regularly balancing one's chakras.

Your chakras will not require a lot of *'maintenance'* once your emotions are balanced and you have released your fears, guilts and other chronic emotions. In the initial phases, however, there is a need for some assistance to unblock the chakras and release trapped energies.

During this initial phase, it would be advisable to seek professional help. There are many different modalities, and therapists available to apply them. Activation can be achieved with crystals, sound healing, reiki, and other energy modality applications.

Maintenance of your chakras can be continued by applying the steps in the following exercise.

Exercise No. 17

- Sit comfortably and in a straight position with your back straight and your chakras aligned.
- Rub your hands together until they generate heat.
- Utilising your stronger hand, activate your Root Chakra (Refer to Chapter 12, Figure 19)
- Bring one of your hands 2 inches away from the groin area and start a circular clockwise movement for approximately 20 circles.
- Repeat this for the remaining chakras.

Do this exercise regularly, with particular emphasis when you have had a difficult day that may have caused one or more of your chakras to malfunction.

Seeking Professional Help

Starting your spiritual journey is not always easy, especially if you have been holding on to the past and you are unable to let go on your own.

Clinical Hypnotherapy uses a variety of tools to help you release past beliefs, fears, and phobias. It will help you to release emotional energy and give you a fresh start in your spiritual journey.

Other modalities can be as equally effective, for example Theta Healing, Reiki, Sound Healing, and so many other techniques. Search for recommended, qualified specialists in your area.

CHAPTER 16

Helpers

People going through depression feel alone. But we are not alone. We have so many spirits around us ready to help us. They love us unconditionally and all we have to do is to ask for their help. They won't help unless they are requested to do so because we all have free will; they won't act without being asked because to do so would interfere with our free will.

I know this from experience. One afternoon, some six months after my awakening, while I was in bed resting during a family holiday, I felt a wonderful warm feeling and my body was vibrating. I felt a little afraid but the voice in my head reassured me that I was safe and there was nothing to worry about. Since that first occurrence, I occasionally experience something similar but not always exactly the same. One time I felt that a light was penetrating the top of my head and I could see it through my closed eyes. Another time I felt as if I was wearing invisible cables on my head and energy was being pumped into my body. On another occasion, through closed eyes, I could feel the presence of two other bright beings in the room, and I felt that they were scanning my body.

I did not tell anyone about this at the time; I thought that people would think I was going mad. When I established contact with my Higher Self, I asked:

D: Every few months I get some sensations, vibrations, feeling energy going through my body. Is it my imagination? Sometimes I think I am going mad!

HS: You are transcending; your vibrations are adjusting.

D: I see ... and another evening, I have seen and felt two beings in my room through my closed eyes. Was that a dream?

HS: No. They are higher beings assigned to help you with your development.

D: They are with me always?

HS: Most of the time.

Until this time, I had never heard the word *'transcend'*. I had to look it up, even though I vaguely understood the meaning. I now understand the meaning; when a person is transcending, he or she is reaching a certain level of soul clarity and their vibrations are adjusting. The beings assigned to us are helping and guiding us through our spiritual journey. They are evolved souls that do not need to reincarnate. They are Spirit Guides. Every one of us has one or more guides assigned to them, depending on their learnings.

Another night, about five years ago, during the time I was at my lowest, as I was asleep, I felt a hand on top of mine. It felt like a human hand, but I knew it wasn't. I kept my eyes closed and a beautiful energy flooded my body. I felt so wonderful that it brought tears to my eyes. Again, I did not tell this to anyone. When I spoke to my Higher Self I asked:

D: A few years ago I felt a hand on top of mine in the middle of the night, and energy was flowing through my body. Was it real or a dream?

HS: It was real.

D: Who was it?

HS: It was your spirit.

D: What do you mean by that?

HS: Your Spirit Guide. It was comforting you.

One must see through the eyes of Lorna Byrne, the author of *Angels in My Hair* (R21). Lorna has a very special gift; she can see angels. In this and several other books, she describes the beautiful, and to most people invisible, angelic realm. Around all of us there are beings ready to help us. Other than our Spirit Guides, we have our Guardian Angels and other angels, who are given specific tasks depending on each of our paths.

Your angels and Spirit Guides send you messages. Notice the synchronicities in your daily lives. There are no coincidences; everything is a well-orchestrated *'plan'* to attract our attentions and direct us towards the right path.

If you have lost loved ones, talk to them. They can hear you. They are there when you need them, and whenever you call them, they will come. You are never alone, even if it seems so.

CHAPTER 17

Conclusion

A Message of Love

During the course of this book, I have highlighted several issues relating to the institution of the Church. You may have also noticed that the whole book was based on the true teachings of Jesus and the great masters, Krishna and the Buddha.

I am not against the Church, or any other religious institution for that matter. The Church plays a very important role in the culture and traditions of a country and should not be ignored or trivialised.

Christianity is a beautiful religion, and one realises this when one reads the New Testament and understands the true teachings of Jesus.

Reading the New and Old Testaments was an eye-opener for me. During the course of this book, I have demonstrated in a number of sections the severe and rigid principles and language adopted in some of the Old Testament books, the religious scriptures written before Jesus.

It was also interesting to observe how Jesus directly challenged those teachings. Why did the Christian Church continue to include those teachings in the Bible when they directly conflict with the teachings of Jesus, as described in the New Testament? There are many examples of this, and some are included in the following pages:

Honouring Your Parents

> *For Moses said, "Honour your father and your mother and, he who curses father or mother, let him be put to death." But you say, "If a man says to his father or mother, whatever profit you might have received from me is Corban" (that is, a gift to God), then you no longer let him do anything for his father or his mother, making the word of God of no effect through your tradition which you have handed down. And many such things you do. (Mark 7:10-13)*

In the above passage, Jesus was not condoning putting people to death. He was pointing out the hypocrisy of choosing when to apply Moses' laws and when not to follow them. He was challenging by asking those who call themselves religious why they were not strictly following Moses' law to the letter. The old Testament states that those who do not honour their parents should be put to death.

An Eye for an Eye

> *You have heard that it was said, 'An eye for an eye and a tooth for a tooth'. But I tell you not to resist an evil person. But whoever slaps you on your right cheek, turn the other to him also. (Matthew 5:38-39)*

Jesus was referring to the Old Testament (Exodus 21:24) - *"eye for eye, tooth for tooth, hand for hand, foot for foot ...."*. Jesus was encouraging meekness, not aggression and brutality. He was an advocate of peace and love.

311

Love Your Enemies

> *You have heard that it was said, you shall love your neighbour and hate your enemy. But I say to you, love your enemies, bless those who curse you, do good to those who hate you, and pray for those who spitefully use you and persecute you, that you may be sons of your Father in heaven; for He makes His sun rise on the evil and on the good, and sends rain on the just and on the unjust. (Matthew 5:43-45)*

Jesus said *"love your enemies and those who cursed you"*. When he said *"you have heard that it was said ... hate your enemy"*, Jesus was referring to the Old Testament Book of Psalms, 139:

> *For they speak against You wickedly; Your enemies take. Your name in vain. Do I not hate them, O LORD, who hate You? And do I not loathe those who rise up against You? I hate them with perfect hatred; I count them my enemies. (Psalms 139:20-22)*

Working On the Day of Rest

When Jesus was challenged for healing on the Sabbath, the rest day, he said:

> *And He said to them, "The Sabbath was made for man, and not man for the Sabbath". (Mark 2:27)*

Jesus was challenging the brutal and narrow-minded view of the Pharisees who punished those who worked on the day of rest by sentencing them to death.

Adultery & The Penalty of Death

This they said, testing Him, that they might have something of which to accuse Him. But Jesus stooped down and wrote on the ground with His finger, as though He did not hear. So when they continued asking Him, He raised Himself up and said to them, "He who is without sin among you, let him throw a stone at her first". (John 8:6-7)

The man who commits adultery with another man's wife, he who commits adultery with his neighbour's wife, the adulterer and the adulteress, shall surely be put to death. (Leviticus 20:10)

In the above passage in the Gospel of John, Jesus challenges the Old Testament passage from Leviticus, which stated that adultery was punishable by death. *"He who is without sin to throw the first stone"*, he said. No one is perfect. We all make mistakes. We are quick to judge others for their mistakes, but we fail to acknowledge ours.

Selling Merchandise at the Temple

And He said to those who sold doves, "Take these things away! Do not make My Father's house a house of merchandise!" (John 2:16)

From an energy perspective, our aura is extended several feet outside of our body. The energy of those selling in the Temple was driven by their physical needs at the time, and this was contaminating and distracting those who were trying to connect with the Divine, by negatively impacting on their auras. This is the reason that all religions disapprove of the practice of trading outside a holy place.

Finally, my book should not be interpreted in any way other than to reconcile the teachings of one of the great masters with those of the institution that represents him.

The Church should be the place where people find solace and discover the path out of darkness. The priests should serve the hungry, the sick, the imprisoned, guiding us all from darkness to the light, just as Jesus did.

A FINAL WORD

I hope that you have found this book practically beneficial as well as educational. I also hope that the knowledge and practical exercises will help with your spiritual development. It is my belief that if you follow the simple principles and activities I have provided, you will live a more peaceful and enjoyable life, one full of love and happiness.

Life will always have its ups and downs. You will be down from time to time; this is inevitable and part of life. Choosing to get up and continue your journey with dignity is what matters.

Just remember that Love is all there was, all there is, and all there will ever be!

Despo Pishiri

GLOSSARY

1. **Baptism:** Baptism is one of the seven sacred mysteries performed in the Church.
2. **Bhagavad Gita**: Bhagavad Gita means the *'Song of God'* and it is one of the most important religious texts of Hinduism. The Gita is the dialogue between Arjuna, a warrior prince, and Krishna.
3. **Canonisation** is the process of accepting and declaring a holy person as a Saint, in Christianity.
4. **Guru:** Guru is a term meaning *'teacher'*, *'guide'* or *'master'*, used by spiritual teachers in India.
5. **Holy Communion**: Also known as *'Eucharist'*, Holy Communion is one of the seven sacred mysteries performed by the Church and symbolises Jesus' Last Supper with his disciples.
6. **Judgement Day:** The Bible refers to judgement day, which is the day, according to the interpretation of the Christian Church, that God will judge all souls to decide whether they will move to Heaven or Hell.
7. **Karma**: Karma is a Sanskrit (G20) word meaning *'action'*, referring to the spiritual principle of cause and effect where intent and actions of an individual influence the future, or future lives of an individual. The philosophy of karma is associated with Eastern religions such as Hinduism, Buddhism, Jainism, Sikhism and Taoism.
8. **Kutastha** is the Third Eye, the chakra in between the eyebrows.
9. **Mantra** is a word or words repeated by a seeker during meditation.

10. **Martyr:** The word '*martyr*' comes from the Greek word μάρτυς (martys), meaning '*witness*' or '*witness of the truth*'. This term was purely used for those who died protecting their faith.

11. **Nirvana:** Nirvana is a Sanskrit word that literally means '*blown out*'. It is the ultimate state, the liberation from repeated death and rebirth.

12. **Paganism** refers to '*polytheism*' (believing in many Gods) in reference to a religion other than one of the main world religions.

13. **Pharisees** were member of a Jewish religious party.

14. **Prana** is the life force energy. Energy is covered in Chapter 12

15. **Rabbi:** A Jewish scholar or teacher.

16. **Relics:** The remains of a saint or a holy person.

17. **Sadducees:** A party of Jewish high priests, aristocratic families, and merchants, active in Judaea from the second century BCE to the first century CE.

18. **Sanskrit** is an ancient Indian language, in which the Hindu scriptures were written.

19. **Second Coming:** According to the teachings of the Christian Church, based on their interpretation of the scriptures, Jesus will return to Earth.

20. **Subtle Body:** '*Subtle body*' and '*energy body*' are the same thing. Energy is covered in Chapter 12.

21. **Sutra:** An Indian religious scripture that contains important religious practices and teachings of key religious figures. Sutras are important in Hinduism, Buddhism and Jainism.

22. **Swami** is an honorific title given to a Hindu religious teacher.

23. **Vedas** are Hindu religious texts.

REFERENCES

1. Many Lives, Many Masters (Dr. Brian Weiss)
2. Holy Science (Sri Yukteswar Giri)
3. Autobiography of a Yogi (Paramhansa Yogananda)
4. Living Buddha, Living Christ (Thich Nhat Hanh)
5. The Heart of the Buddha's Teachings (Thich Nhat Hanh)
6. Crossing the Threshold of Hope (Pope John Paul II)
7. Biology of Belief (Dr. Bruce Lipton)
8. The Second Coming of Christ: The Resurrection of the Christ Within You (Paramhansa Yogananda)
9. Between Death and Life (Dolores Cannon)
10. Witness of Hope: The Biography of Pope John Paul II (George Weigel)
11. Vine's Expository Dictionary of New Testament Words (William Edwy Vine)
12. Dying to Be Me (Anita Moorjani)
13. Love (Dr. Leo Buscaglia)
14. The Emotion Code (Dr. Bradley Nelson)
15. Zero Limits: The Secret Hawaiian System for Wealth, Health, Peace, and More (Joe Vitale & Dr. Ihaleakala Hew Len)
16. Emotional Intelligence (Daniel Goleman)
17. Origen (Fr. Tadros Y. Malaty)
18. Journey of Souls (Dr. Michael Newton)
19. Destiny of Souls (Dr. Michael Newton)
20. The Hidden Messages of Water (Dr. Masaru Emoto)

21. Angels in My Hair (Lorna Byrne)
22. The Enlightened Gardener (Sydney Banks)
23. Energy Medicine (Donna Eden with Dr. David Feinstein)
24. DMT: The Spirit Molecule (Dr. Rick Strassman)

CPSIA information can be obtained
at www.ICGtesting.com
Printed in the USA
BVHW072119080821
613897BV00002B/3

9 781982 265373